PROFESSIONAL REGULATION AND MEDICAL GUIDELINES

PROFESSIONAL REGULATION AND MEDICAL GUIDELINES

The Real Forces Behind the Development of Evidence-Based Guidelines

Friso Johannes JANSEN

INTERSENTIA

Intersentia Ltd
8 Wellington Mews
Wellington Street | Cambridge
CB1 1HW | United Kingdom
Tel.: +44 1223 736 170
Email: mail@intersentia.co.uk
www.intersentia.com | www.intersentia.co.uk

Distribution for the UK and Ireland:
NBN International
Airport Business Centre, 10 Thornbury Road
Plymouth, PL6 7PP
United Kingdom
Tel.: +44 1752 202 301 | Fax: +44 1752 202 331
Email: orders@nbninternational.com

Distribution for Europe and all other countries:
Intersentia Publishing nv
Groenstraat 31
2640 Mortsel
Belgium
Tel.: +32 3 680 15 50 | Fax: +32 3 658 71 21
Email: mail@intersentia.be

Distribution for the USA and Canada:
Independent Publishers Group
Order Department
814 North Franklin Street
Chicago, IL 60610
USA
Tel.: +1 800 888 4741 (toll free) | Fax: +1 312 337 5985
Email: orders@ipgbook.com

Professional Regulation and Medical Guidelines. The Real Forces Behind the Development of Evidence-Based Guidelines

Image on cover: S_L – Shutterstock

ISBN 978-1-78068-819-0
D/2020/7849/1
NUR 820

British Library Cataloguing in Publication Data. A catalogue record for this book is available from the British Library.

For Sarah

ACKNOWLEDGEMENTS

Firstly, I would like to thank all the participants who willingly took the time to answer all my various questions. Without your cooperation this book could never have been completed. The supervisors of my PhD thesis, on which this book is based, Dr Marina Kurkchiyan and Dr Christopher Decker were always generous with their time and constructive in their comments. Their help was instrumental in refining the approach of the study and the theoretical approaches adopted. Their patient reading and re-reading of the manuscript made a vital difference in strengthening the final work.

At the Centre for Socio-Legal Studies many were generous with their advice, and many more with their friendship. I would like to particularly thank Naomi whose warmth and friendship provided a constant source of support and laughter, lots of laughter. I would like to thank Petra, Rogier, Inginio, Paulo and Christina for their encouragement and friendship.

Fellow students who made my DPhil a collective endeavour and to whom I would like to show my immense gratitude are, in no particular order: Po-Hsiang, Paul, Owain, Matilde, Christina and Felix, as well as all the others that I was fortunate to meet in Oxford.

I would like to thank Doede Joustra for his help with accessing some of the Dutch sources in this book. Sarah, my vrouw, has been instrumental in pushing me to pursue a DPhil and I would be lost without her. Her critical mind and probing questions have improved this book time and time again. I hope to return the favour and give some of the love back she has given me over the years. My agent Ann-Christin Maak-Scherpe and editor Ahmed Hegazi were instrumental in turning the manuscript into a publishable work and their support is gratefully acknowledged.

CONTENTS

LIST OF ABBREVIATIONS

ACCORD	Action to Control Cardiovascular Risk in Diabetes
ACM	Authority for Consumers and Markets
ADVANCE	Action in Diabetes and Vascular Disease
AGREE (II)	Advancing Guideline Development, Reporting and Evaluation in Healthcare
BEAM	United Kingdom Back Pain Exercise and Manipulation Randomised Trial
CBO	National Association for Quality Assurance in Hospitals
CCG	Clinical Commission Group
COMPare	Centre for Evidence-based Medicine Outcome Monitoring Project
CQC	Care Quality Commission
EBM	Evidence-based Medicine
EBRO	Evidence-based Guideline Development
EU	European Union
GDG	Guideline Development Group
G-I-N	Guidelines-International-Network
GP	General Practitioner
GRADE	Grading of Recommendations Assessment, Development and Evaluation
HSCA 2012	Health and Social Care Act 2012
HTA	Health Technology Assessment
ICER	Incremental Cost-effectiveness Ratio
IGZ	Dutch Health Inspectorate
ISO	International Organization for Standardization
ISDA	International Swaps and Derivatives Association
KNMG	Royal Dutch Federation of Medicine
LHV	The National Association of General Practitioners
NCC	National Collaborating Centre
NHG	The Dutch Royal College of General Practitioners
NHG-Standaarden	The Dutch Royal College of General Practitioners Guidelines

NICE	National Institute for Care and Health Excellence
NZA	Dutch Healthcare Authority
OMS	Order of Medical Specialists
RCT	Randomised Control Trail
QALY	Quality-adjusted Life-year
UKPDS	United Kingdom Prospective Diabetes Study
VADT	Veteran Affairs Diabetes Trial
Zorginstituut	The (Dutch) National Health Care Institute

CHAPTER 1
INTRODUCTION

This book is a socio-legal enquiry into the development of medical practice guidelines that provides insights into professional self-regulation and the 'black box' of guideline making. We all would like to receive the best medical care possible. When we see our general practitioner (GP) we expect to receive the best possible care, independent of location.

In response to increasing calls for the accountability of medical professionals, consensus-based medical practice guidelines were developed in the latter part of the 1970s in the United States of America[1] and quickly spread to the Netherlands and England.[2] The aim of these guidelines was to reduce practice variation by achieving consensus among a large group of medical professionals on the best care for medical conditions. If guidelines would be widely followed, treatments would, in principle, have to be the same.

However, in the 1990s, the fact that these guidelines were developed on the basis of consensus among experts was questioned and there was a call to base guidelines on a systematic appraisal of all available scientific evidence: one that would provide universal knowledge on which to base medical decisions. This 'evidence-based medicine'[3]

---

1 While the problem of practice variation has always existed, there were no guidelines prior to the 1970s. With the rationalisation of medical knowledge and the increasing availability of the computer, it became possible to share medical knowledge more easily than ever before. Guidelines themselves were the result of pressure from the US Government for more 'value for money' in the field.

2 JJE van Everdingen, *Consensusontwikkeling in de geneeskunde* (Bohn, Scheltema en Holkema 1988).

3 An approach to medicine that promotes the use of clinical epidemiology and stresses the importance of Randomised Control Trials to inform treatment decisions in medicine. Among many: David L Sackett and others, 'Evidence Based Medicine: What It Is and What It Isn't' (1996) 312 *BMJ* 71; Frank Davidoff and others, 'Evidence Based Medicine' (1995) 310 *BMJ* 1085; David Armstrong, 'Clinical Autonomy, Individual and Collective: The Problem of Changing Doctors' Behaviour' (2002) 55 *Social Science & Medicine* 1771; GH Guyatt, 'Evidence-Based Medicine' [1991]

movement[4] had a profound effect on the medical world and is suggested by some to be one of the most important developments in modern medicine.[5] As a result of this movement, all medical practice guidelines are now described as evidence-based and it is these guidelines that will be considered here.

The motivation here lies in the observation that when comparing evidence-based medical guidelines across countries, the same diseases are often treated in different ways.[6] There is no obvious reason to suspect, for example, that the populations of England and the Netherlands are so different that this could explain these differences. As evidence-based medicine endorses the systematic use of the best available evidence and both countries have access to the same (English-language) medical studies, it would be expected that the guidelines would reflect these similarities? So, the question that follows is how do differences in medical guidelines occur despite access to the same evidence? Or conversely, how is it that some elements are similar between countries despite these guidelines referring to very different evidence to support their recommendations?

While examining similarities and differences in guidelines is an appropriate starting point, it does not explain the mechanisms behind the development of guidelines. So, here, medical guidelines are used to study and analyse the process of policy and regulatory development. Guidelines are extensively debated within the medical literature, however, a book that approaches them from a socio-legal perspective is still missing. Understanding guideline development in a socio-legal sense can further add to ongoing debates about the role of law in society and the role of experts in promulgating law and other normative orderings, as these guidelines are part of the regulatory system of healthcare governance. Further, these insights provide food for thought to the debate around the value of evidence-based medicine as a method. Beyond medical or health

ACP J Club A; Evidence-Based Medicine Working Group, 'Evidence-Based Medicine: A New Approach to Teaching the Practice of Medicine' (1992) 268 *JAMA* 2420; Alvan R Feinstein MD and Ralph I Horwitz MD, 'Problems in the "Evidence" of "Evidence-Based Medicine"' (1997) 103 *The American Journal of Medicine* 529.

4 Catherine Pope, 'Resisting Evidence: The Study of Evidence-Based Medicine as a Contemporary Social Movement' (2003) 7 *Health* 267.

5 Eric Mykhalovskiy and Lorna Weir, 'The Problem of Evidence-Based Medicine: Directions for Social Science' (2004) 59 *Social Science & Medicine* 1059.

6 Bart W Koes and others, 'Clinical Guidelines for the Management of Low Back Pain in Primary Care: An International Comparison' (2001) 26 *Spine* 2504; Jako S Burgers and others, 'Inside Guidelines Comparative Analysis of Recommendations and Evidence in Diabetes Guidelines from 13 Countries' (2002) 25 *Diabetes Care* 1933.

subjects, insights into the process of the development of guidelines is important for wider debates about self-regulation and policy. Opening the 'black-box' of guideline development may help uncover broader lessons about the use and construction of scientific knowledge by experts.

This builds on earlier work which studied the process of guideline formation using ethnographic methods, as well as empirical studies of the group process of guideline production using interviews, quasi-experiments or surveys.[7] Although these earlier studies provide an important understanding of some of the elements of guideline formation and negotiation, research on the topic has so far been relatively piecemeal, with various aspects considered in isolation. It draws together case study findings and tries to explore all relevant factors in as much detail as possible to provide transferable lessons for guideline development.

1.1. A SOCIO-LEGAL ENQUIRY

To understand the mechanisms that drive guideline development a detailed qualitative analysis of the drafting process of two sets of guidelines in the Netherlands and England is provided.

These countries have been selected because they share similar characteristics; nonetheless, this has resulted in different recommendations in medical guidelines:

- Both countries subscribe to the same ideas of evidence-based healthcare and refer to the same sources for evidence. This can be seen in the use of the same medical databases for searching medical evidence and the restriction to English (or Dutch) language publications and not French, German or Spanish publications.

---

7 Tim Hopthrow, Gene Feder and Susan Michie, 'The Role of Group Decision Making Processes in the Creation of Clinical Guidelines' (2011) 23 *International Review of Psychiatry* 358; Claudia Pagliari and Jeremy Grimshaw, 'Impact of Group Structure and Process on Multidisciplinary Evidence-Based Guideline Development: An Observational Study' (2002) 8 *Journal of Evaluation in Clinical Practice* 145; Rosalind Raine and others, 'An Experimental Study of Determinants of Group Judgments in Clinical Guideline Development' (2004) 364 *The Lancet* 429; Harry Hemingway and others, 'Appropriateness Criteria for Coronary Angiography in Angina: Reliability and Validity' (2008) 149 *Annals of Internal Medicine* 221; Lou Atkins and others, 'The Process of Developing Evidence-Based Guidance in Medicine and Public Health: A Qualitative Study of Views from the Inside' (2013) 8 *Implementation Science* 101.

- Policy makers participate in international collaborations on healthcare innovations and regulation: examples of this are the G-I-N network that collaborates on medical guidelines and medical collaborations between hospitals in the Netherlands and England.[8]
- Academic hospitals in the Netherlands, especially those attached to universities, have explicit relationships with hospitals in England and collaborate on several research projects. In addition, Dutch medical personnel often visit England (admittedly much less so the other way around) and practice as doctors there; when they return, they bring knowledge of the English healthcare system back with them.

In addition, the two countries have similar general characteristics: both are considered among the best healthcare systems in the world.[9] Both systems are located in rich Western European, developed countries with a long tradition of trying to improve the quality of healthcare.

The two areas of medical practice guidelines that have been chosen are lower back pain and Type II Diabetes. Guidelines on both conditions have a long history, going back to the early 1990s and affect a large part of the population. The treatment regimens are also comparable. Given the fact that these conditions are so prevalent, gaining an insight into how the medical advice for these conditions is determined is of particular interest.

The key question is: What factors and mechanisms explain the differences between the development of the 'evidence-based' guidelines? However, in exploring this question, the book also identified and addresses several sub-questions: What role does evidence play in creating differences and similarities in guidelines and what types of 'evidence' are used? How do institutional framings impact on guideline development? What is the role of group decision making in the development of guidelines? What is the role of evidence on cost and cost-effectiveness in the formation of guidelines? How do external factors determine choices made in guideline

8 Among many: <https://www.elixir-europe.org/about-us/collaborations, eyehospitals.eu>.

9 Sarah Thomson and others, 'International Profiles of Health Care Systems, 2013' (Commonwealth Fund). Available at: <http://www.commonwealthfund.org/~/media/Files/Publications/Fund%20Report/2013/Nov/1717_Thomson_intl_profiles_hlt_care_sys_2013_v2.pdf>; Health Consumer Powerhouse, 'European Health Consumer Index'. Available at: <http://www.healthpowerhouse.com/files/EHCI_2015/EHCI_2015_report.pdf>; 'Mirror, Mirror on the Wall, 2014 Update: How the U.S. Health Care System Compares Internationally – The Commonwealth Fund'. Available at: <http://www.commonwealthfund.org/publications/fund-reports/2014/jun/mirror-mirror>.

development? How do these factors and mechanisms impact on guidelines as a form of professional self-regulation?

1.2. SETTING THE SCENE

1.2.1. GUIDELINE MAKERS

So, who are the guideline making organisations at the centre of this book?

The situation in England is quite straightforward: no-one can escape the dominance of NICE (National Institute of Health and Care Excellence) as a producer of guidelines. In contrast, in the Netherlands, there are several organisations of medical professionals that produce guidelines. Among them are the KNMG (Royal Dutch Federation of Medicine), NHG (Royal College of General Practitioners) and several organisations of medical consultants across the medical specialists: for example, surgeons, anaesthesiologists and paediatric doctors. Of these organisations, the NHG has had a long history of producing guidelines: since the 1980s they have produced both a guideline on back pain as well as on diabetes.[10] Choosing to focus solely on the NHG in the Dutch context facilitates a meaningful comparison because the comparison is limited to two different institutions.

In both countries, the medical professionals involved in drafting the guidelines were identifiable through the published guideline documents and a total of 16 guideline drafters were interviewed (eight per country). In addition to interviewing medical professionals, two pilot interviews were held in the Netherlands with a specialist in medical guidelines and a compliance officer in a rural hospital to test the feasibility and appropriateness of the topic list. Furthermore, pilot interviews were held with a senior official at NICE and two officials at the Zorginstituut Netherlands to discuss broader aspects of the work of guideline groups.

The interviews with the members of the guideline groups provided valuable information about the process of drafting a guideline, nonetheless, it is vital to also scrutinise the wording of the final guideline document and draft versions where available: In England, NICE publishes a comprehensive list of documents that outline the guideline process, including documents on the scope of the guideline, meeting notes, appendices with background studies and draft versions and also comments received from registered stakeholders. In the Netherlands, only the final guideline document

10 So-called NHG-standaarden, more detail is provided in Chapter 2.

is available. However, there are responses to the guidelines published in medical journals and general press that provide further insights. Bringing these various elements together, the supplemental guideline documents provide an integral part of this book. A critical analysis of these documents helps to provide the impetus to describe the gap between the 'law in the books' and the 'law in action'.

The text in these documents is not approached as definitive and no attempt is made to discover their absolute meaning in the sense that some legal research purports to when analysing text in a system of law. Instead, the focus of this research is on the text as the embodiment of the compromises struck in the process of negotiation. In addition to looking at what is said in the guideline, it is also important to understand what is not said. Issues not dealt with or recommendations not made might say a lot about the drafting process. When these omissions were spotted (through comparing various guideline documents), this fed into the interview process. Given the focus here on the process and development of medical guidelines, less attention is paid to their implementation, though it will be briefly covered where necessary.

A description of guidelines and guideline-making organisations might give the impression that this will be a tedious, even boring, study of mundane technical documents that could hardly throw up any novel or noteworthy insights. However, gladly dispensing with any apprehensions that the reader may have at this stage, this author can confirm that beneath the surface of mundane tranquillity a struggle both for power and meaning is hidden. It seems that the longer and more technical the guideline document becomes with, in some cases, long lists of annexes, the more intense the debate that took place during its development. The various developmental processes that took place and influence the final text of a guideline will be unpacked to show the complicated way in which 'facts' are created in a political process of meaning making.

1.2.2. THE ROLE OF MEDICAL EVIDENCE

The overarching argument in this book is that medical evidence plays a more limited and nuanced role in guideline construction than might be expected and that guidelines are manifestations of professional (self-)regulation. Guidelines are written not only to inform and provide guidance to healthcare professionals but also to embody a desire to control (an aspect of) medical clinical practice. Importantly, this work also establishes that institutions contribute to the shaping of guidelines in a multitude of ways, ironically through guidelines of their own. Institutional factors have been shown to be essential elements in guideline development, influencing all aspects of development through institutional cultures of practice.

In this way, a more nuanced understanding of evidence than is prevalent within the medical literature is presented thus conceptualising evidence as part of a process of a social and institutional construction. It is argued that medical evidence – or any knowledge for that matter – often does not speak for itself but only speaks in relation to the social environment in which it is used. This process of listening to, silencing, selecting and crafting knowledge lies at the heart of the interaction of science and regulation which this book investigates.

Construction of evidence is used within a collaborative and communicative process aimed at creating 'objective facts.' Contrary to existing scholarship, it is argued that evidence merely informs the understanding of members of guideline groups while a range of economic, cultural, institutional and political factors, that together form cognitive frames, provide the driving force behind the development of guidelines. In this way, an attempt is made to holistically demonstrate how choices are made time and time again in developing these specific forms of self-regulation. The book concludes with the argument that calling guidelines evidence-based is an important rhetorical instrument, which helps to conceal and legitimise some of the normative choices that are inherent in guideline making.

1.2.3. THE ROLE OF MEDICAL EXPERTS

Different conceptual frames emerged from interviews undertaken with those directly involved in creating the guidelines. The varied stories of negotiating, debate, conflict and compromise form the backbone of this book. Through careful exposition of these evolving and multi-faceted stories it is possible to reconstruct some of the important decisions taken during the construction of a guideline. This shows convincingly how this process is messy, but also surprisingly fruitful, in bringing together various perspectives to create a normative guideline document.

A clearer understanding of the mechanisms behind the development of medical guidelines can shed light on an aspect of healthcare governance that has not been given sufficient attention. As a healthcare professional, having an insight into the development of a guideline can lead to a better understanding of the basis for some of the choices within it. This might also lead to a greater feeling of ownership of these guidelines and reduce the feeling they are made 'far-away' and detached from practice. From the perspective of organisations like the National Institute for Health and Care Excellence (NICE) and the Nederlands Huisartsen Genootschap (NHG), understanding the workings of guideline groups will provide opportunities to further improve their practice. These institutions are responsible for the institutional structuring of guideline development processes, but they then leave the detailed development to independent guideline groups. A close look at how these groups develop guidelines will provide valuable insights in a better balance between institutional control and professional independence. For healthcare insurers, especially in the Netherlands, this book will show some of the complexities and carefully thought out compromises that go into a medical guideline. This will inform informal and formal discussions on contracts for the delivery of healthcare where guidelines can be used as tools for budgetary control or as minimum quality standard. Finally, for regulators such as the IGZ and Zorginstituut in the Netherlands and the CQC and Healthcare Improvement in the UK, this work can help contextualise some of the uncertainties in the practice of medicine and hopefully lead to a style of enforcement of medical standards that is mindful of this.

The role of medical experts in developing medical guidelines tells a wider story about the role of experts in society. While Michael Gove might have had enough of experts,[11] their increasing role in society cannot easily be wished away. Rules made by a great variety of experts deserve critical consideration, the analysis that these rules are technical and therefore unimportant is too limited. This book explores how experts use science to construct regulation that influences society and points out that the technocratic is political. While the influence of experts is only likely to grow, as our society becomes increasingly complex, our scrutiny of their efforts should likewise grow. Insight into an important aspect of the regulation of medical care opens the door to similar efforts in other fields.

Transparency initiatives already undertaken must be further strengthened as one of the possible ways of providing more legitimacy for guidelines (and other instruments) created by experts. They are also important mechanisms for enabling criticism of and accountability for

11 Interview with Faisal Islam, Sky News, 3 June 2016.

guideline makers. Such mechanisms are important to maintain a careful balance between the need to involve experts in technical evaluations that require their expertise, while at the same time setting boundaries for the exercise of their power.

When experts dominate a field there is always a danger that a disconnect could inadvertently arise between them, their patients and the citizens who fund healthcare. Guidelines could act as a bridge between experts and patients, helping to mediate the divide of power in their relationship. Patients and citizens understanding the role of medical guidelines would enable more informed conversations and, as a result, provide information on what can be expected of medical professionals in charge of care. Efforts towards 'shared decision-making'[12] should be encouraged; patients being informed in new accessible ways about the content of guidelines[13] would go some way to help achieve this. While patients are not the focus here and their role is not systematically scrutinised, that does not mean that they are somehow unimportant. Patients are central to the choices made in guidelines, but they are only indirectly involved in their construction, through patient representatives. How guideline-makers deal with these influences is explored here. In this way, a holistic look at the development of medical guidelines and its impact on medical governance, regulation and society is provided.

---

12 Glyn Elwyn and others, 'Shared Decision Making: A Model for Clinical Practice' (2012) 27 *Journal of General Internal Medicine* 1361.

13 Initiatives like <www.thuisarts.nl> and NHS Choices provide good examples of successful approaches.

CHAPTER 2

UNDERSTANDING GUIDELINES IN THEIR ACADEMIC CONTEXT

2.1. INTRODUCTION

This chapter presents the existing scholarship which engages with medical guidelines. The issues the literature presents are discussed with the aim of presenting the field of study. It is important to connect the research featured here with literature from different disciplines to allow for a broad analysis of the development of medical practice guidelines in a comparative perspective. The literature that is instrumental in understanding the process of development of medical guidelines can be positioned under four broad categories: evidence, regulation, institutions and group decision making.

An important element here is an engagement with the notion of evidence. Evidence is used in the medical field in a specific technical sense. It is understood to refer to a body of *knowledge*; not just (medical) knowledge but knowledge that conforms to standards in the methods that were used to create it. This is important for understanding the development of evidence-based medical guidelines because those responsible for drafting the guidelines will be influenced by their conception of evidence. This influence comes in at least three ways: a conception of what evidence is informs what drafters see as informing a guideline; it shapes their understanding of the process of making a guideline; and it influences their ideas about what constitutes a good guideline. The debates in the literature about what counts as evidence, the process of using evidence and measures of success in drafting guidelines will be explored.

Regulatory literature is a second source of information that helps to understand the drivers and the processes that influence the development of medical guidelines. It will be argued that guidelines are not just forms of advice which can be easily ignored, but rather they are regulatory tools used by professionals for two distinct purposes: to ward off the influence of the state on the profession; and to influence other professionals and steer the quality of their practice of medicine. The regulatory literature provides interesting theories and debates on the nature of self-regulation by professionals; this book will be positioned as a contribution to a better understanding of these aspects of the regulatory state.

At least in theory, the work of a guideline group, purports to be independent. An essential aspect of the development of guidelines can be explained by specific features of its institutional embedding within a guideline-making organisation. The institutional literature informs our approach here by examining the interplay and tensions between institutions and the guideline groups who work for them.

Finally, guideline-making groups will also be studied at the micro level. The interaction between guideline makers and their processes of decision making form the heart of this work. Accordingly, several different theories and approaches that analyse group decision making will be explored so that this can add to the important scholarship in this field.

2.2. EVIDENCE-BASED GUIDELINES

Guidelines are commonly defined as 'systematically developed statements to assist practitioner and patient decisions about appropriate health care for specific clinical circumstances'.[1] In practice, they can have different names: protocols, standards, practice statements or guidelines. Here, medical practice guidelines, or just guidelines, will be used to describe all the above.

Medical practice statements are described as 'systematically developed'. This description points to two types of guidelines: consensus- or evidence-based guidelines. Consensus-based development refers to those adopted in the 1980s, when large conferences were held during which healthcare professionals decided, by consensus, to adopt recommendations and to draft guidelines.[2] This approach has gradually been replaced by a focus on evidence-based development. This historical

---

1 Marilyn J Field and others, *Clinical Practice Guidelines Directions for a New Program* (National Academy Press, 1990) 38.

2 Nick Black and others, 'Consensus Development Methods: A Review of Best Practice in Creating Clinical Guidelines' (1999) 4 *Journal of Health Services Research & Policy* 236; van Everdingen (Chapter 1, n 2).

development and its description in the literature is directly relevant here as it colours the perception guideline developers have about the correct way of making a guideline. Medical practice guidelines did not move to being described as evidence-based without the impetus of a broader movement that has had (and still has) an effect on medicine. To understand how guideline group members might approach the task of developing a medical guideline, an analysis of the evidence-based medicine movement and its central philosophy is appropriate.

The term 'evidence-based medicine' was coined in 1991 by Guyatt.[3] It describes an approach to clinical decision-making that builds on findings from clinical epidemiology and the promotion of the Randomised Control Trial (RCT) by Cochrane.[4] This approach set out to challenge doctors who would take decisions based on clinical expertise or knowledge gained from other professionals and started promoting the systematic use of medical studies in clinical decision making. Sackett describes this approach in the following terms: 'The practice of evidence-based medicine means integrating individual clinical expertise with the best available external clinical evidence from systematic research.'[5] Its take up has been dramatic: journals,[6] research institutes[7] and medical training[8] have all been reformed based on these ideas. Evidence-based medicine has not been interpreted in a uniform way. While Sackett stresses the need to select the appropriate evidence for the clinical question at hand, one of the defining features of evidence-based medicine is the introduction of an evidence hierarchy in medicine.

The background to the term evidence-based medicine lies in the medical discipline of epidemiology, a discipline that studies diseases on the level of populations. RCTs are a type of scientific experiment to

---

3 Guyatt (Chapter 1, n 3).

4 Iain Chalmers, 'The Cochrane Collaboration: Preparing, Maintaining, and Disseminating Systematic Reviews of the Effects of Health Care' (1993) 703 *Annals of the New York Academy of Sciences* 156; A L Cochrane, J Glyn Cox and T Francis Jarman, 'Pulmonary Tuberculosis in the Rhondda Fach' (1952) 2 *British Medical Journal* 843; AL Cochrane, *Effectiveness and Efficiency: Random Reflections on Health Services* (Nuffield Provincial Hospitals Trust 1972).

5 Sackett and others (Chapter 1, n 3) 71.

6 Davidoff and others (Chapter 1, n 3).

7 The Oxford Centre for Evidence-Based medicine is but one of many examples.

8 JH Shin, RB Haynes and ME Johnston, 'Effect of Problem-Based, Self-Directed Undergraduate Education on Life-Long Learning' (1993) 148 CMAJ: *Canadian Medical Association Journal* 969.

determine whether a treatment is effective by placing randomly assigned participants into either a control group (who receive no treatment) or an intervention group (who receive treatment) to establish causal links. RCTs are seen as being scientifically more rigorous, thus they are labelled as a more valuable way of assessing treatments and diagnosis. When RCTs are coupled with an emphasis on the need to consult and appraise the scientific literature in making clinical decisions they can improve the evidence base of those decisions.[9] Other forms of scientific evidence are also included in producing medical guidelines, such as expert opinion, cohort studies and case studies. Cohort studies are a form of longitudinal prospective study used to establish a correlation between risk factors and a certain disease. Case studies test for a predefined causal attribute, such as smoking, in a group of people with a disease, say lung cancer, compared to a group of people without lung cancer. If a significantly greater amount of people in the group with lung cancer smoke, there is a strong correlation but no causation between smoking and lung cancer. Critically, as these types of studies are observational, they can only provide correlations while randomised control trials, if conducted properly, can establish causal links.

In evidence-based medicine, forms of evidence are ranked by type and placed in a hierarchy of quality of evidence: with RCTs given most weight, cohort and case studies are given a medium ranking and expert opinion is ranked as being of lowest value. As such, evidence-based medicine proposes a hierarchy of evidence, as displayed in Figure 1 below.

Evidence-based guidelines use all of forms of evidence and the relative assessment of their value, to produce recommendations for treatment. From this we can deduce that there is a preference in evidence-based medicine to favour knowledge that is the result of statistical inferences for population-level research on diseases. It is precisely this hierarchy that is innovative in evidence-based medicine; no one would go so far as to say that earlier decisions in medicine were not based on any evidence, only that an explicit hierarchy of evidence is new. This approach to medical knowledge is true to its foundations in epidemiological research, but therefore also imports a specific epidemiological view of medicine into mainstream thinking.

To further understand the precise nature of evidence in specific evidence-based medical guidelines it is important to outline the

[9] Evidence-Based Medicine Working Group (Chapter 1, n 3); Roger L Sur and Philipp Dahm, 'History of Evidence-Based Medicine' (2011) 27 *Indian Journal of Urology* 487.

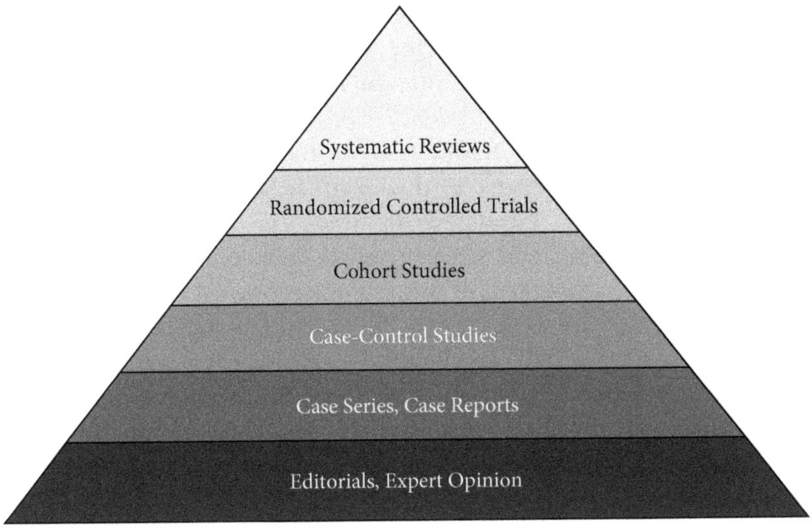

Figure 1. The Evidence Hierarchy[10]

broader canvas of scientific knowledge and use of evidence by scientific communities. The use of knowledge, falsifiability of scientific claims, paradigms and the Duhem–Quine thesis, will be discussed briefly to understand the foundations of evidence-based medicine, certain critiques formulated against it and its relevance here.

The use of evidence in science has been discussed extensively by Thomas Kuhn and Karl Popper: in general, Popper is interested in the logic of science, while Kuhn focused on its history.[11] Kuhn contends that it is a scientist's work within a paradigm that structures how they see their data; this means that our observations are always theory-laden and can never reveal the 'natural order' of things. These theorists are relevant for the formulation of guidelines as their work examines the nature of science in society and opens up 'scientific procedures' to critical scrutiny by social scientists.

10 © Some Rights Reserved CC-BY-NC-SA 3.0 licence. Available at: <https://creativecommons.org/licenses/by-nc-sa/3.0/>. Levels of Evidence, Evidence-Based Practice in the Health Sciences Tutorials, Information Services Department of the Library of the Health Sciences-Chicago, University of Illinois at Chicago. Available at: <https://uic.blackboard.com/courses/1/cont.library_tutorials.jamied.1/content/_4166951_1/dir_NursingResearchDesign.zip/index.html>.

11 Thomas S Kuhn, *The Structure of Scientific Revolutions* (University of Chicago Press 1970).

Popper's claim that scientific knowledge depends on the falsifiability of statements established a specific way of looking at the logic of knowledge. By introducing this criterion, he intended to provide a way of demarcating science from non-science.[12] Progress in science can therefore be achieved through the falsification of theories of knowledge and their subsequent replacement by theories that have greater explanatory power to explain the phenomena to which the theory relates. Many have critiqued Popper and his distrust of induction as a method of science, but a full assessment of this critique is beyond the scope of this book.[13] Popper's work is important for our discussion as randomised controlled trials (RCTs), an important element of evidence-based medicine, are based on a logic that looks for falsifiable statements. This work explores how members of guideline groups evaluate evidence based on an understanding of science informed by these philosophical critiques.

Lakatos has extended both Popper's and Kuhn's work by identifying research programmes, comparable to Kuhn's paradigms, which consist of a 'hard core' together with auxiliary hypotheses.[14] He suggests that auxiliary hypotheses can be abandoned without threatening the theoretical core of a theory. Only when this hard core is refuted does a paradigm (or research programme) shift occur; this is in line with Kuhn's historical view of science. Lakatos' auxiliary hypotheses were inspired by the work of Duhem. Duhem[15] and Quine[16] extended Lakatos' theory, by stating that it is impossible to test a scientific hypothesis in isolation because it requires background assumptions about other hypotheses, which must be correct. So, if one falsifies a single hypothesis it is not known whether this was because the hypothesis is indeed false or because one of the background assumptions or auxiliary hypotheses are false. Again, this is relevant for the analysis of evidence-based medicine because RCTs aim precisely to do what Duhem and Quine suggest is impossible: to test a hypothesis in isolation. They suggest that it is possible

---

12 Karl Raimund Popper, *The Logic of Scientific Discovery* (Psychology Press 2002).

13 For example: Paul Feyerabend, *Against Method* (Verso 2010); David Miller, 'Some Hard Questions for Critical Rationalism' (2014) 15 *Discusiones Filosóficas* 15.

14 Imre Lakatos, *The Methodology of Scientific Research Programmes* (Cambridge University Press 1999).

15 Pierre Maurice Marie Duhem, *The Aim and Structure of Physical Theory* (Princeton University Press 1991).

16 WV Quine, 'Main Trends in Recent Philosophy: Two Dogmas of Empiricism' (1951) 60 *The Philosophical Review* 20.

to falsify a theory, or a bundle of hypotheses as a whole, so, in this sense, their work is congruent with that of Kuhn and Lakatos. Equally, it could be argued that guideline group members may not want to evaluate evidence in isolation but instead may wish to examine groups of medical studies to help them decide whether a change of clinical practice is warranted. As a result, these philosophical concerns may feed directly into the development process of a medical guideline. Understanding academic thinking on philosophy of science is directly relevant here.

2.2.1. CRITIQUES OF THE EVIDENCE HIERARCHY

An epidemiological approach has not been accepted uncritically within medicine: there are several critiques that are important in considering the role of evidence. To understand the role evidence plays for guideline makers we need to understand how doctors and policymakers understand and use knowledge.

Evidence-based medicine has been challenged within the literature on the grounds of its selectiveness and conservative employment of knowledge.[17] For example, Chin-Yee[18] is insightful in his critique of the limited nature of knowledge in evidence-based medicine and addresses 'underdetermination'. This is the idea that 'empirical evidence alone provides insufficient grounds for acceptance or rejection of scientific theories and therefore underdetermines our beliefs about the world.'[19] The relevance of this argument for our study is his contention that we need several different forms of knowledge to overcome the problem of underdetermination. Chin-Yee rightly draws attention to the fact that 'evidence-based medicine' is quite a specific way of conceptualising

---

17 Among many: Abhaya V Kulkarni, 'The Challenges of Evidence-Based Medicine: A Philosophical Perspective' (2005) 8 *Medicine, Health Care and Philosophy* 255; Benjamin H Chin-Yee, 'Underdetermination in Evidence-Based Medicine' (2014) 20 *Journal of Evaluation in Clinical Practice* 921; Aaron Michael Cohen, P Zoë Stavri and William R Hersh, 'A Categorization and Analysis of the Criticisms of Evidence-Based Medicine' (2004) 73 *International Journal of Medical Informatics* 35; Maya J Goldenberg, 'On Evidence and Evidence-Based Medicine: Lessons from the Philosophy of Science' (2006) 62 *Social Science & Medicine* 2621; John Worrall, 'What Evidence in Evidence-Based Medicine?' (2002) 69 *Philosophy of Science* S316; Edwin Harari, 'Whose Evidence? Lessons from the Philosophy of Science and the Epistemology of Medicine' (2001) 35 *Australian and New Zealand Journal of Psychiatry* 724.

18 Chin-Yee, ibid.

19 Ibid, 922.

medicine and that there are other complementary ways of generating knowledge, in his words:

> Such an epistemic attitude imposes limitations on medical research: by failing to probe core beliefs regarding the mechanisms of disease and therapeutics, EBM fails to generate a theoretical framework that is necessary for hypothesis generation and integrating knowledge to develop new treatments. Although clinical studies are an important component of medical research, clinical trials are not the sole epistemic authority in medical knowledge nor are they effective as a singular research heuristic.[20]

While these arguments are mainly directed towards clinical science and the epistemological underpinnings of research, these ideas can be neatly transposed into the domain of guideline construction. This literature reminds us that there are competing knowledge claims at play and that the evidence hierarchy as envisaged by evidence-based medicine is not the only way of conceptualising evidence in medicine. In the formation of guidelines, two complementary critiques of 'evidence' generated by randomised clinical trials are possible: one draws attention to the fact that there might be methodological limitations in conducting an RCT, and the second that highlights that some knowledge claims cannot be made by using clinical trials. Both elements are relevant if we want to conceptualise the nature of evidence use in guideline creation.

If we take the first point about the methodological limitations of RCTs, we can see a real challenge for the use of evidence in medicine. We can challenge whether the results of an RCT are valid in the 'real' world and whether these results should lead to the conclusion that a causal relationship exists between the intervention and the alleviation of symptoms. Existing empirical research suggests that this is a pertinent point in many guideline group discussions.[21] Critiques on the methodological limits of RCTs reveal the number of assumptions necessary before we can infer a causal relationship between Treatment X helping to cure Disease Y. It also helps us to understand that appraisal of evidence is vital in deciding to what extent a certain study can dislodge an entrenched idea about a given disease or condition. A parallel with

---

20 Ibid, 921.

21 T Moreira, 'Diversity in Clinical Guidelines: The Role of Repertoires of Evaluation' (2005) 60 *Social Science & Medicine* 1975.

Kuhn's paradigm is appropriate here; in that one study that disproves a 'theory' about how a disease should be treated does not immediately necessitate a change, but if a body of knowledge exists that points in a different direction this might dislodge the orthodox position and lead to a new paradigm.

The second critique by Chin draws attention to the fact some knowledge cannot be established by RCTs. It is also necessary to understand disease pathology and rely on basic science to help establish the effectiveness of treatments because they reveal the underlying mechanisms of disease.[22] The evidence-based medicine approach thus fails to ask *why* treatments work and focuses only on the fact that they do appear to work. Clinical knowledge about disease pathology is necessary, however, to distinguish between classes or groups of patients for which a certain study is relevant and others for which that is not the case. This helps us to understand the postulated objective nature of evidence-based medicine. The evidence hierarchy suggests that higher quality evidence is more objective and thus better; however, we now know normative assumptions about the nature of knowledge underpin this hierarchy. In this context, knowledge is neither 'natural' nor complete, but rather based on several normative assumptions about the nature of knowledge; it is, in essence, politically and socially constructed.

This political nature of knowledge deserves further scrutiny. This book will address these arguments about knowledge and engage with these philosophical concerns in an empirical way. It will provide an important addition to this strand of the evidence-based literature because, so far, the question of whether these philosophical doubts about the theoretical underpinnings has any effect on how clinicians think of evidence-based medicine has not been addressed. By combining the literature which paints a normative picture of what evidence-based medicine should look like, with knowledge on how this is brought into practice, a more detailed understanding of the role of evidence-based medicine in influencing the development of medical guidelines can be reached. This can be seen as filling a gap in the literature because these arguments have not been brought to bear in the empirical study of guidelines.

---

22 Ibid, 926.

2.2.2. OBJECTIVITY AND EVIDENCE

Evidence-based medicine is not only analysed from a medical viewpoint; the literature in the tradition of science and technology studies understands guidelines in a broader sense as an attempt to create objectivity. A different strand stresses the normativity of the use of instruments such as guidelines and it is helpful to contrast these two different approaches. The (postulated) objectivity of evidence has been problematised in this literature as socially bound, context dependent and historically shifting. The literature behind this claim sits largely in the field of science and technology studies, which build on Latour's actor-network theory.[23] For example, Cambrosio et al have shown how evidence-based medicine sits within a broader tradition of shifting ways of creating objectivity in medical science which is based on the collective production of evidence.[24] The authors chart an historical transformation of what objectivity means in science, culminating in what they call 'regulatory objectivity'. They posit that different forms of objectivity are in play concurrently:

> As previously noted, recent historical studies have transformed scientific and medical objectivity into a subject of historical inquiry. They have shown how different historical periods have produced different types of objectivity that have subsequently persisted either as autonomous forms or in combination with other types of objectivity. Thus, whereas the objectivity of a statement was once guaranteed by the knowledge and experience of the author of the statement, later periods have tended to privilege mechanical or instrumental objectivity that replaces experts' subjectivity with mechanically produced inscriptions.[25]

This shift from expert to mechanical objectivity can be taken one step further; as Cambrosio et al explain, current arrangements are a combination of human expertise and objects:

> There has therefore been a reversal of objectivity: whereas mechanical objectivity displaces the bearer of objectivity from the human expert to the object, regulatory objectivity turns the focus away from objects towards collective

---

23 Bruno Latour, *Reassembling the Social: An Introduction to Actor-Network-Theory* (Oxford University Press 2005).

24 Alberto Cambrosio and others, 'Regulatory Objectivity and the Generation and Management of Evidence in Medicine' (2006) 63 *Social Science & Medicine* 189.

25 Ibid, 193.

> forms of expertise combining people (clinicians, researchers, administrators, patients, etc.) and objects (entities, instruments, tools, techniques, etc.) connected by specific coordination regimens.[26]

These specific 'coordination regimens' that make the collective production of regulatory objectivity possible include medical guidelines. This approach does not stress the intricate detail of what is created, but rather focuses on the external effect of that creation; as such, the impression of objectivity is created for people viewing the guidelines. One thing we can take from this discussion of regulatory objectivity is the collective nature of considering and creating evidence. Note that the evidence that goes into an evidence-based guideline is transformed through a collective process to produce 'objective scientific facts' at the end of the exercise. This approach categorically highlights the social nature of the process of guideline construction and the social choices that are made within this process. While Cambrosio et al claim a clear shift to regulatory objectivity, suggesting that coordination regimens play a vital role, they leave unanswered exactly how these would function and how it is that people would see the result of this process as objective. These questions are addressed here. This strand of argument is important because it provides insight into a possible way to conceptualise how members of guideline groups might work with medical knowledge and how they can create guidelines that are accepted by medical professionals.

The literature on evidence-based medicine and the use of evidence in guidelines presents a varied picture. On the one hand, evidence-based medicine is heralded as a fundamental change in doing medicine while, on the other hand, others such as Chin-Yee show the importance of 'traditional' sources of knowledge. While much of the medical literature, in its nature, presents evidence-based medicine as a fact and devotes itself to understanding the best way of implementing it, the philosophical and science and technology studies literature provide a more critical engagement with this movement and the conceptual language it has introduced. Here, evidence will play a major role because it describes a large part of the language that is used in guideline documents and the discourses surrounding them. This book will address *evidence* in a socio-legal enquiry and interrogates what evidence means for people, how they use it and what the effects are of

26 Ibid, 194.

this particular language. It seems plausible that the way people negotiate the meaning of a technical term such as evidence will expose a gap between the textbook definition of evidence and the reality of its socially constructed use.

2.3. REGULATION AND THE NATURE OF MEDICAL GUIDELINES

Guidelines are, in contrast to their names, not mere forms of voluntary guidance that can be ignored without consequence, but rather a specific form of professional self-regulation. Before developing this argument further, it is helpful to set out an analysis of the regulatory literature and the position self-regulation has within it. This starts with a look at the development of the regulatory state and presents an analysis of the changing nature and conception of the role regulation plays in society, before going on to establish arguments that view guidelines as regulatory tools which play a role in the regulatory state. This literature helps us explore the argument that guidelines as a regulatory tool can be seen as a method to ward off (undue) influence of the state on a given profession. The second body of relevant literature here deals with issues of professionalisation and professionalism. From this, we can develop ideas about how guidelines are used as a regulatory tool by medical professionals and how they are aimed at achieving behavioural change in clinical practice. The contribution this book aims to make to debates in these two fields is to show how they are connected and bring these disparate literatures together, in such a way that it illuminates how this form of medical regulation functions in a western welfare state. A separate section is devoted to the issue of transparency and the insight the regulation literature provides on the importance of the transparency of regulatory initiatives.

Regulation as a discipline can be approached through an exploration of the literature that is concerned with the changing nature of western states. The regulation literature developed as a response to the (perceived) changing nature of the state's power and the way the state regulates the behaviour of its citizens. One influential definition is Black's 'decentred' definition of regulation:

> Regulation is the sustained and focused attempt to alter the behaviour of others according to defined standards or purposes with the intention of producing a

> broadly identified outcome or outcomes, which may involve mechanisms of standard-setting, information-gathering and behaviour-modification.[27]

The classical model of regulation of citizens' behaviour would consist of law-making in the form of concrete laws that ban certain conduct and contain detailed rules on how to achieve certain societal goals that legislation would promote or, as was common in the former communist East-European States, centralised planning measures. The contribution of the regulation literature is to focus on how, in reality, the state governs its citizens, its governance arrangements and to discuss how this has shifted from a command-and-control type of regulation to a regulatory state now achieving its goals through regulatory action. This shift is first explored and argued in relation to the EU by Majone.[28] He contends that the EU should be thought of as a regulatory state because, instead of centralised administration of policies, it now attempts to change behaviour through independent regulatory agencies.

Majone's article created a watershed in the thinking about the role of the state and his thesis has been confirmed and modified in subsequent work: the Regulatory State,[29] the Audit Society,[30] Regulation Inside Government,[31] the New Regulatory State,[32] the British Regulatory State[33] and Regulatory Capitalism.[34] All these, despite differences in approaches and language, refer to the central phenomenon of the regulatory state, which is analysed by Wincott as the shift 'typically interpreted through conceptual oppositions that have taken us from government to governance, rowing to steering, providing to facilitating, national sovereignty to post-nationalism after the sovereign state and the welfare

27 Julia Black, 'Critical Reflections on Regulation' (January 2002) 20. Available at: <http://www.lse.ac.uk/CARR>.

28 Giandomenico Majone, 'The Rise of the Regulatory State in Europe' (1994) 17 *West European Politics* 77.

29 Ibid.

30 Michael Power, *The Audit Society* (Oxford University Press 1997).

31 Christopher Hood and others, *Regulation inside Government: Waste Watchers, Quality Police, and Sleaze-Busters* (Oxford University Press 1999).

32 John Braithwaite, 'The New Regulatory State and the Transformation of Criminology' (2000) 40 *British Journal of Criminology* 222.

33 Michael Moran, *The British Regulatory State: High Modernism and Hyper-Innovation: High Modernism and Hyper-Innovation* (Oxford University Press 2003).

34 D Levi-Faur, 'The Rise of Regulatory Capitalism: The Global Diffusion of a New Order' (2005) 598 *The Annals of the American Academy of Political and Social Science* 200.

state to the regulatory state'.[35] Recently as a result of the economic crisis and its aftermath, there have been voices in the literature that question the validity of Majone's thesis for the EU today – but that analysis falls outside the scope of this work.[36]

The model of the regulatory state also brought with it changing ideas on how to best govern professions that enjoyed a great deal of autonomy. The work by Power on the audit society deals with this component particularly well. He provides an account of how the regulation of banking has changed from a form of 'club government'[37] to a far more formal relationship in which the banking profession is more clearly regulated and its conduct prescribed through detailed rules within a wider web of detailed governmental rules. In return for this (relative) freedom the government prescribes detailed policy outcomes that this regulation by the profession was meant to satisfy. Governments police this new arrangement by establishing independent regulators, who set standards and monitor the compliance of the profession. A result of these developments is central to this study: the increase of *mandated self-regulation*. This means that a collective group, such as medical professionals, is designated to formulate rules within a broadly defined framework set by the government.[38] The profession is subject to this mandated regulation in both England and the Netherlands, in England directly through the National Institute for Health and Care Excellence (NICE), in the Netherlands as a result of the Act on the Medical Treatment Contract.[39] Guidelines can be developed independently but must fit within this broader framework. These developments are directly relevant to this project as the medical profession is confronted by the broader regulatory changes: medical guidelines play an essential role in a system of mandated self-regulation and warrant further investigation.

---

35 Daniel Wincott, 'European Political Development, Regulatory Governance, and the European Social Model: The Challenge of Substantive Legitimacy' (2006) 12 *European Law Journal* 743.

36 James A Caporaso and others, 'Still a Regulatory State? The European Union and the Financial Crisis' (2015) 22 *Journal of European Public Policy* 889.

37 Moran (n 33).

38 Anthony Ogus, 'Rethinking Self-Regulation' (1995) 15 *Oxford Journal of Legal Studies* 97; Julia Black, 'Constitutionalising Self-Regulation' (1996) 59 *Modern Law Review* 24.

39 Wet op de geneeskundige behandelovereenkomst 1994 (Stb 1994, 837).

2.3.1. THE IMPACT OF HEALTHCARE REGULATION IN ENGLAND AND THE NETHERLANDS

Regulatory developments are not just confined to the financial sphere; they have affected healthcare regulation as well. A good account of the changing landscape of English medical regulation is provided by Wright. He describes the regulation of the NHS as a result of the Labour reforms between 1997 and 2007 using the themes: 'the division of labour between state and society, the division of state, the codification of relationships, the development of meta-regulatory techniques for enforced self-regulation'.[40]

The emergence of NICE in 1999 as a special health authority fits well with the trend described in the regulatory literature and the themes described by White. NICE changed the division of labour between state and society (as it then fell) to within the realm of the state to support the regulation of the medical profession through medical guidelines. This is covered in the literature on self-regulation, which notes how professionalisation was the result of a further division within the state, moving from direct ministerial control to a model with several bodies at arm's-length with various levels of independence. For example, NICE formed a codification of the relationship with the medical profession, moving from an informal settlement with the General Medical Council and the Royal Colleges, who used to be in charge of guidelines, to a formalised relationship with a government body. NICE is now an essential link in a chain of self-regulation that fits neatly with White's thesis on the development of meta-regulatory techniques for self-regulation. It can be described as using meta-regulatory techniques precisely because it facilitates (rather than drafting itself) the production of medical practice guidelines. In turn, these form part of self-regulatory regime, one which is mandated through processes of compliance involving auditing and financial incentives. By overseeing guideline production, NICE is not merely facilitating but also controls – as a regulator – guideline production. It could be said that NICE tries to shape the production of guidelines through these controls, which do not take the form of formal rules but are themselves guidelines in the form of manuals on guideline production.

---

40 John SF Wright, 'The Regulatory State and the UK Labour Government's Re-Regulation of Provision in the English National Health Service' (2009) 3 *Regulation & Governance* 334, 337.

In the Netherlands, the NHG is a professional body of GPs and, as such, produces self-regulation in the form of guidelines.[41] This is an important institutional and regulatory difference between the two countries: the NHG is independent from the state and the production of guidelines is not directly state regulated in the Netherlands. Does this mean that the Netherlands has not become a regulatory state and that we should describe its model as that of the 'old' welfare state? This would be to misunderstand the Dutch healthcare system.

The Dutch healthcare system is as much a part of a regulatory state as the British healthcare system. The Dutch system is based on private hospitals and private healthcare insurers who compete to attract patients/the insured. It is managed by the *Nederlandse Zorgautoriteit* and *Zorginstituut Nederland* who, similar to the English system, regulate the (quasi) market in healthcare. The details of the Dutch healthcare system are covered in greater detail in chapter 3. The key point for the current discussion is that the NHG and its guideline functions is one area where medical practitioners, it seems, have retained autonomy. There is no central institution in the Netherlands for the production of guidelines, but rather a multitude of which the NHG is one. Other institutions, such as the *Zorginstituut*, point towards the conclusion that the Netherlands is much like England and there is mandated self-regulation at play, even if it initially appears more dispersed in its operation. The complicated, precise interrelation between these elements of healthcare systems, institutions and guidelines is further explored in chapters 4 and 5.

2.3.2. GUIDELINES AS REGULATORY TOOLS

The changes that the rise of the regulatory state has brought to the regulatory systems and institutions of healthcare in both the Netherlands and England is relevant because it provides one of the reasons why we have seen a multiplication of guidelines. It feeds a demand for accountability partly fuelled by the different arrangement of healthcare governance due to the rise of the regulatory state in (western) Europe. Of course, the position is more nuanced than that; endogenous developments in medicine have also played a role.[42] The proliferation of

41 Called NHG-standaarden. Available at: www.nhg.org.

42 Ruud van Herk, Rita Schepers and Anton F Casparie, 'Huisartsen en zelfregulering. De ontwikkeling van intercollegiale toesting en standaarden voor huisartsen tussen 1970

guidelines as such is not of central relevance here, but importantly this growth has led to such a change in the role of guidelines that this author would claim that they can now be seen as *regulatory tools*. As far as this author is aware, this argument has not been advanced in the scholarly literature before, but it follows from the existing regulatory literature and would place medical guidelines in the same category as the International Swaps and Derivatives Association (ISDA) master-agreement, International Organization for Standardization (ISO) standards and financial standards developed by the Basel Group.[43]

To support the argument that guidelines are attempts at standard-setting, information gathering and behaviour modification to achieve certain outcomes, a short history of their development is set out. When they were initially developed in the Netherlands and England, guidelines were measures to ensure that scientific medical knowledge was widely available and was kept up to date. Guidelines were also designed to support internal auditing of medical professionals by other medical professionals, as Everdingen and Klazinga describe in detail.[44] They quickly developed a broader appeal and became instruments to improve the quality of care.[45] With this development it also became possible for external parties to use guidelines as a transparency mechanism over what the profession regards as 'good quality care'.[46] In both England and the Netherlands the government uses guidelines as a tool to reduce practice variation and increase quality, while simultaneously saving costs by further rationalising care.[47]

---

en 1990' (1994) <https://lirias.kuleuven.be/handle/123456789/161090>; Cornelia de Vos, 'Kwaliteit, disciplinering en sturing. Een historisch sociologisch onderzoek naar de vormgeving van kwaliteit van zorg in ziekenhuizen = Quality, discipline and governance. A historical sociological study into the design of quality of care in hospitals' (Erasmus Universiteit Rotterdam 2014).

43 Julia Black, 'Constructing and Contesting Legitimacy and Accountability in Polycentric Regulatory Regimes' (2008) 2 *Regulation & Governance* 137; Julia Black and David Rouch, 'The Development of the Global Markets as Rule-Makers: Engagement and Legitimacy' (2008) 2 *Law and Financial Markets Review* 218.

44 van Everdingen (Chapter 1, n 2); N Klazinga, 'Quality Management of Medical Specialist Care in the Netherlands. An Explorative Study of its Nature and Development' (Erasmus Universiteit Rotterdam 1996).

45 R van Herk, 'Artsen onder druk. Het kwaliteitsbeleid van de medische beroepen in Groot-Brittannië, Nederland en België tussen 1970 en 1996, als gevolg van de interne en externe druk op de zelfregulering van artsen.' (Erasmus Universiteit Rotterdam 1997); de Vos (n 42).

46 N Klazinga, 'Compliance with Practice Guidelines: Clinical Autonomy Revisited' (1994) 28 *Health Policy* (Amsterdam, Netherlands) 51.

47 de Vos (n 42).

Guidelines have become central objects in the complex interplay between the internal regulation of the profession and external control and oversight of self-regulation by the government. They are thus tools of mandated self-regulation used as a form of professional self-regulation and *at the same time* an instrument of control for governments to co-opt professionals to fulfil government aims such as, standardisation of care, cost-effectiveness, rationalisation and patient involvement.[48]

A crucial result of these developments is the fact that guidelines always suffer from a *tension* between these two interconnected aspects: a regulatory tool for control over clinicians and regulatory tool to satisfy and *limit* government control. By defining autonomy for the clinician in medical guidelines the profession tries to prevent the government controlling this aspect of their professional role. Does this tension have an effect on the development of guidelines and how this might be reflected in their text?

To explore in greater depth what guidelines as regulatory tools for professionals might mean and how they are employed, we must look beyond the regulatory literature to academic work on the sociology of professions.

2.3.3. PROFESSIONALISATION

The sociology of professions provides us with a framework with which to address the importance of guidelines as a project of professional regulation. Evetts provides a useful description of three central concepts in this sociological sub-field: profession, professionalisation and professionalism.[49] Where profession refers to 'a distinct and generic category of occupational work',[50] Evetts notes there is no generic definition that demarcates a profession from a mere occupation. Professionalisation, however, is referred to 'as the process to achieve the status of profession and has been interpreted as the process to pursue, develop and maintain the closure of the occupational group in order to maintain practitioners own occupational self-interests in terms

48 In Chapter 3, the history of guideline development will be considered in greater depth in relation to the specific case studies under consideration. Transparency and its importance in understanding guidelines will be explored separately below.

49 Julia Evetts, 'Sociological Analysis of Professionalism: Past, Present and Future' (2011) 10 *Comparative Sociology* 1.

50 Ibid, 6.

of their salary, status and power as well as the monopoly protection of the occupational jurisdiction'.[51]

Medicine has always been regarded as a profession (notwithstanding the failure to arrive at a generic definition) and its professionalisation has been described in terms of the 'medical dominance' thesis advanced by Freidson,[52] but also in more pessimistic terms as suffering from 'proletarianization and de-skilling.'[53] The most relevant element of this literature for our discussion of guidelines, however, is the sub-field that engages with professionalism and its link to trust. As Evetts states:

> Professionalism in occupations and professions implies the importance of trust in economic relations in modern societies with an advanced division of labour. In other words, lay people must place their trust in professional workers (electricians and plumbers as well as lawyers and doctors) and some professionals must acquire confidential knowledge.[54]

Guidelines are a part of this process in a couple of interrelated ways. They are part of making trust more explicit in some aspects of the relationship between doctor and patient: because they mediate the doctor–patient relationship by making explicit what advice the doctor relies on (whether the patient is aware of this is another question) and introducing an external source of knowledge that both parties rely on. Furthermore, guidelines relate to the 'confidential knowledge' Evetts refers to because they make explicit previously 'implicit' knowledge understood without codification by medical practitioners. By publishing the guidelines, some of the knowledge healthcare professionals use has become (more) public and is now open to criticism by external parties. The focus for this enquiry is the possibility that professionals (and by extension the doctor–patient encounter) can be controlled through guidelines. Fournier provides a good assessment of this process in describing professionalism as a disciplinary tool 'which inscribes "autonomous" professional practice within a network of accountability and governs professional conduct at a distance'.[55]

---

51 Ibid.

52 Eliot Freidson, *Professionalism, the Third Logic* (University of Chicago Press 2001).

53 John B McKinlay and Joan Arches, 'Towards the Proletarianization of Physicians' (1985) 15 *International Journal of Health Services* 161; John B McKinlay and John D Stoeckle, 'Corporatization and the Social Transformation of Doctoring' (1988) 18 *International Journal of Health Services* 191.

54 Evetts (n 49) 4.

55 Valérie Fournier, 'The Appeal to "Professionalism" as a Disciplinary Mechanism' (1999) 47 *Sociological Review* 280.

Guidelines used by NICE or the NHG, irrespective of the differences in institutional context we might observe, both strive for 'professionalisation'. This aim, of course, is not described in direct terms using the language of disciplinary tools; rather it is presented as part of a broader mission of improving the quality of care. Based on this literature, one element that is likely to play a role in the deliberations of guideline makers is what 'image' they have of their audience (healthcare professionals) and the fact that they will have to respond to what healthcare professionals want from a guideline. Guidelines can be more or less ambitious depending on the level of change they demand in the working practices of healthcare professionals. While attention is paid to the micro-politics of guideline production[56] within a guideline group and research exists on the political consequences of guideline making for other healthcare actors like the government,[57] this relationship between professionals within the guideline group and those outside is neglected. There is reason to include this here because the way a guideline group defines their role in the regulation of professionals, by the use of guidelines, directly influences the amount of leeway they have to adopt recommendations that change clinical practice. It is likely, but as yet unclear, that the room for change in clinical practice correlates with the specific position of the guideline-producing organisation in relation to the professional associations of the various medical professionals affected. In a more corporatist healthcare system, such as the Dutch system, one could expect less room for clinical change than in a more top-down organised guideline-making process in England. So, it is plausible that in a system with more dispersed guideline making, the relationship between the healthcare professionals who must follow the guidelines and those who draft them are closer than in a system where guidelines are always made by a multidisciplinary group of professionals. This book will explore whether these assumptions hold true.

2.3.4. TRANSPARENCY AS A STRUCTURING FORCE INFLUENCING GUIDELINES

An important element that drives the success of guidelines as regulatory tools is the transparency of the process of developing the guideline.

---

56 Ruth McDonald and Stephen Harrison, 'The Micropolitics of Clinical Guidelines: An Empirical Study' (2004) 32 *Policy & Politics* 223.

57 Moreira (n 21).

Transparency has several different functions and shapes the development of guidelines in various ways. Understanding how calls for transparency are described in the regulatory literature and the debates surrounding this concept will provide further pointers for an empirical examination of the process of guideline development.

Transparency is closely connected to processes of accountability in modern regulatory states. Evidence-based medicine and tools surrounding its rise, quality assessments, performance indicators, rankings, clinical audits and guidelines, are all in various ways aimed at creating a greater transparency of professional practice for outside observers.[58] Some of the literature on this topic paints the response of professionals in negative terms and suggests active resistance by professionals to these transparency initiatives.[59] Levay and Waks, however, shine a light on a more positive engagement of professionals with these transparency initiatives in the Swedish healthcare setting:

> Professional involvement in transparency technologies in the two cases developed despite initial resistance, largely in response to outside pressures. Professionals perceived the need to *legitimize [stress in original]* their work in the face of external demands … However, the transparency techniques also seemed to correspond to professionals' own conceptions of how to *develop [stress in original]* quality in modern healthcare organizations. Accreditation and national quality registries could be used both to assure minimal quality levels and standardized procedures and to develop new ways of organizing work.[60]

Their argument is interesting because they show how by working with these initiatives professionals retain control over the criteria of their own evaluation: 'On the contrary, they still managed to control many of the premises and criteria of evaluation. Professionals were neither independent in evaluating their own work, nor in the hands of external evaluators, but enjoyed a negotiated, "soft" professional autonomy.'[61]

This literature suggests that transparency projects can lead to resistance and a loss of autonomy but at the same time can strengthen autonomy

58 Power (n 30); Charlotta Levay and Caroline Waks, 'Professions and the Pursuit of Transparency in Healthcare: Two Cases of Soft Autonomy' (2009) 30 *Organization Studies* 509.

59 Haridimos Tsoukas, 'The Tyranny of Light: The Temptations and the Paradoxes of the Information Society' (1997) 29 *Futures* 827; Marilyn Strathern, 'The Tyranny of Transparency' (2000) 26 *British Educational Research Journal* 309.

60 Levay and Waks (n 58) 519.

61 Ibid, 523.

within the new boundaries set as a result of the interaction between state and profession. This book will explore whether the argument that medical guidelines are used in such a positive way, to establish autonomy is valid and builds on the work of Levay and Waks by exploring transparency in guidelines. Transparency that is specific to medical guidelines has not received attention in the literature so far.

How transparent guideline makers are during their drafting may help to provide an explanation for some of the differences in guidelines between countries. For example, in England, recent guidelines by NICE all follow the GRADE-approach to grade evidence.[62] This is a process developed to help guideline makers consider which studies should be included in the evidence base of a guideline. This works through a process of developing an assessment of the strength of the certainty that the result of the study is not a coincidental result but represents a casual relation. In other words, this instrument helps make explicit the potential sources of bias in the studies that underpin guidelines. The results of the GRADE analysis are available online and are open to the public: this improves the visibility of the guideline drafting process in England. Other guidelines might not follow this approach, which might explain some of the differences we observe between them. The specific relevance of this literature will be examined in the context of the case studies in the following chapters.

Through the construction of evidence tables, the GRADE-methodology tries to improve the visibility of the relevance and strength of the evidence used to base recommendations on in guidelines. This is an important aspect of the claim that guidelines are evidence-based: it provides for a possibility to check the basis for every recommendation made in a guideline and assess, as a reader, whether you agree with the analysis. Knaapen places this development in the key of the 'EBM-ness' of guidelines: 'Not (quantitative) Evidence but specific procedural rules are the central feature of "being EBM", reflecting a new type of objectivity that Cambrosio and colleagues … have called "regulatory objectivity".'[63] This has been identified as important because the GRADE approach leads to the adoption of evidence that is placed higher in the evidence hierarchy.

---

62 Gordon H Guyatt and others, 'GRADE: An Emerging Consensus on Rating Quality of Evidence and Strength of Recommendations' (2008) 336 *BMJ* 924; ibid, 'Grading Quality of Evidence and Strength of Recommendations' (2004) 328 *BMJ* 1490.

63 Loes Knaapen, 'Being "Evidence-Based" in the Absence of Evidence: The Management of Non-Evidence in Guideline Development' (2013) 43 *Social Studies of Science* 681, 701.

These guidelines might differ from those that do not adopt this approach and use less systematic ways of selecting evidence.

Another example of a transparency tool that has gained prominence in the field of guidelines is the Appraisal of Guidelines for Research and Evaluation (AGREE) tool, alongside the updated AGREE II.[64] This defines several procedural criteria that guidelines have to meet, making it possible to compare guidelines on different diseases and in different countries.[65] The claim that guidelines that score highly on these procedural criteria are also high-quality guidelines is questioned within the literature.[66] The AGREE tool promotes transparency of procedures for developing guidelines, as it is online and available for public review.

A final example is the Centre for Evidence-Based Medicine Outcome Monitoring Project (COMPare) in which the authors research the prevalence of reporting bias: the incorrect reporting of the outcomes of clinical trials,[67] which could lead to clinical differences being due to chance or the effects being exaggerated.[68] If guideline drafters are aware of these errors in reporting, this could influence the confidence they have in the results of these studies. This also highlights the risks that could flow from human error in negative influencing the evidence guideline makers use to make decisions.

These attempts at improving the transparency of guidelines could have an indirect effect on guideline makers and explain guideline differences because they help steer a process of evidence selection and define criteria for attaching weight to some evidence (studies with low degrees

64 AGREE Collaboration, 'Development and Validation of an International Appraisal Instrument for Assessing the Quality of Clinical Practice Guidelines: The AGREE Project' (2003) 12 *Quality and Safety in Health Care* 18; Melissa C Brouwers and others, 'AGREE II: Advancing Guideline Development, Reporting and Evaluation in Health Care' (2010) 63 *Journal of Clinical Epidemiology* 1308.

65 Pablo Alonso-Coello and others, 'The Quality of Clinical Practice Guidelines over the Last Two Decades: A Systematic Review of Guideline Appraisal Studies' (2010) 19 *Quality and Safety in Health Care* 1.

66 Joseph C Watine and Peter S Bunting, 'Mass Colorectal Cancer Screening: Methodological Quality of Practice Guidelines is not Related to their Content Validity' (2008) 41 *Clinical Biochemistry* 459.

67 Which means not reporting them in accordance with the guidelines for those as contained in the CONSORT-statement. Kenneth F Schulz, Douglas G Altman and David Moher, 'CONSORT 2010 Statement: Updated Guidelines for Reporting Parallel Group Randomised Trials' (2010) 340 *BMJ* c332.

68 Ben Goldacre and others, 'COMPare: A Prospective Cohort Study Correcting and Monitoring 58 Misreported Trials in Real Time' (2019) 20 *Trials* 118; Ben Goldacre and others, 'COMPare: Qualitative Analysis of Researchers' Responses to Critical Correspondence on a Cohort of 58 Misreported Trials' (2019) 20 *Trials* 124.

of bias and so a high degree of confidence in the result). If these criteria are followed, this might lead to different choices in what is defined as 'evidence' and, as a result, different recommendations between guidelines. Plausibly, this could also lead to more consistency in selecting evidence in response to the transparency brought about by these instruments. As a result, the role transparency initiatives have on guideline decision-making will be discussed here.

2.3.5. MAKING SENSE OF GUIDELINES AS REGULATION

The regulatory and sociological literature enable the argument that guidelines are a particular form of professional-mandated self-regulation which straddles the divide between regulation to control professionals and regulation to control (further) state intervention by controlling the criteria of evaluation. How those two, sometimes contradictory, rationales play out in practice and in this way contribute to the literature in both the field of sociology as well as regulation is discussed here. Furthermore, the role of the transparency initiatives identified in this process will be considered.

2.4. INSTITUTIONAL LITERATURE ON GUIDELINE-PRODUCING ORGANISATIONS

So far, we have mainly considered guidelines and guideline drafters in isolation, as if guidelines are produced in a vacuum. However, we should not neglect the institutional environment in which guideline drafting takes place: we should consider the impact of institutions on guideline drafting. To date, the institutional context of guideline drafting has not been considered explicitly in the main body of medical guideline literature. This represents an important gap in the literature and more research is needed to draw attention to the institutional dimensions of guideline drafting. Institutional understandings offer a more nuanced understanding of the ways in which guidelines differ, allowing us to see the role institutions have in promoting specific guidelines.

This book will focus on the mechanisms that structure institutions and their relationships to actors within those institutions. It does not aim to provide a full institutional history of medical regulation. By focusing on the institutional element of guideline drafting it is expected that new insights might be gained about the factors that influence guideline drafting by bringing to the fore elements that have so far been neglected in their discussion. The comparative design is particularly suited to bring more clarity to this issue by enabling a comparison between relatively similar medical communities, one in the Netherlands and one in England. This section will present three different institutional literatures that are particularly relevant for the study of the development of guidelines: sociological institutionalism, the institutional regulation of conflicts of interest and the institutional role of cost and cost-effectiveness as a factor that influences the development of guidelines.

2.4.1. INSTITUTIONAL THEORY

Central to the development of guidelines are guideline groups. These are presented as being independent in their operation and it is perhaps for that reason that an institutional focus is absent in the literature. While attention is paid to the micro-level of guideline development by Pagliari et al,[69] and to European cooperation between different guideline makers,[70] the relationship between guideline-making institutions and guideline groups and how they could potentially influence each other often goes unquestioned.

Modern sociological institutionalism,[71] the term used by Meyer,[72] provides a way of conceptualising organisations and their relation to other actors. In this strand of the organisational literature, actors are both empowered and constricted by the institutional context of organisations and institutional forces provide a rationale for action. Meyer describes this in these terms:

> Here, actors are substantially empowered and controlled by institutional contexts, and these contexts go far beyond a few norms or network structures …

69 C Pagliari, J Grimshaw and M Eccles, 'The Potential Influence of Small Group Processes on Guideline Development' (2001) 7 *Journal of Evaluation in Clinical Practice* 165.

70 Loes Knaapen, 'European Regulation and Harmonization of Clinical Practice Guidelines' in Scott L Greer and Paulette Kurzer (eds), *European Union Public Health Policy: Regional and Global Trends* (Routledge 2013).

71 Paul J DiMaggio and Walter W Powell, 'The Iron Cage Revisited: Institutional Isomorphism and Collective Rationality in Organizational Fields' (1983) 48 *American Sociological Review* 147; Walter W Powell and Paul J DiMaggio, *The New Institutionalism in Organizational Analysis* (University of Chicago Press 1991).

72 John W Meyer, 'Reflections on Institutional Theories of Organizations', *The SAGE Handbook of Organizational Institutionalism* (SAGE 2008).

> Institutions, in these conceptions are packages or programs of an expanded sort. "Regimes" is a term employed in political science for the idea – organizational packages infused with cultural meaning.[73]

Actors do not act in an unconstrained way out of self-interest,[74] but are instead within bounds that constrain certain courses of action and legitimise others. In this realist (or constructivist) perspective, actors are not only influenced by their institutional environment but also constructed by it.[75] This approach will be adopted and built on because it allows for a more nuanced understanding of the conflicting forces of actors and institutions.

In exploring the notion of the actor in modern society, Meyer and Jepperson provide an interesting account of a specific future of modern 'actorhood', one that provides a useful description.[76] They present the notion of 'agentic actors' who not only work for, or because of, their immediate interest, but also work towards becoming a more effective agent for himself and others.[77] These actors are highly standardised through a process of isomorphism,[78] where organisations become structurally similar and the way actors behave within them conforms to standardised models of individualism. In describing a society made up of these 'agentic actors' they suggest how collective action and social status is bound up with pretence about the interests of others, by which they mean the expression of cultural ideals. They describe the role of professionals in these terms:

> The great enhancement of the centrality of "disinterested" professionalized others is a notable development of modern society, one difficult to account for in terms of interests or functional requirements. (Indeed, demonstrations of functionality are conspicuous for their absence.) The definers and carriers of social agency – especially those more removed from direct responsibility for mundane self-interested actorhood – are granted substantial authority and prominence. The most canonical authority is that of the professional who

---

73 Ibid, 791–792.

74 An axiomatic feature of economic models of human agency.

75 This book does not, therefore, seek to engage with the work of Foucault or that of Luhmann, even though the relevance of their thinking for a potential construction of the role of actors in institutions is acknowledged.

76 John W Meyer and Ronald L Jepperson, 'The "Actors" of Modern Society: The Cultural Construction of Social Agency' (2000) 18 *Sociological Theory* 100.

77 Ibid, 107.

78 DiMaggio and Powell (n 71).

> serves no actor but rather the high truths of the rationalized natural and moral universe: pure other-hood (…).[79]

Restating their argument more simply: they describe that for individuals to be accorded a high social status in society, they are required, at least putatively, to describe their endeavours to be directed towards the achievement of cultural goals, rather than self-interest. This provides interesting new insights for conceptualising the process of developing medical guidelines. This literature suggests that actors might be self-interested and act to further these interests but, when confronted by the necessity of the institutional scripts that are connected to this activity, they must present themselves as being disinterested, neutral, enactors of scientific knowledge[80] to further the interests of medicine.

A sociological institutionalist approach will be used here to understand and interpret the experiences of collectively producing medical guidelines, while at the same time accounting for the cultural scripts produced and maintained by the guideline-making organisations of which they form a part. This theory will be useful in trying to see how the development of guidelines might be a contextualised and socially constructed process of collective organisation.

2.4.2. INSTITUTIONAL REGULATION OF CONFLICTS OF INTEREST

While sociological institutionalism has provided a general approach to conceptualising the role of institutions in the development of guidelines, a more detailed analysis of the institutional regulation of conflicts of interest is particularly relevant here. The prevailing medical norms (or scripts in the institutional literature) mandate that (medical) organisations have a policy to deal with (actual or perceived) conflicts of interest. Here we can observe a form of institutional isomorphism, as described earlier, in so far as the NHG and NICE adopt very similar institutional procedures and policies in this area.

Potential conflicts of interest have led to an institutional response in medical regulation: both NICE and the NHG recognise that conflicts

---

79 Meyer and Jepperson (n 76) 115.

80 The 'evidence' as described in detail earlier.

of interest might occur and require disclosure. The NICE guideline manual[81] and the NHG 'procedure book'[82] require both financial as well as non-financial conflicts of interest to be reported on disclosure forms before the making of a guideline and these declarations must be kept up to date. The NHG procedure book states that if there is doubt about the independence of a guideline group member, he/she can be excluded.[83] The NICE policy on conflicts of interest states that if there is a specific financial interest, the person cannot attend the meeting the interest relates to; this might also be the case for specific non-financial interest. All other types of non-specific interest must be declared but do not preclude participation.[84] In this way both institutions try to find a balance between including the experts and profiting from their expertise while avoiding a biased guideline. Both institutions allow someone with a conflict of interests to participate, but prevents that person from influencing decisions where there is a direct financial conflict of interest. The conflicts of interest literature lays the groundwork to analyse whether these policies are only adhered to on paper rather than in practice and whether we are able to discern any association between a conflict of interest and the recommendations in a guideline. The underlying assumption of much of this literature is that without such institutional controls on participation, guideline groups will draft guidelines that are biased towards the pharmaceutical industry. This book will endeavour, as far as possible, to uncover whether this can be said to be the case or whether this institutional regulation provides an effective bulwark against such undue influence.

The concept of 'regulatory capture' expresses the idea that guideline-making bodies could be biased on an institutional level.[85] Regulatory capture literature suggests that NICE and the NHG could be 'captured' by the pharmaceutical companies to produce and promote guidelines that favour their products, in contrast to generic medication made by

---

81 NICE, 'Developing NICE Guidelines: The Manual' (2014) <https://www.nice.org.uk/process/pmg20/resources/developing-nice-guidelines-the-manual-2014-edition-pdf-6596134525>.

82 NHG, 'Procedureboek 2010' <https://www.nhg.org/sites/default/files/content/nhg_org/uploads/procedureboek_versie_090810.pdf>.

83 Ibid, 15.

84 NICE, 'Code of Practice for Declaring and Managing Conflicts of Interest' 7 <https://www.nice.org.uk/Media/Default/About/Who-we-are/Policies-and-procedures/code-of-practice-for-declaring-and-managing-conflicts-of-interest.pdf>.

85 George J Stigler, 'The Theory of Economic Regulation' (1971) 2 *The Bell Journal of Economics and Management Science* 3.

competitors, to give an example. Regulators would then no longer work in the 'public interest' making evidence-based guidelines to increase the quality of medicine, but instead work to further the private interests and profits of companies.

The fact that NICE and NHG have policies on paper aimed at dealing with individual conflicts of interest of guideline group members, does not preclude this form of bias. Direct funding of NICE and NHG would be one way in which regulatory capture could occur. There are, however, no direct financial links between the industry and the guideline-making bodies, as both are funded by the state or through a combination of private professional fees and state funding. Another way in which these bodies could be 'captured' is termed 'cognitive capture':[86] here, guideline-making institutions start to identify (too) strongly with the interests of industry instead of keeping a professional distance. This might be a factor that could explain differences in guidelines between countries. The role of pharmaceutical companies in the construction of guidelines and their contacts with NICE and NHG will be analysed to assess the strength of this factor.

2.4.3. THE ROLE OF COSTS IN MEDICAL GUIDELINES

It is important to make the role of the costs of medical treatment more explicit and to highlight the influence this has on building consensus in a guideline group in order to understand how this issue can steer the evaluation of evidence and how institutional factors influence the importance of cost considerations.

An extensive literature that evaluates cost in healthcare exists, mainly emerging from the fields of economics and health policy. A strand of this literature is concerned with designing and validating economic models to use in cost–benefit analysis,[87] while others apply these models in systematic

86 Daniel P Carpenter and David A Moss (eds), *Preventing Regulatory Capture: Special Interest Influence and How to Limit It* (Cambridge University Press 2014).

87 Joan Costa-Font, Christophe Courbage and Alistair McGuire, *The Economics of New Health Technologies* (Oxford University Press 2009); Karl Claxton and others, 'Discounting and Cost-Effectiveness in NICE – Stepping Back to Sort out a Confusion' (2006) 15 *Health Economics* 1; Andrew J Palmer and others, 'The CORE Diabetes Model: Projecting Long-term Clinical Outcomes, Costs and Cost-Effectiveness of Interventions in Diabetes Mellitus (Types 1 and 2) to Support Clinical and Reimbursement Decision-Making' (2004) 20 Suppl 1 *Current Medical Research and Opinion* S5.

reviews of the cost-effectiveness of specific treatments.[88] The use of these cost-effectiveness and cost–benefit analyses techniques has been most prominent in the growing field of health technology assessment.[89]

To give a sense of the scale of this literature, for one disease (diabetes) in one journal (*Health Technology Assessment*) 44 health technology assessment reports have already been published.[90] Health technology assessments are used in evaluating whether new drugs or technologies should be covered by the healthcare system and decision makers rely partly on these economic models to help their decision making. In England, the literature has critically engaged with the cost-effectiveness thresholds NICE uses in its decision making.[91] This suggests that, within NICE, cost-effectiveness has a central place in the drafting of guidelines through its use in health technology assessments. These assessments use an economic threshold above which they will usually not recommend a technology or drug. The expression of this threshold is in ICER's, incremental cost-effectiveness ratio, per quality-adjusted life year (QALY) gained. This threshold is set at £20,000–£30,000 per QALY gained.[92] NICE is careful to say that cost-effectiveness is not the only reason for treatment selection and that it also funds technologies or drugs with higher costs.

---

88 E Loveman and others, 'The Clinical and Cost-Effectiveness of Patient Education Models for Diabetes: A Systematic Review and Economic Evaluation' (2003) 7 *Health Technology Assessment*; WC Peul, 'ZonMw – A Randomised Cost-Effectiveness Study on the Surgical versus Conservative Treatment of Sciatica' <http://www.zonmw.nl/nl/projecten/project-detail/a-randomised-cost-effectiveness-study-on-the-surgical-versus-conservative-treatment-of-sciatica/hoe-nu-verder/>.

89 HTA Commissioning Board, 'Standing Group on Health Technology' (1998) 2 Health Technology Assessment; Pascale Lehoux and Stuart Blume, 'Technology Assessment and the Sociopolitics of Health Technologies' (2000) 25 *Journal of Health Politics, Policy and Law* 1083; Patricia W Stone, Christine R Curran and Suzanne Bakken, 'Economic Evidence for Evidence-Based Practice' (2002) 34 *Journal of Nursing Scholarship* 277; David Banta, 'The Development of Health Technology Assessment' (2003) 63 *Health Policy* 121; Carl May, 'Mobilising Modern Facts: Health Technology Assessment and the Politics of Evidence' (2006) 28 *Sociology of Health & Illness* 513.

90 Available at: <https://www-journalslibrary-nihr-ac-uk./collections/diabetes/>.

91 Centre for Health Economics, The University of York, 'NICE Threshold' <http://www.york.ac.uk/che/research/teehta/thresholds/>; Nancy Devlin and David Parkin, 'Does NICE Have a Cost-Effectiveness Threshold and What Other Factors Influence Its Decisions? A Binary Choice Analysis' (2004) 13 *Health Economics* 437; Karl Claxton and others, *Methods for the Estimation of the NICE Cost Effectiveness Threshold* (University of York, Centre for Health Economics 2013) <http://www.york.ac.uk/media/che/documents/reports/resubmitted_report.pdf>.

92 NICE, 'Guide to the Methods of Technology Appraisal 2013' (2013) para 6 <https://www.nice.org.uk/process/pmg9/chapter/1-foreword>.

While in the field of health technology assessment cost and cost-effectiveness are analysed and extensively debated this has not been true of the use of these methods within guidelines. This is even more surprising because cost-effectiveness modelling is such an important rationale, at least in England. It influences not only health technology assessments but also guidelines through the reference to cost-effectiveness in the NICE guideline manual.[93] It is likely that the effect on drafting a guideline of cost-effectiveness considerations can be considerable. Cost-effectiveness considerations require guideline drafting groups to consider (complex) cost–benefit economic modelling of particular technologies and drugs and a sophisticated cost–benefit weighing exercise against clinical values, patient preferences and other considerations. An attempt is made here to partly fill this gap by evaluating how cost-effectiveness models and considerations feature, if at all, in the development of guidelines and how and to what extent this is reflected in those that are produced. This element of guideline development might also allow for an interesting comparison with the Netherlands because cost-effectiveness considerations are unlikely to play the same role there. While the NHG recognises costs as a factor and recommends prescribing the cheapest medication if the effectiveness is the same,[94] no methodology to integrate cost considerations in guidelines is in use there. This can be explained by the fact that, in the Netherlands, the health technology assessments are performed by the Zorginstituut Netherlands, an advisory body to the Secretary of State for Health, Social Care and Sport.[95] The Dutch NHG has no direct involvement with health technology assessment and, unlike in England there is no relation between a recommendation in a guideline and the funding of treatment, as these decisions are taken by two separate and independent bodies. Given these differences, the question is do cost considerations force English guideline makers to recommend cheaper medication or technologies, whilst the Dutch guideline makers are free to prescribe more expensive medication or technologies regardless

93 NICE, 'Developing NICE Guidelines: The Manual' (2009) ch 7 <http://www.ha-ring.nl/download/literatuur/The_NICEguidelines_manual_2009_-_All_chapters.pdf>.

94 NHG (n 82).

95 Zorginstituut Nederland, 'Kosteneffectiviteit in de Praktijk' <https://www.zorginstituutnederland.nl/binaries/content/documents/zinl-www/documenten/publicaties/rapporten-en-standpunten/2015/1506-kosteneffectiviteit-in-de-praktijk/1506-kosteneffectiviteit-in-de-praktijk/Kosteneffectiviteit+in+de+praktijk.pdf>.

of the cost? These assumptions will be empirically analysed through a comparative assessment of the role of cost in Dutch and English guidelines.

Could the way that the issue of the cost of treatment is handled have a real influence on the development of guidelines? The institutional environment of guideline making in England forces guideline groups to consider cost considerations. In the Netherlands, guideline groups do not have to confront the issue of cost in this way because these decisions are taken by the Zorginstituut, a separate and independent body.

2.5. FACTORS SHAPING GROUP DECISION-MAKING IN GUIDELINE GROUPS

To analyse the development of guidelines from a socio-legal perspective, the consideration of a range of factors that shape group-decision making processes in constructing medical guidelines is important. At the outset, it is essential to state that this book does not purport to give an ethnographic or sociological account of the exact nature of the discussion in guideline groups. The research does not strive to establish a precise account of the discussion of the guideline group members, rather the focus lies on the results these discussions have had on the text of the guideline documents. To this end this section will analyse several literatures that can provide potential factors to influence the decision-making in guideline groups and the subsequent text of the guideline that is constructed as a result of this process.

Guidelines are a product of consensus within a group of professionals. Naturally the process of reaching consensus will influence the guideline. Social psychology literature on group-processes paints a picture of the pitfalls that exist within this process. Status hierarchies that exist outside of the group might be reproduced within the guideline group;[96] minorities and women might be underrepresented in the discussion,[97] the group might suffer from the social influence from one individual to the

96 JE Driskell and B Mullen, 'Status, Expectations, and Behavior: A Meta-Analytic Review and Test of the Theory' (1990) 16 *Personality and Social Psychology Bulletin* 541.

97 Alice H Eagly, 'Gender and Social Influence: A Social Psychological Analysis' (1983) 38 *American Psychologist* 971.

detriment of the collective decision making,[98] there might be majority pressure to conform,[99] as well as outcomes suffering from 'groupthink.'[100]

The potential influence of group dynamics on guidelines has not gone unnoticed in the literature. Several authors have discussed these factors in some detail. Pagliari and colleagues[101] have observed that status hierarchies are indeed reproduced to some extent in guideline groups, through the fact that there is more discussion among high status individuals. Berg et al have drawn attention to the fact that not all group members contribute equally.[102] Hopthrow et al have highlighted four areas that influence the functioning of guideline groups and have suggested ways to make sure groups are effective. These are: '(1) information sharing, (2) systematic processing, (3) group formation and (4) process loss.'[103] For all these areas, Hopthrow et al provide suggestions on how to improve the process. Examples they give include: a diversity of opinions and expertise, providing group socialisation activities to enhance bonding, promote group norms that provide for critical thinking, sufficient time and matching people to specific (sub-)tasks.[104]

If we consider the guideline working groups in the Netherlands, there is a study by Zuiderent-Jerak and others on the variation between guidelines.[105] In this study the authors conduct interviews with different guideline developers which shed some light on parts of the process of guideline development. Some guideline groups have patient involvement while others do not;[106] there are sometimes tensions between evidence- and consensus-based approaches within a working group and monetary constraints play a role in deciding the scope of a guideline.[107]

---

98 S Milgram, 'Some Conditions of Obedience and Disobedience to Authority' (1965) 18 *Human Re*lations 57.
99 Solomon E Asch, 'Opinions and Social Pressure' (1955) 193 *Scientific American* 31.
100 Irving L Janis, *Victims of Groupthink: A Psychological Study of Foreign-Policy Decisions and Fiascoes* (Houghton Mifflin 1972).
101 Pagliari, Grimshaw and Eccles (n 69); Pagliari and Grimshaw (Chapter 1, n 7).
102 Marc Berg, Ruud ter Meulen and Masja Van den Burg, 'Guidelines for Appropriate Care: The Importance of Empirical Normative Analysis' (2001) 9 *Health Care Analysis* 77.
103 Hopthrow, Feder and Michie (Chapter 1, n 7) 359–60.
104 Ibid, 360–364.
105 Teun Zuiderent-Jerak and others, 'Variatie in richtlijnen. Wat is het probleem?' <http://www.pgosupport.nl/mailings/FILES/plugin_content/176/Regieraad_rapport_variatie_in_richtlijnen.pdf>.
106 Ibid.
107 Ibid.

Considering the guideline groups in England, Atkins et al paint a detailed picture in their study of three working groups of NICE.[108] The authors establish that some participants see guideline recommendations as aspirational statements, while others prefer directly implementable recommendations.[109] This study lends more substance to the claim the professional expertise and status influence group discussions, where higher status professionals have a greater voice, as well as the importance of vested interests of health professionals (in a certain procedure or treatment) in influencing recommendations.[110]

One message that emerges clearly is that the group process involved in creating a guideline is a complex one: a process requiring very specific tasks, which necessitates a large amount of expertise and must be completed within a limited time frame.

Here, we can build further on this literature by establishing whether the differences that exist in the group composition and the way that the groups function, does indeed lead to differences in assessment and differences in decision making and whether the factors that Hopthrow et al suggest play a role. It is not immediately clear whether the factors they identify will always be present in the same way in different guideline groups. These factors could be present, but not to such an extent that they explain differences in guidelines. This book will use a comparative approach to gain insight on this question.

While this literature gives a general sense of some of the difficulties that group members might face during the processes of developing a guideline, a more specific account given some of the political and normative elements of guideline drafting are also of interest here. Understanding potential political and normative considerations in guideline drafting will help to uncover the potential motivations of group members and help shine a light on the process that feeds a guideline text. These also provide arguments to question the orthodox view of evidence-based guidelines as 'the application of evidence to decision-making' and suggest ways in which that picture is more complicated than some of the medical literature allows for.

---

108 Atkins and others (Chapter 1, n 7).

109 Ibid, 106.

110 Atkins and others, ibid; Raine and others (Chapter 1, n 7); Andrew Hutchings and Rosalind Raine, 'A Systematic Review of Factors Affecting the Judgments Produced by Formal Consensus Development Methods in Health Care' (2006) 11 *Journal of Health Services Research & Policy* 172; Pagliari and Grimshaw (Chapter 1, n 7).

First, we will consider the politics inherent in evidence-based medicine itself, following the critique expressed in the philosophy of science literature discussed earlier. To be able to apply this knowledge to a study of participants in developing guidelines, we then turn to the sociology of situated judgement to provide insights into the form of repertoires of action that members of guideline groups might employ.

2.5.1. MEDICAL POLITICS AND EVIDENCE

The study of medical politics and the role of medical guidelines is predicated upon understanding the link between knowledge and power in healthcare. The possession of scientific knowledge is the key to power. Belkin describes this link as the 'technocratic wish.'[111] In his treatment of managed care he suggests that there is an intimate relation between the scientific justifications given for actions and shifts in power within healthcare. So the shift in evidence-based medicine to favour generalisable data about populations, in the form of RCTs, over uncontrolled studies or clinical experience, is the result of contingent coalition of interests that shape the success of this claim for truthfulness over other competing claims.[112] The way that managed care – and evidence-based medicine by extension – is successful is in its claim to 'scientific obviousness'[113] and as a result is accepted as right and correct, thereby hides the essentially cultural nature of the choices made to arrive at these scientific claims. Scientific knowledge claims are therefore socially constructed and contestable.

Rodwin observes how evidence-based medicine neatly transposes questions of ideology, values and standards, into technical questions of evidence. He draws a parallel with the progressive era in 1890's American politics which strove to replace 'governance by politics with governance by experts' and describes this as a search for a 'technocratic fix.'[114] Goldenberg, following Rodwin, formulates this succinctly:

> The configuration of policy considerations and clinical standards into questions of evidence conveniently transform normative questions into technical ones. Political issues are not resolved, however, but merely disguised in technocratic

111 Gary S Belkin, 'The Technocratic Wish: Making Sense and Finding Power in the "Managed" Medical Marketplace' (1997) 22 *Journal of Health Politics, Policy and Law* 509.

112 Ibid, 511.

113 Ibid, 512.

114 Marc A Rodwin, 'Commentary: The Politics of Evidence-Based Medicine' (2001) 26 *Journal of Health Politics, Policy and Law* 439, 441.

> consideration and language. Thus the goals of medicine and other normative considerations lie just below the surface of these evidentiary questions, and evidence becomes an instrument of, rather than a substitute for, politics.[115]

This literature suggests that evidence-based medicine and evidence-based guidelines can be political but still claim to be objective and scientific because the political questions are masked as technical questions that only require medical expertise. Understanding how evidence-based medicine produces objectivity claims will help us understand how guideline group members are likely to understand their own work and how they relate their work to medicine as a whole.

While regulatory objectivity stresses the guideline as an instrument and looks at it as a whole, work by Berg et al inverts this perspective and looks at the normativity inside a guideline and the choices that are made by the participants.[116] Normativity occurs where values are assigned that are inherently 'good' or 'bad' (or other social values) to a choice: this choice is then dictated by those values based on what is perceived to be 'normal' or correct. Berg et al provide a classification of types of normativity in guidelines that are useful in this regard: 'I: The normativity implied in the instrument itself, II: The assumptions and translations that have to be made each time the instrument is developed for a specific problem, III: The assumptions and translations that are specific to the medical situation addressed by the instrument.'[117]

The second type of normativity here is particularly relevant for this book on guidelines. Normative choices are often judgements that involve weighing costs against effects – and making choices about which costs count.[118] When applying this to evidence, normativity can be seen in the choices made around the following questions: does this study count as evidence, is the result of the study relevant to my population of patients and should the study lead to a change in recommendation? The use of evidence is thus an activity that is imbued with a series of more and less normative choices, which provides a filter to achieve the link between medical knowledge and recommendations in a guideline. The choice to include one medical study over another, even if driven by seemingly objective criteria, remains a normative choice.

115 Goldenberg (n 17) 2630.
116 Berg, ter Meulen and Van den Burg (n 102).
117 Ibid, 80.
118 Ibid, 81.

To be able to link elements of normativity more directly to the activity of members of the guideline group we turn now to the sociology of situated judgement:[119] an approach that stresses the social nature of coordinated action by individuals. The 'sociology of situated judgement' refers to sociological and evaluative studies of how actors reach consensus through discursive methods in a discrete social situation. Moreira has applied this approach specially to show how groups deal with evidence based on his in-depth observation of several guideline groups. His approach is valuable for this study as it draws together wider concerns about normativity of guidelines in an abstract sense, with the practical knowledge of observation of social action. Furthermore, he is one of the few authors who base their findings in detailed ethnographic observations of guideline group meetings; this makes his work particularly valuable. He distinguishes four repertoires of evaluation, drawing upon theories of situated judgement.

Moreira's repertoire of evaluation is 'a recurrent form of judgement deployed by social actors in considering the worth of an object … as means of harmonizing their actions with others'.[120] As Moreira explains, these types of judgement employed by members of guideline groups serve the specific purpose of creating meaning through the use of (medical) knowledge as a mediation of social action.[121] One of these 'recurrent forms of judgement' is called 'Science' and forms the first 'repertoire of evaluation'. Moreira describes this repertoire as one where guideline group members are evaluating the technical robustness of evidence in light of possible criticisms of health researchers, specialists and other guideline groups.[122]

This accords well with our discussion of evidence-based medicine and its attempts to enhance the use of appropriate medical knowledge, such as clinical trials, to influence clinical medicine. However, what Moreira shows convincingly is that this is only part of what happens in a guideline group when clinicians discuss evidence. Considering research that is methodologically sound and satisfies the requirements of evidence-based medicine is not enough: the next step is to analyse this evidence considering the argumentative forum it is going to be

---

119 Luc Boltanski and Laurent Thévenot, 'The Reality of Moral Expectations: A Sociology of Situated Judgement' (2000) 3 *Philosophical Explorations* 208.

120 Moreira (n 21) 1977.

121 Ibid.

122 Ibid, 1978.

used in. This might affect whether a change that is based on a technical assessment of scientific studies is translated into a recommendation to change practice. Using this sociological approach has the advantage of not stating what guidelines ought to be, but rather analysing how they are made.

The second repertoire Moreira discusses is that of practice. In his words: 'where members are concerned with the practical usability of the knowledge in debate in view of routine patient care.'[123] This repertoire stresses the need for the guideline to be useful in the direct clinical encounter between health professional and patient. Moreira explains that guideline group members have discussions involving reference to experiences of clinical practice, where one tries to square the 'typified health knowledge' embodied in statistical relations that come out of scientific studies in various forms and sizes and the uniqueness of the individual encounter between patient and clinician. This repertoire provides an important addition to the debate as it draws attention to the necessary tension that is inherent in the drafting of a guideline. When drafting a general guideline, one tries to give general guidance which necessarily cannot cover every individual application. This sits well with the findings on the implementation of evidence-based guidelines and underscores the contested nature of integrating biomedical science with clinical knowledge. Moreira presents two further repertoires, politics and process, which will be discussed in the following sections. What we can conclude from his repertoires of science and practice is that evidence only becomes evidence through social debate and iterative discourse which includes perspectives outside evidence alone.

Moreira has also commented on the professional aspect of guideline production, styling it as the repertoire of 'politics'. In Moreira's words: 'where members are concerned with the acceptability of their recommendation in relation to public health policies and stakeholder views on the condition in question.'[124] This repertoire highlights that recommendations recommending certain treatments or medication will influence an existing balance of power within a (sub)discipline and the existing configuration of responsibilities and arrangement in a given (sub)discipline that the guideline affects. The wider interests of pharmaceutical industry or even government policy might be at stake. As Moreira rightly argues, the need to be seen to act as a guideline

123 Ibid.

124 Ibid, 1981.

group and make recommendations, needs to be balanced with the acceptability of a political position and the need to achieve consensus within the group.[125] This accords well with our wider discussion about guidelines as self-regulation and the role of the sociology of professions. While Moreira seems to stress the political role of guidelines in wider institutional fora, he only implicitly discusses the professionalisation consequences of guidelines where recommendations affect individual health professionals. This is not a material distinction, however, because, in practice, it is likely that discontent with guidelines will often be expressed through the mediation of a Medical Association or Royal College due to (perceived) political choices.

The final repertoire that Moreira distinguishes is that of process. 'Process' here speaks to the means of constructing the methodological reliability of knowledge claims which emerge from the guideline group discussions and are represented in the text of the guideline. As Moreira explains, this involves separating the group from the 'outside' and constructs the group as a separate social world. Making sure there are no conflicts of interest is an example of how this can be achieved. A further element, according to Moreira, is to make sure that the evaluation of the evidence is not distorted by the social ties of expert members of the group.[126] It shows an interesting ambiguity, in that concerns regarding how people's interest outside the group might influence their decision within it are coupled with efforts to establish the group as an independent institution with its own identity. This would preclude external influences from intervening in debates within the group. The process repertoire suggests a new way of assessing the influences of conflicts of interest depending on the group dynamics: by linking this to the external interests of the group. This is a potentially fruitful way of discussing conflicts of interest that will be pursued further in the case studies.

Such a lengthy discussion of Moreira's work is justified here as it provides a multitude of good conceptual tools to help strengthen the empirical approach adopted here. However, this book hopes to go further and to take a broader approach to understanding the development of guidelines as a complex process where understanding can be strengthened through a combination of various approaches.

The politics of evidence-based medicine are important rationales influencing the conception of guidelines. The evidence hierarchy has

[125] Ibid, 1982.
[126] Ibid, 1983.

been influential and currently and at least formally, underpins the evidence gathering and appraisal for making evidence-based guidelines. It is, however, not an exclusive epistemological foundation of medical knowledge, so other types of knowledge claims are used in the production of guidelines. Likewise, knowledge claims will always be normative, if only in the limited sense envisioned by Berg.[127] How evidence is used and conceptualised and to what extent reference is made to the evidence-based hierarchy of evidence, will be the subject of this research. What is not well understood is how exactly the interplay between the formal evidence-based medicine logic, medical politics and other considerations in a guideline group will play out, or to what extent evidence-based medicine provides an overriding logic for the consideration of evidence. The sociology of situated judgement might provide the tools to analyse these questions, but in this research further attention will be paid to the concrete ways in which the different 'repertoires' might interact and collide with each other. This literature has also hinted of the importance of considering conflicts of interest as an important factor that could influence the negotiations in guideline groups and thus could shape the text of a guideline. This literature will be explored below.

2.5.2. CONFLICTS OF INTEREST AND TIES BETWEEN THE PHARMACEUTICAL INDUSTRY AND CLINICIANS

There is a large literature that deals with various conflicts of interest between the medical profession and the pharmaceutical industry.[128] Conflicts of interest are viewed as problematic because of the fear that commercial interests will dictate the availability of medication and priorities in research: this clashes with the view that healthcare is a public good delivered for the benefit of all. Avoiding undue influence is particularly relevant for medical guidelines as the strength of their advice would be perceived as weaker if this advice was seen as biased;

---

127 Berg, ter Meulen and Van den Burg (n 102).

128 Committee on Conflict of Interest in Medical Research, Education and Institute of Medicine (US), *Conflict of Interest in Medical Research, Education, and Practice* (Bernard Lo and Marilyn J Field (eds), National Academies Press 2009); Marc A Rodwin, 'Conflicts of Interest, Institutional Corruption, and Pharma: An Agenda for Reform' (2012) 40 *The Journal of Law, Medicine & Ethics* 511; Robert Steinbrook and Bernard Lo, 'Medical Journals and Conflicts of Interest' (2012) 40 *The Journal of Law, Medicine & Ethics* 488.

not driven by scientific knowledge but by other commercial agendas. Likewise, guidelines based on a conflict of interest would be seen to benefit those parties who influenced it; this may provide concessions the pharmaceutical industry.[129] To establish whether conflicts of interest have a role to play in guideline construction we first need to understand the literature on the scope of conflict of interest and what kind of regulation exists to manage it. Furthermore, this review highlights the possibility of 'regulatory capture', where the guideline institution itself, such as NICE and NHG, would work at the behest of outside interests and no would longer be impartial.

Goldacre has provided a comprehensive overview of some of the problems in medicine and presents some of the ways in which a conflict of interest might occur, why it matters and ways to respond to it.[130] Goldacre identifies that studies by pharmaceutical companies have a higher likelihood of being published, while those containing negative results are far less likely to be published, leading to bias. He goes on to identify several ways in which pharmaceutical companies influence clinicians: drug reps from pharmaceutical companies visit clinicians to promote their drugs, there are industry-funded education courses and congresses on new drugs, clinicians have paid consultancy positions with pharmaceutical companies, ghost-writers are employed to write publications for academics – and the list goes on.

The question, of course, is whether these financial ties between practitioners and industry have been shown to affect guidelines. There is some evidence that this has indeed been the case. Several studies have examined guidelines on the same medical condition and found a correlation between more positive recommendations and the number of conflicts of interest present in the guideline group.[131] One obvious solution to this problem, presented by some of the literature, might be

---

129 Edwin AM Gale, 'Conflicts of Interest in Guideline Panel Members' (2011) 343 *BMJ* d5728; Susan L Norris and others, 'Conflict of Interest in Clinical Practice Guideline Development: A Systematic Review' (2011) 6 PLoS ONE.

130 Ben Goldacre, *Bad Pharma: How Drug Companies Mislead Doctors and Harm Patients* (Fourth Estate 2012); Ben Goldacre and Carl Heneghan, 'How Medicine Is Broken, and How We Can Fix It' (2015) 350 *BMJ* h3397.

131 James N George, Sara K Vesely and Steven H Woolf, 'Conflicts of Interest and Clinical Recommendations Comparison of Two Concurrent Clinical Practice Guidelines for Primary Immune Thrombocytopenia Developed by Different Methods' (2014) 29 *American Journal of Medical Quality* 53; Gisela Schott and others, 'Does the Pharmaceutical Industry Influence Guidelines?: Two Examples from Germany' (2013) 110 *Deutsches Ärzteblatt International* 575; Norris and others (n 129).

to categorically exclude people with a (financial) conflict of interest from taking any part in developing a guideline. Other authors, however, point to the fact that this might lead to guidelines that are not based on sufficient expertise of the condition at hand.[132] This debate has led many to conclude that the best way forward is to 'manage' conflicts of interest: by allowing participation but restricting involvement at certain moments during guideline development. Different organisations have developed different rules along these lines: some are stricter than others in how they deal with conflicts of interest.

Through an analysis of the factors shaping decision making in guideline groups, conflicts of interest, medical politics and group dynamics, we can complement our analysis of the development of guidelines. By linking these micro-level concerns to the text of the guideline it will be possible to trace linkages between aspects of the development of guidelines and the text of the final guideline product. We seek to engage with this literature and use them as a basis for developing a more nuanced comparative understanding of medical guidelines.

2.6. CONCLUSION: THE RELEVANCE OF EXISTING LITERATURE

In this concluding section of this chapter, the various strands of literature that have been discussed will be pulled together. The main issues will be analysed in more detail in chapter 3. The analysis of the literature has covered four main areas: evidence, regulation, institutions and factors affecting decision making.

Of central concern in this book is the concept of evidence. This is used in the specific technical sense of the use of medical knowledge contained in scientific studies which are ranked according to a hierarchy of evidence. Philosophy of science, especially the work of Chin[133] and Goldenberg,[134]

---

132 Derek J Jones and others, 'Conflicts of Interest Ethics: Silencing Expertise in the Development of International Clinical Practice Guidelines' (2012) 156 *Annals of Internal Medicine* 809; Caroline Price, 'NICE Risks Making Itself a "Laughing Stock" over Guidance on Metformin Alternatives, Say Experts' (*Pulse Today*) <http://www.pulsetoday.co.uk/clinical/diabetes/nice-risks-making-itself-a-laughing-stock-over-guidance-on-metformin-alternatives-say-experts/20009139.article>.

133 Chin-Yee (n 17).

134 Goldenberg (n 17); Maya J Goldenberg, 'Iconoclast or Creed?: Objectivism, Pragmatism, and the Hierarchy of Evidence' (2009) 52 *Perspectives in Biology and Medicine* 168.

has illuminated how evidence-based medicine has both methodological and epistemological limits. These critiques are taken seriously; we will build further on their findings by providing a robust empirical account of the practical understanding and use of evidence by guideline groups. Science and technology studies have examined evidence and place it at the heart of the attempt (through guidelines) to create objectivity.[135] This literature examines objectivity as a concept to show how it is purposefully socially constructed. An empirical assessment of the strength of these arguments is currently lacking; here we will attempt to address this gap in the literature through a comparative study of guidelines. A sole focus on evidence would, however, risk adopting the viewpoint of the medical literature in this book. This might limit the opportunity to criticise the underlying assumptions of evidence-based medicine, while asking searching questions about its role in society.

Analysing medical guidelines as regulatory tools to some extent addresses these concerns and at the same time purports to add to the extensive regulatory literature on the nature and role of (mandated) self-regulation in the current governance of the state.[136] This book takes the position that guidelines are a specific form of regulation that both regulates professionals and, at the same time, tries to ward off the encroaching state by fulfilling a mandate for self-regulation. It will break new ground in putting this duality of purpose of guidelines centre stage.

Literature from the sociology of professions, especially Evetts[137] helped conceptualise the duality of guidelines. A critical engagement with some of their earlier findings on the nature of banking regulation, international private regulatory actors like ISO and the Basel group will enrich this position further. It is thought that medical guidelines might have unique features that have not been addressed in the literature before. The specific role of transparency initiatives in shaping the development of guidelines has the potential to add interesting new elements to this field. Guidelines are also used as regulatory tools of persuasion in relation to medical professionals that, as Evetts suggests, might in some circumstances be instruments of control. This book will seek the views of guideline drafters and hopes to ascertain how they see the relationship between a guideline and the wider medical profession. In this way, it adds to and builds on Evetts' work.

135 Cambrosio and others (n 24).
136 John Braithwaite, 'Enforced Self-Regulation: A New Strategy for Corporate Crime Control' (1982) 80 *Michigan Law Review* 1466; Ogus (n 38); Black (n 27).
137 Evetts (n 49).

These combined perspectives on the role of evidence and guidelines as specific regulatory tools will be further complemented by an understanding of the institutional literature. This area has been neglected so far in the study of guidelines and here we hope to contribute to this field by exploring in-depth aspects of the institutional context shaping both guideline drafters and the text of guidelines in different countries. A sociological institutionalism approach has been adopted, championed by Meyer.[138] This approach allows for a nuanced understanding of the role of actors (drafters), who are both constrained and shaped by specific institutional scripts, such as conflicts of interest.

Cost-effectiveness and its potentially major role in negotiating guidelines, especially in England, is also explored. An extensive literature that deals with cost in relation to health technology assessments exists.[139] This book will build on this literature by exploring whether these types of studies apply to medical guidelines – so far research of this nature has been absent. Cost-effectiveness considerations have the potential to interact with assessments based on evidence: we hope to bring these literatures together and explore any potential interactions between them.

Finally, this book draws on literature that has engaged with the micro-level of guideline construction, through observations and ethnographic academic research. The work of Pagliari,[140] Hopthrow,[141] Berg,[142] Rodwin[143] and Moreira[144] all have shown in various ways that discussions within guideline groups have strong normative dimensions and can be said to represent the political process, at the micro-level; again, the issue of conflicts of interest and its potential corrupting influence coming to the fore.[145] Interesting questions will need to be asked: how can such a supposedly political process lead to objectivity, as science and technology scholars claim? Several different academic disciplines are drawn on to provide a broad and detailed discussion of the development of medical guidelines in the Netherlands and England.

---

138 Meyer and Jepperson (n 76); Meyer (n 72).
139 Lehoux and Blume (n 89); May (n 89).
140 Pagliari, Grimshaw and Eccles (n 69).
141 Hopthrow, Feder and Michie (Chapter 1, n 7).
142 Berg, ter Meulen and Van den Burg (n 102).
143 Rodwin (n 128).
144 Moreira (n 21).
145 Goldacre (n 130).

CHAPTER 3
GUIDELINES IN THE NETHERLANDS AND ENGLAND

This chapter provides the background and context to help us to understand the emergence of medical practice guidelines. Section 3.1 describes the emergence of medical practice guidelines in the Netherlands and England. It explores the different trajectories that the guideline development process has followed in the two countries – particularly the shift from consensus-based to evidence-based guidelines – while drawing out the implications that this might have for this book. Section 3.2 introduces the relevant professional associations and other actors involved in drafting and negotiating guidelines in these two countries and explores differences in the composition of guideline working groups and practices in negotiating guidelines. Section 3.3 discusses guidelines in the broader institutional context of healthcare delivery, the role of the institutional and regulatory context on guidelines and the financing of guidelines. Section 3.4 discusses the role of guidelines in the wider governance of healthcare in the Netherlands and England. Concluding remarks are presented in section 3.5 in the form of a cross-country comparison.

3.1. HISTORICAL PERSPECTIVES: FROM CONSENSUS TO EVIDENCE-BASED

It is important to trace the history of the development from consensus-based to evidence-based guidelines in both countries and assess when and to what extent, the shift from consensus-based to evidence-based guideline development occurred, as this will enable us to understand the current developments in both countries.

3.1.1. THE NETHERLANDS

In the Netherlands, the production of so-called 'consensus statements' began in 1982, when the National Association for Quality Assurance in Hospitals (CBO)[1] produced a set of clinical practice guidelines describing a 'state of the art' procedure a health professional should follow when confronted with a situation the guideline describes.[2] These consensus statements were produced in response to increasing government pressure to cut budgets, which led to fears that cost considerations might endanger the quality of care.[3] The scientific council of the CBO, who produced these initial guidelines, consisted of representatives of the various scientific organisations of medical specialists. The CBO aimed to improve the quality of care in hospitals and the guidelines were meant to reduce practice variation and provide a way to audit care.[4] In 1987, the National Association of General Practitioners (NHG) followed suit by producing the NHG-Standaarden: clinical practice guidelines aimed at illnesses prevalent in GP surgeries.[5] Klazinga provided a survey of the first 12 years of the CBO clinical guideline programme and established three clusters of reasons for their (more widespread) use: professionalisation, accountability and efficiency.[6] Klazinga argued that guidelines help doctors deliver state-of-the-art care as well as potentially delivering transparency about treatments to patients, insurers, management and the government and possibly helping to ration care and control costs.[7]

The Cochrane Centre was set up in the Netherlands (following England) to conduct reviews of RCTs.[8] Initially, the CBO and the Cochrane Centre started working together, followed by a great many other scientific associations of doctors who later joined the collaboration.[9] The shift from consensus-based to evidence-based guidelines, however,

---

1 In Dutch: Centraal begeleidingsorgaan intercollegiale toetsing.

2 Klazinga (Chapter 2, n 44).

3 Michael I Harrison, *Implementing Change in Health Systems: Market Reforms in the United Kingdom, Sweden, and the Netherlands* (SAGE 2004) 144.

4 Zuiderent-Jerak and others (Chapter 2, n 105).

5 JS Burgers and JJE van Everdingen, 'Evidence-based richtlijnontwikkeling in Nederland: het EBRO-platform' (2004) 148 *Nederlands Tijdschrift voor Geneeskunde* 2057.

6 Klazinga (Chapter 2, n 44).

7 Ibid.

8 'Dutch Cochrane Centre'. Available at: <http://dcc.cochrane.org/>.

9 Burgers and van Everdingen (n 5).

was not a radical 'paradigm shift' as some literature suggests.[10] Rather, in the Netherlands, it meant that evidence-based methods became part of the consensus-based approach to development of a guideline.[11] It follows that although the term 'evidence-based' is often used to describe the guideline development process in the Netherlands, a more accurate description of the process would focus on the role of consensus in establishing what the power and relevance is of certain scientific evidence.[12] This has not prevented evidence-based guideline development from becoming the preferred term to describe guidelines. A good example of this point is the EBRO-platform,[13] which brought together organisations involved in evidence-based guideline development. The platform was financed by the Order of Medical Specialists (OMS) and launched in 2001. Since then, all clinical practice guidelines strive to be evidence-based and advances were made to further formalise the procedure for drafting guidelines.[14] Furthermore, textbooks have been produced that promote evidence-based guideline development as the new standard and suggest a (normatively) correct way of making a guideline.[15]

Guideline production remained in the hands of the professional associations from the 1980s until the present day. However, an interesting recent development in the Netherlands is the stronger involvement of the government in guaranteeing guideline quality; a quality assurance institute has been set up as a part of the *Zorginstituut*, a body functioning at arm's-length from government.[16] This quality assurance institute has opened a register in which quality instruments, such as guidelines, can be entered. Before guidelines will be allowed on this registry, they are

---

10 Evidence-based Medicine Working Group (Chapter 1, n 3).

11 Zuiderent-Jerak and others (Chapter 2, n 105).

12 Loes Knaapen and others, 'Pragmatic Evidence and Textual Arrangements: A Case Study of French Clinical Cancer Guidelines' (2010) 71 *Social Science & Medicine* (1982) 685.

13 Evidence-based guideline development.

14 An example is the 'procedurebook' used by the National College of General Practitioners: 'procedureboek voor de ontwikkeling van NHG-standaarden, NHG 2010'.

15 JJE van Everdingen, *Evidence-based richtlijnontwikkeling: een leidraad voor de praktijk* (Bohn Stafleu Van Loghum 2004); JJE van Everdingen, *Handboek evidence-based richtlijnontwikkeling: een leidraad voor de praktijk* (Bohn Stafleu van Loghum, Springer Media 2014).

16 Zorginstituut Nederland, 'Kwaliteit' (*Quality*). Available at: <http://zorginstituut nederland.nl/kwaliteit>.

assessed by the *Zorginstituut*.[17] In the Dutch healthcare system, guidelines are now ubiquitous; all scientific associations of doctors have their own guideline programme. As a result, the number of NHG-standards has grown to 91.[18] The NHG, however, is only one of a multitude of organisations involved in guideline production: they are also produced by associations of medical specialists and several para-medical professions.[19] The total number of guidelines is hard to establish, but it is clear that the figure is in the region of hundreds: several databases give some indications,[20] but it is hard to specify a number.

3.1.2. ENGLAND

In England, consensus-based guidelines were also developed in the late 1980s, although these efforts mainly produced guidelines aimed at specific health districts where NHS trusts worked together.[21] There are several examples here of guidelines using this model: the Royal College of Physicians guidelines on stroke provide an example of a development of a national guideline in the early 1990s.[22] The Clinical Standards Advisory Group, set up by the NHS executive board, produced early guidelines on back pain to reduce practice variation,[23] while the Centre for Health Services Research of the University of Newcastle also produced

17 This development dates from after the development of the Dutch guidelines in this study, so these developments do not play a role in discussing the Dutch guidelines in this book.

18 On 14 February 2019. 'NHG-Standaarden' (*Standards of the Dutch Scientifc Association of General Practicioners*). Available at: <https://www.nhg.org/nhg-standaarden>.

19 Artsennet a Dutch website for doctors indicates that around 75 organisations are involved in guideline production. 'Medische Richtlijnen per Organisatie' (*Medical Guidelines by Organisation*). Available at: <http://www.artsennet.nl/Richtlijnen/Per-organisatie.htm>.

20 'Richtlijnendatabase'. Available at: <http://kims.orde.nl/het-kennisinstituut-voor-u/richtlijnen/richtlijnendatabase.html>; 'International Guideline Library – Guidelines International Network' <http://www.g-i-n.net/library/international-guidelines-library>; 'Richtlijnen//Diliguide.Nl' <http://www.diliguide.nl/>; 'Oncoline' <http://www.oncoline.nl/>; 'Pallialine' <http://www.pallialine.nl/>.

21 D Armstrong and others, 'Development of Clinical Guidelines in a Health District: An Attempt to Find Consensus' (1992) 1 *Quality in Health Care* 241.

22 Jako S Burgers and others, 'Towards Evidence-Based Clinical Practice: An International Survey of 18 Clinical Guideline Programs' (2003) 15 *International Journal for Quality in Health Care* 31.

23 Clinical Standards Advisory Group, *Back Pain* (HMSO, 1994).

guidelines aimed at improving medical research.[24] The real impetus for guideline production, however, came when the government established the National Institute for Health and Care Excellence (NICE),[25] set up in 1999 as a special health authority which was part of the NHS. Its aim was to reduce variation in the availability and quality of NHS treatments and care.[26] With the advent of NICE, guideline production became more formalised. It became a statutory body as a result of the HSCA 2012.[27] To date,[28] 202 clinical guidelines are available, with 57 in development.[29] The procedure to develop these guidelines is based on the evidence-based guideline development model discussed earlier. NICE has a clear national remit; its guidelines are disseminated to all NHS trusts. It has therefore largely replaced the previous local initiatives. This has also meant that because NICE started out using the evidence-based model of developing guidelines, it does not have an institutional history of consensus-based methods, which were used in the 1980s and early 1990s.

The establishment of NICE, an independent non-departmental public body, has caused a shift from professional control over guidelines to a situation of (at least on paper) large government influence over guideline production, albeit at arm's-length. The establishment of NICE has meant direct government involvement in the financing off and priority-setting for guideline making.

3.1.3. SIMILARITIES AND DIFFERENCES

The history of medical guidelines in the Netherlands and England show some important commonalities: there is a trend towards more formalised guideline production and international cooperation on guidelines through the so-called Guidelines International network (G-I-N).[30] In the

24 Burgers and others (n 22).

25 National Institute for Health and Care Excellence, previously the National Institute for Clinical Excellence.

26 Available at: http://www.nice.org.uk/aboutnice/whoweare/who_we_are.jsp; National Institute for Clinical Excellence (Establishment and Constitution) Order 1999, SI 1999/220.

27 Health and Social Care Act 2012, s. 232.

28 14 February 2019.

29 'Published Clinical Guidelines'. Available at: <https://www.nice.org.uk/guidance/published?type=cg>.

30 Knaapen (Chapter 2, n 70).

Netherlands, the consensus-based models used in developing the first guidelines still play a role, while within NICE there is no institutional history of using consensus-based methods to develop guidelines. Evaluating the precise relationship between consensus-based and evidence-based methods in this book, through interviews and the analysis of guideline documents helps to understand the process of negotiation of a guideline and the nature of the choices that are made.

There are further differences if we consider the ownership of medical guidelines. In the Netherlands, the various professional organisations develop their own guidelines and are therefore more likely to feel ownership of them and follow their own disciplinary outlook in deciding on what to include. In England, because NICE has ownership of guidelines, control is removed from professional associations and moved to (representatives) of the state. The practitioners who are asked to implement the guideline are further removed from its conception.

A final point of apparent difference is the fragmentation of guidelines production in the Netherlands as compared to the more centralised approach in England. It remains to be seen whether this fragmentation has any meaningful effect on the development of guidelines. One potential way this fragmentation could affect the content in guidelines is through a need to coordinate the advice in guidelines between different medical professionals.

3.2. PROFESSIONAL ASSOCIATIONS AND OTHER GUIDELINE ACTORS

We have seen that both professional associations as well as government bodies play a role in guideline production and that guidelines are developed within working groups. To help to create a detailed understanding of how these guideline groups work and how they contribute to the development of medical guidelines we need to understand who is involved. The specific institutional environment varies between countries. Understanding of how these environments operate will help the analysis of the development of medical guidelines.

3.2.1. THE NETHERLANDS

In the Netherlands, healthcare professionals are organised into numerous scientific and professional associations. These associations have always played an important role in shaping the healthcare system. Under the corporatist model of the 1970s and 1980s, doctors (under the umbrella of their associations) negotiated directly with the government on tariffs for their care and displayed a great amount of autonomy in the way they practised their profession. The three most influential associations will be included in this book and the way they develop guidelines and their wider influence on healthcare will be discussed: the Royal Dutch Medical Association (KNMG), the National Association of General Practitioners (LHV) and the Dutch Order of Medical Specialists (OMS).

The Royal Dutch Medical Association, established in 1999, is a federation of seven associations of health professionals.[31] The KNMG is very influential through various regulatory and non-regulatory activities. It is responsible for the regulation of the fitness to practice licence for physicians and their five-year revalidation process, subject to agreement of the minister of health.[32] The KNMG also produces guidelines on various topics – the most comprehensive being on end-of-life care, including euthanasia.[33] Its process for producing guidelines is to establish a commission that consists of representatives from all the various medical disciplines directly involved in the topic of the guideline, who participate based on their expertise, not as representatives of a professional association. After a draft guideline is produced, there is a consultation in which stakeholders can comment. In practice, these are often the professional associations most closely involved with the topic of the guideline. In addition to its involvement in guidelines, the KNMG carries considerable political clout, as it actively lobbies parliament and

31 'The federation consists of the Association of Public Health Physicians (KAMG), the National Association of Salaried Doctors (LAD), the National Association of General Practitioners (LHV), the Dutch Association for Occupational Health (NVAB), the Association for Elderly Care Physicians (Verenso), the Dutch Association of Insurance Medicine (NVVG), the Dutch Order of Medical Specialists (Orde van Medisch Specialisten) and a group of individual KNMG members and students.' Available at: <http://knmg.artsennet.nl/Over-KNMG/about-knmg.htm>.

32 One example is the ratification of the decision by a commission of the KNMG to set the training requirements for GPs. 'Goedkeuringsbesluit Kaderbesluit En Drie Specifieke Besluiten van de CHVG Betreffende Huisartsgeneeskunde, Verpleeghuisgeneeskunde En Medische Zorg Voor Verstandelijk Gehandicapten' (*Ratification of the Decision by the Commission for GP Care, Social Care and Care for the Mentally Disabled on the Training Requirements*). Available at: <http://wetten.overheid.nl/BWBR0017529>.

33 KNMG/KNMP, 'KNMG/KNMP Richtlijn Uitvoering Euthanasie En Hulp Bij Zelfdoding.' Available at: <https://www.knmp.nl/praktijkvoering/richtlijnen/multidisciplinaire-richtlijnen/richtlijn-uitvoering-euthanasie-en-hulp-bij-zelfdoding>.

the health minister.[34] Elements of the Dutch '*poldermodel*'[35] still dictate that measures are preferably taken when there is support in the field; the KNMG often acts as the voice of health care professionals, so it can provide or withdraw this support.

Two other relevant Dutch professional bodies are the LHV, the National Association of General Practitioners and the OMS (the Dutch Order of Medical Specialists). The LHV works through its sister organisation the NHG. This promotes the scientific foundation of the work of GPs, by publishing the NHG-standards, medical guidelines for GPs: a selection of which will be included here.[36] The NHG guideline process is very similar to that of the KNMG, the obvious difference being that the members of the guideline development group are mostly GPs. The consultation is carried out by sending the concept of the guidance to 50 randomly selected GPs; references are sought from other professional associations. After this the guideline is presented to the 'authorisation committee', which has the final word on whether the guideline should be published and to what extent it might need modification before authorisation would be granted. This committee is composed of several professors of primary care medicine in the Netherlands and tasks itself with providing a final 'quality check' of the guideline that is developed. The LHV has a membership rate of about 98 per cent of all GPs in the Netherlands,[37] is a vocal supporter of 'GP-care' (*huisartsgeneeskunde*) and actively lobbies to that effect.

The OMS provide a very similar role for 'specialists', the Dutch term for consultants and surgeons in hospitals. The OMS sponsored the EBRO-platform that works on evidence-based guideline development and various different scientific organisations of medical specialists come together on this platform informally to work on guidelines.[38] Currently, the

---

34 Examples can be found on its website, where comments on new legislative initiatives appear and letters being sent to the parliament and reports of meetings with the health ministry are published.

35 The *poldermodel* describes a tradition of consensual decision making especially prevalent in the Netherlands during the purple coalition years when the Labour Party, the Liberal Democrats and the Conservatives formed a government, but is also used to describe earlier consensual styles of government all the way back to the Republic of the Seven United Provinces of the Netherlands. The use of the word 'polder' is appropriate, as it describes the forming of an area of land reclaimed from the sea and protected by dikes that can only come about through cooperation.

36 'NHG-Standaarden' (Chapter 2, n 41).

37 'Boeterapport NMa' (*Rapport of a Fine by the Dutch Competition Authority*) note 3. Available at: <https://www.acm.nl/sites/default/files/old_publication/bijlagen/4595_6888BLD.pdf>.

38 Burgers and van Everdingen (n 5).

OMS supports various professional organisations of specialists through its knowledge centre, which promotes and supports working with the evidence-based guideline development method and maintains a database of guidelines produced according to the EBRO method.[39] OMS does not produce guidelines itself, rather it acts as an umbrella for various scientific organisations of specialists and experts from its knowledge institute participate in guideline production.

From this brief overview, we can see that professional bodies in the Netherlands combine various roles: they are regulators who set standards for the education of professionals, guideline developers and they provide advocacy services. Guideline production is not an activity in isolation, but part of a broader drive for quality improvement by the professional bodies. The knowledge institute of OMS explains this well: 'guidelines are the basis of a policy of quality [in healthcare] of medical specialists and form a bridge between science and practice.'[40] These three professional associations, although influential, represent only a very partial picture of all organisations involved in guideline production. As a result, guideline production in the Netherlands is highly decentralised and fragmented with no clear leader and no hierarchical ordering of guidelines.

An important feature of these arrangements is that guidelines are produced by professional associations primarily for their use. There are exceptions to this, for example where multidisciplinary groups work on guidelines across professional boundaries, such as guidelines made by CBO.[41] Nonetheless, a primary driver for guideline production is provided by the wish to maintain (and improve) the quality of care provided by distinct groups of medical professionals. These guideline efforts seem to be mainly driven by the wish to self-regulate and are not primarily driven by government intervention. Competition between professional groups with the medical profession is also a part of this picture. Klazinga[42] and de Herk[43] show how guidelines are a response to changing government

---

39 'Richtlijnendatabase' (n 20).

40 'Kennisinstituut van Medisch Specialisten – Het Belang van Een Goede Richtlijn' (*Knowledge Institute of Medical Specialists – The importance of a good guideline*). Available at: <http://kims.orde.nl/het-kennisinstituut-voor-u/richtlijnen/het-belang-van-een-goede-richtlijn.html>.

41 BW Koes, RJ Sanders and MK Tuut, 'CBO-Richtlijn Voor Diagnostiek En Behandeling van Acute En Chronische Aspecifieke Lage Rugklachten' (2004) 148 *Nederlands Tijdschrift voor Geneeskunde* 310.

42 Klazinga (Chapter 2, n 44).

43 van Herk (Chapter 2, n 45).

pressures and, in that sense, are an attempt to ward off the (implicit) threat by government bodies to regulate the profession more directly. Guidelines in the Netherlands are developed because of an independent wish to further regulate professional standards and improve the quality of care, while at the same time, providing assurance to the government that, through these efforts, the profession can still be trusted to regulate its own affairs.

Guidelines in the Netherlands therefore have features of both professional self-regulation and government (mandated) self-regulation. Seeing this on a spectrum between the two extremes of 'pure' self-regulation and 'pure' government regulation, Dutch arrangements would lean towards professional self-regulation.

One further player needs to be discussed: healthcare insurers.[44] There are around 36 different insurers' labels active on the Dutch market, these labels refer to insurance companies or their agents marketing under their own name. This represents around 26 different insurance companies: the four largest conglomerates cover 95 per cent of the market.[45] Healthcare insurers play no direct role in the drafting of guidelines. They do, however, influence healthcare professionals through policies that refer to these guidelines. If a patient is insured by a healthcare insurer, he agrees to their specific policy for reimbursing healthcare costs. Whether certain costs are reimbursed sometimes depends on whether the treatment provided conforms to their guidelines. One example is the policy of the Friesland Health Insurer, which only reimburses bariatric surgery for cases of obesity if this conforms to the relevant medical practice guidelines.[46] This could potentially make guidelines into more than a quality instrument and extend its range to influence decisions on reimbursement of costs. Given the fact that guideline drafters will likely be aware of the way guidelines are used by healthcare insurance companies it is plausible they would be influenced by how insurers use their guidelines in practice. While healthcare insurers

---

44 These health insurers are insurance companies who solely provide insurance for health care.

45 'Zorgverzekeraars in Nederland' (*Health Insurers in the Netherlands*). Available at: <http://www.zorghulpatlas.nl/zorghulpwereld/zorgverzekering/zorgverzekeraars-in-nederland/>; 'Overzicht Zorgverzekeraars in Nederland' (*List of Health Insurers in the Netherlands*) <http://www.zorginstituutnederland.nl/binaries/content/documents/zinl-www/documenten/rubrieken/verzekering/1302-overzicht-zorgverzekeraars-in-nederland/Overzicht+zorgverzekeraars+%28in+Nederland%29.pdf>.

46 De Friesland Zorgverzekeraar, 'Basisverzekering Online Verzorgd Polis 2014' (*Basic Health Policy Online Care Policy 2014*). Available at: <https://www.defriesland.nl/Images/Basisverzekering-Online-Verzorgd-Polis-2014-11650.pdf>.

are thus not central to this research, they need to be mentioned to create an overall picture of the Dutch healthcare system.

3.2.2. ENGLAND

In England, NICE functions as the central body for the production of guidelines. It employs formal methods to decide who the actors are that are involved in guideline production. It explains on its website that the structure of guideline development has eight steps. After referral by the Department of Health, stakeholders can register their interest. These stakeholders can be national organisations of patients or carers, health professionals or representatives of the pharmaceutical industry and they are consulted during the process. The National Collaborating Centre (NCC), an independent guideline centre funded by NICE, which consists of representatives of several royal colleges of medicine, then prepares the scope of the guideline. Only then is the guideline development group established: consisting of medical professionals, representatives of patient groups and technical experts (mainly health economists, but some may also be medical information specialists). Guidelines are therefore always made by multidisciplinary groups of medical professionals. A draft guideline is produced by the group and opened for public consultation; only registered stakeholders can comment. The NCC produces the guidance and finally NICE authorises the guideline and disseminates it.[47] This process is highly structured and formalised and NICE therefore scores very high on the AGREE scale, which measures the rigorousness of the methods employed in guideline production and is used by academics and other experts to compare guideline institutions.[48] A further important characteristic of NICE is the mandatory involvement of a health economist in guideline development and an explicit requirement to take cost-effectiveness into account when developing a guideline as stated in the guideline manual used by NICE.[49]

This shows a picture of NICE replacing more informal attempts to make guidelines with a more rigid and formalised structure. Professional

---

47 'Developing NICE Clinical Guidelines'. Available at: <http://www.nice.org.uk/aboutnice/howwework/developingniceclinicalguidelines/developing_nice_clinical_guidelines.jsp>.

48 G Leng and M Baker, 'NICE Accredits Guidelines Using International AGREE Criteria' (2013) 347 *BMJ* f4771.

49 NICE, 'Developing NICE Guidelines: The Manual' (Chapter 2, n 81) ch 7.

associations are not completely excluded from the process as they can influence who will be part of the working group in the National Collaborating Centre; in this indirect way they remain in control of the process. The arrangements are closer to a form of state regulation, as the professional associations can only participate in the guideline-making process on the terms set by NICE. The mandatory involvement of a health economist, for example, also points in that direction. NICE has not completely replaced other bodies in making guidelines. There are still Royal Colleges who produce their own guidelines, but they often take the form of documents providing a more localized or contextualised version of a NICE guideline. It would be fair to say that NICE guidelines have the greatest authority in the medical field in England.

3.2.3. COMPARING INSTITUTIONS IN ENGLAND AND THE NETHERLANDS

While the historical trajectories of guideline development in the Netherlands and England started out looking very similar, with the advent of NICE the actors in the guideline field have taken on a different shape. In the Netherlands, professional associations control the development of guidelines and they invite members of their own associations to participate in producing them. In England, NICE sets priorities for guideline developments and members of associations have a more indirect role in the process through participation in Guideline Centres who provide the working groups developing guidelines. Whether these differences on paper turn out to be relevant when it comes to the process of developing a guideline is something this book will explore.

Another clear institutional difference is the fact that NICE makes it mandatory for its guideline groups to consider the patient's perspective through the requirement that the guideline development group includes a member from a patient organisation. In the Netherlands, patients are not always included in guideline groups, but other methods are sometimes used to establish the patient perspective such as questionnaires.[50]

The more fragmented nature of guideline production in the Netherlands opens up the possibility that several specialities might produce guidelines

---

50 'Richtlijnendatabase' (n 20). An analysis of a selection of the guidelines in this database shows various ways of including the 'patient perspective' in guideline production.

that are not fully joined up, for example, when GPs might provide different advice from consultants in hospitals because they refer to different guidelines. This, in turn, might affect the drafting of guidelines if different parties aim to avoid those differences and strive for harmonisation. NICE guidance is less likely to lead to conflicting results in this way because it is always multidisciplinary in nature, where everyone in the chain of care is involved in the drafting process. For NICE guidelines a potential pitfall would be to ensure the *internal* consistency of the guidelines it produces. The potential impact of these differences will be included in the assessment of guidelines in this book.

Cost-effectiveness considerations and their role in the development of guidelines and the way that these elements of the guideline development process are institutionally embedded, differ between the two countries. In England, NICE, through its guideline manual, ensures a role for cost-effectiveness considerations in the development of guidelines. Any such reference is absent in the Netherlands. This difference might have a significant impact on the development of guidelines and we will consider how these prima facie differences work out in practice.

3.3. THE REGULATORY ENVIRONMENT OF GUIDELINES

We have identified the various organisations that play a role in the healthcare system and have the potential to influence, or work with, guidelines. The broader institutional and regulatory context in which 'the world of guidelines' is located are those institutions that make up the healthcare system: hospitals, regulators, the Department of Health and parliament. A description of the relevant bodies will enable us to establish where potential relationships between guidelines and policy in the wider context of the healthcare system take place. In the Netherlands this means the healthcare system as it stands after the last major reform in 2006, while in England the health care system after the reform of the Health and Social Care Act 2012 will be considered. In describing these two healthcare systems, no attempt is made to be fully comprehensive, rather only those aspects of the healthcare systems that could plausibly influence the development of guidelines will be discussed. By placing a stress on both the institutions and their regulatory functions a good picture of these aspects of the context of guideline development will emerge.

3.3.1. THE NETHERLANDS

This chapter will describe the situation in the Netherlands up to 2014 when the research undertaken for this study started. It will not address in detail more recent developments.[51] In the Netherlands, the healthcare system can be described as one of managed competition. Healthcare insurers play a central role as they contract care with providers to make sure the insured get the healthcare they are entitled to. Furthermore, there is a contractual relationship between the insured/patient and the healthcare insurer through an insurance policy. A further relationship is the relationship between the patient and healthcare professional, where the Act on the medical treatment contract plays a role.[52]

This system of competition is regulated and managed through several bodies who are (to a greater or lesser extent) independent from the government: ACM, NZA, IGZ and Zorginstituut Nederland. The ACM (Authority for Consumers and Markets) is the competition regulator who works in conjunction with the NZA (Dutch Healthcare Authority), who is the specialised healthcare competition regulator. The IGZ (Health Inspectorate) oversees the quality of healthcare.

The *Zorginstituut Nederland* (the National Health Care Institute) addresses various health insurance aspects such as the risk-adjusted compensation payments to insurers,[53] enforcement of the mandatory

---

51 In relation to medical guidelines, two recent developments are noteworthy: the establishment of a quality institute as part of the Netherlands Health Institute and the codification of the medical standard as positive norm in article 7:453 of the Dutch Civil Code, which now includes a reference to the register of quality standards kept by the quality institute. These two developments signal a shift from reliance on professional self-regulation to more state regulation in the field of quality of care. While in the past professional standards were purely a matter for professional bodies, the healthcare institute now has a role in authorising standards and can, as last resort, require healthcare parties to draw up standards if insufficient action is taken. It is also made more explicit by the state that healthcare professionals should follow guidelines or explain why they deviate from them, through this explicit reference to the register of standards. These developments started in response to professionals failing to reach consensus on guidelines in various areas of practice, which happened after the guidelines discussed in this book had been published.

52 Wet op de geneeskundige behandelovereenkomst.

53 To achieve community-rated insurance premiums, a sophisticated risk-adjustment payment is made between insurers through *Zorginstituut Nederland*, to compensate for 'bad risks' (i.e. people who have high healthcare needs). This task has recently been moved to the CAK (centraal administratiekantoor). These changes are not further detailed here.

insurance requirement. Through its quality institute, it facilitates medical guideline production and dissemination and is responsible for deciding on the limits of the insured package of care on behalf of the government and making cost-effectiveness judgements based on the principles of evidence-based medicine. This explains why cost-effectiveness considerations do not feature prominently in Dutch guidelines, as these issues are decided elsewhere by the Zorginstituut (and its predecessor institutions). Of these institutions only the Zorginstituut has any active involvement in guidelines, but most of its work in this area started after 2014, so did not play a role in the development of the guidelines discussed here.

Finally, the Ministry of Health has 'system responsibility' for the overall healthcare system, making sure that it delivers affordable, high-quality, care. But this 'responsibility' is rather different from that of the Secretary of State for Health and Social Care in England as is not a direct legal obligation to provide for a comprehensive healthcare service. The Ministry of Health might be described as a 'meta-regulator' encouraging and steering independent parties towards the goal, but not providing any healthcare directly. Politicians are at a greater distance from healthcare delivery; this has been a deliberate choice in the design of the healthcare system as a result of the 2006 reforms.

The Dutch healthcare system might be described as an attempt to strike a balance between the opposing interests of medical professionals, who strive to provide the maximum amount of healthcare for the highest possible remuneration and healthcare insurers, who strive to keep the premiums they have to charge their customers (all Dutch citizens) as low as possible to maximise their market share.[54] The Dutch government, through its regulators, acts as referee and by providing detailed regulation of this 'market' creates a level 'playing field' (to stay with an economic analogy).

What is interesting about these arrangements is the fact that none of them seem to directly affect the development of guidelines. This organisation of healthcare leaves the responsibility for producing, maintaining and updating guidelines in the hands of professional associations. This seems to be the result of the fact that most of the regulatory interventions in the Dutch healthcare systems are concerned more with price than with issues of quality.

---

54 Healthcare insurers can make a profit but have to reinvest this into healthcare (through lower premiums) and are not allowed to distribute this to shareholders or other external parties.

This leaves open the issue of financing of medical practice guidelines in the Netherlands. This financing comes from various sources and often has an ad hoc nature. Some guidelines are financed through the Foundation for the Financing of Quality of Medical Specialists,[55] some through payments by hospitals for their use (e.g. the guidelines developed by the working group for infection prevention).[56] In some cases, such as those of the former EBRO platform, guideline production is funded by subsidies from the Ministry of Health. Finally, most of the guidelines are financed out of the budget of the scientific or professional organisation who produce it, such as the NHG-Standaarden who are financed by the NHG itself.

3.3.2. ENGLAND

The situation in England is described in relation to the most recent 2012 healthcare reforms. The Secretary of State for Health and Social Care and NHS England can give direction to NICE on which clinical guidelines to produce and in this way can potentially actively steer which guidelines are produced. However, the government cannot influence the content of a guideline. This aspect is left to professional self-regulation, as the guideline development groups employ medical professionals who negotiate on the content of the guideline.

The English healthcare system has features of competition, but this takes place within an 'internal market'. It mimics features of a market within the bureaucratic system of the nationalised hospitals that exists in England. It is clear that the state plays a more active role in this system, by steering actively how the 'market' functions within the existing structures through several arm's-length bodies. The government is also actively involved through its control of NICE. This allows for the setting of the topics that need to be covered by guidelines. Furthermore, the government controls the budget of NICE and in this way is directly in control of the financing of guidelines and can potentially choose areas for guideline development.

Although there are no healthcare insurers in the NHS, this does not mean that 'contract' does not play a role: this arrangement is established

---

55 'Orde van Medisch Specialisten – Stichting Kwaliteitsgelden Medisch Specialisten (SKMS)' <http://www.orde.nl/over-oms/wat-doet-de-oms/stichting-kwaliteitsgelden-medisch-specialisten-skms.html>.

56 Which was disbanded in June 2017 but these guidelines are still in use pending a new financing structure being agreed. 'Werkgroep Infectiepreventie (WIP)' <http://www.rivm.nl/Onderwerpen/W/Werkgroep_Infectiepreventie_WIP>.

through NHS England and clinical commission groups (CCGs) who act as commissioners and so mimic a market situation. The Standard NHS contract between a CCG and a provider of healthcare, say an NHS Foundation Trust, can require adherence to clinical guidelines.

NICE, however, does not have a monopoly on guideline production: the Royal Colleges and various associations of doctors produce guidelines independent from NICE.[57] The General Medical Council, in its publication *Good Medical Practice*,[58] provides ethical guidelines to doctors.

The English healthcare system is now based on the Health and Social Care Act 2012 (HSCA). This opens by changing the role of the Secretary of State from providing a comprehensive healthcare service to *only securing that* a comprehensive healthcare service is provided for.[59] This might look like a small change in wording but it embodies a radical shift in the conception of how the NHS should be run. The Secretary of State now delegates the function of providing a comprehensive health service to the NHS Health Commissioning Board, clinical commissioning groups and local authorities. However, the Secretary of State remains responsible to parliament for providing a comprehensive health service.[60] This set-up inevitably causes tension between the independence of the arm's-length bodies and the responsibility of the Secretary of State when something goes wrong and the promise in the 2010 white paper to liberate the NHS (from day-to-day political control).[61] The Department of Health still plays a central role in the NHS, despite the 2012 reforms that nominally seemed to reduce its influence; it appears it has only gained in importance. Before we consider the Secretary of State and the Department of Health, we must describe the arm's-length bodies.

The NHS Commissioning board, operating under the name NHS England, is the central body responsible for commissioning specialised

57 The Royal Colleges as well as associations of specialists and nurses.

58 General Medical Council, 'Good Medical Practice (2013)' (2013). Available at: <https://www.gmc-uk.org/-/media/documents/good-medical-practice---english-1215_pdf-51527435.pdf?la=en>.

59 Health and Social Care Act 2012, s. 1: 'The Secretary of State must continue the promotion in England of a comprehensive health service designed to secure improvement – (a) in the physical and mental health of the people of England, and (b) in the prevention, diagnosis and treatment of physical and mental illness. (2) For that purpose, the Secretary of State must exercise the functions conferred by this Act so as to secure that services are provided in accordance with this Act.'

60 Health and Social Care Act 2012, s. 1(3): 'The Secretary of State retains ministerial responsibility to Parliament for the provision of the health service in England.'

61 Department of Health, *Equity and Excellence: Liberating the NHS*. (Stationery Office, 2010).

nationalised services, primary care and care for offenders and for overseeing the 211 new clinical commissioning groups (CCGs). It provides commissioning support to the CCGs, authorises them and can place conditions on their authorisation.[62]

These CCGs are the 'new form' of practice-based commissioning, formed by groups of general practices in a specified area, who commission healthcare for that area. They have been given a large part of the commissioning budget and, through their local knowledge, are seen to be suited to commission services based on the needs of the local population.[63] In making decisions on commissioning care, the CCGs must pay due regard to competition law, as required by section 75 of the HSCA 2012 and are not allowed to engage in anti-competitive behaviour.[64] This brings us to NHS Improvement[65] and its extended role under the Health and Social Care Act 2012. NHS Improvement now fulfils several roles: it protects choice for patients and prevents anti-competitive behaviour, it licenses NHS healthcare providers, it sets the national tariff and it has a duty to enable integrated care delivery. It is therefore a specialised healthcare competition authority,[66] as well as the price-setting body in conjunction with NHS England. At the same time, NHS Improvement licences a broad range of providers so as to require them to follow basic transparency and competition criteria.[67] Reducing healthcare inequalities and improving healthcare quality through integrated care delivery also falls to NHS Improvement, which might lead to tensions with its role as competition authority. The Health and Social Care Act 2012 simply states that NHS

---

62 NHS England, 'CCG Authorisation'. Available at: <https://www.england.nhs.uk/2012/09/auth-decision/>.

63 £65 billion of the £95 billion budget, the remaining £30 billion is spent by NHS England.

64 Section 76(1) states: 'Regulations may impose requirements on the National Health Service Commissioning Board and clinical commissioning groups for the purpose of securing that, in commissioning health care services for the purposes of the NHS, they – (a) adhere to good practice in relation to procurement; (b) protect and promote the right of patients to make choices with respect to treatment or other health care services provided for the purposes of the NHS; (c) do not engage in anti-competitive behaviour which is against the interests of people who use such services. (3) Regulations under this section may, in particular, impose requirements relating to – (a) competitive tendering for the provision of services.'

65 Previously known as Monitor (from July 2012 until April 2016) and more previously as the Independent Regulator for Foundation Trusts (from January 2004).

66 With a duty to cooperate with the Competition and Markets Authority.

67 Health and Social Care Act 2012, s. 94, standard conditions (for a licence).

Improvement should resolve these tensions and publish how they have achieved this.[68] These arm's-length bodies all report to the Secretary of State for Health.

The Secretary of State has several levers to influence the arm's-length bodies it has created: it sets the mandate for the NHS commissioning board,[69] gives guidance to NHS Improvement about its functions,[70] provides guidance on the improvement of quality of services,[71] has wide powers to intervene when a body fails to act in the interests of the health service,[72] has a greater role in the reconfigurations of NHS (Foundation) Trusts[73] and claims strong oversight over the National Institute for Health and Care Excellence that produces guidelines and quality standards.[74] This list is far from comprehensive.[75] It is of course not self-evident that just because the Secretary of State has these powers it means he/she will use them and it is too early to draw firm conclusions in this regard, but there are some suggestions that the Secretary of State might be micro-managing the NHS.[76] The last player on the government stage we have to consider is the National Institute for Health and Care Excellence (NICE) whose role has largely already been covered in the section on the history of medical guidelines.

3.3.3. CONCLUSIONS

In both countries, the institutional environment is aligned with a system of managed competition and the specialist competition regulators (NMA, NHS Improvement) now play a prominent role. However, there

68 Ibid, s. 67.
69 Ibid, s. 23.
70 Ibid, s. 63.
71 Ibid, s. 23.
72 Ibid, s. 71.
73 Ibid, ss 174–178.
74 Ibid, s. 237.
75 It does not list powers of local authorities for example, nor does it list powers in any other Healthcare Act.
76 Denis Campbell, '"Control Freak" Jeremy Hunt Accused of Manipulating NHS for Political Ends' *The Guardian* (27 March 2014). Available at: <http://www.theguardian.com/society/2014/mar/27/jeremy-hunt-control-freak-manipulating-nhs>; Daniel Boffey, 'NHS Chief Admits to Dismay at Jeremy Hunt's Meddling' *The Guardian* (21 December 2013). Available at: <http://www.theguardian.com/society/2013/dec/21/nhs-service-jeremy-hunt-malcolm-grant>.

are differences in the way in which competition is seen to operate in the two countries. In the Netherlands, all hospitals are private not-for-profit foundations, while in the NHS, the hospitals are nationalised. Therefore, competition in the NHS has a more internal and bureaucratic nature compared to the Dutch healthcare system. These differences are significant insofar as they suggest that the government in the Netherlands takes a more 'hands-off' approach to the healthcare system and claims only a residual responsibility while in England, government is more directly involved in shaping the system of managed competition. Therefore, labels such as 'managed competition' might hide more than that they reveal, as these discussions are necessarily in the form of broad strokes.

These more generic differences are reflected in the approach taken to the development of guidelines in both countries. While the development of guidelines is in the hands of professional associations in the Netherlands, in England, NICE, a statutory body, has a large role. Potentially, this institutional difference might have some effect on the development of guidelines. Where guidelines in the Netherlands might plausibly reflect the priorities of healthcare professionals, those in England might more closely align with the interests and priorities of the government of the day.

Guideline financing is another area of difference between the two countries. In the Netherlands there is no single source to finance guidelines. Sometimes professional associations pay, sometimes private or government subsidies cover the cost. In England the financing of guidelines is provided centrally through the NICE budget and, in this way, it is guaranteed and controlled by the government.

3.4. THE IMPLICATIONS OF GUIDELINES FOR THE GOVERNANCE OF HEALTHCARE

To fully understand the environment of guidelines and explain why understanding the development of guidelines is of interest it is necessary to consider the implications guidelines have for the governance of healthcare. Guidelines have as their stated aim to influence clinical decision-making in daily medical practice, but there at least four other ways in which guidelines could affect the governance of healthcare in the Netherlands and England: through financing decisions, medical tribunals and enforcement of standards, organisation of healthcare and remuneration of healthcare professionals. These areas will be further explored for both countries.

3.4.1. THE NETHERLANDS

In the Netherlands the contract with a Healthcare Insurer determines whether you receive a refund (or your healthcare insurer pays for) your medical treatment. These insurers are regulated and the 'package' of care they must provide is primarily determined by law.[77] While the broad strokes are set through legislation, the healthcare insurers still have some discretion; this is where guidelines play a role. A few examples will suffice to illustrate this. Healthcare Insurer Menzis pays for an amount of test strips to measure blood sugar based on an interdisciplinary guideline created by various diabetes professionals,[78] while De Friesland restricts bariatric surgery to those cases conforming to a guideline[79] and the list goes on. This shows how guidelines have an impact on the rules surrounding the financing of treatment. The implication is that is it possible in the Netherlands that a guideline recommends certain treatment that falls outside insured care, for which a patient would have to pay. At the same time, a more expensive definition of care in a guideline can filter through into a larger insured package of care. So, guidelines, while being made for clinical care, are being used more widely by healthcare insurers in the Netherlands. This use of guidelines in decisions on the financing of care adds a further dimension to the work of guideline groups as their guideline potentially has a wider remit than the clinical setting for which it is written.

Guidelines also plays an important role in the enforcement of what is called the 'professional standard', defined by Hout as: 'the legal requirements, jurisprudence, professional codes and rules of conduct, professional-technical regulations, standards, guidelines and protocols'.[80] This professional standard is upheld through statutory disciplinary medical tribunals. These tribunals consist of lawyers and healthcare professionals.[81] The judgments of these tribunals on what the professional standard requires of a medical professional is strongly influenced by the guidelines

77 Besluit and Regeling Zorgverzekering.

78 EADV/NAD, 'Een Multidisciplinaire Richtlijn over Zelfcontrole van Bloedglucose-waarden Door Mensen Met Diabetes.Pdf' <http://www.venvndiabeteszorg.nl/kennisbank%20documenten/Kennisbank-open-zelfcontrole/Een%20multidisciplinaire%20richtlijn%20over%20zelfcontrole%20van%20bloedglucosewaarden%20door%20mensen%20met%20diabetes.pdf>.

79 De Friesland Zorgverzekeraar (n 46).

80 FAG Hout, 'The Dutch Disciplinary System for Health Care: An Empirical Study' (Institute for Research in Extramural Medicine (EMGO institute) at the dept of Public and Occupational Health VU University Medical Center (VUMC) 2006) 9.

81 Wet op de beroepen in de individuele gezondheidszorg, art. 55.

that regulate their conduct. A general statement that is found in many Medical Tribunal judgments is:

> The medical tribunal points out first of all that the disciplinary assessment of professional conduct is not aimed to establish whether this conduct could have been better, rather it is aimed at answering whether the medical professional has stayed with the boundaries of reasonably competent medical practice, paying attention to the scientific standard at the time of the conduct in issue and what was accepted within the profession as norm or standard at the time.[82]

The standard or norm referred to is often found in a medical guideline. A very cursory analysis shows that the word 'guideline' is mentioned in 1,693 of the 8,360 judgments published.[83] Given that guidelines are described using a wide variety of terms (standard, opinion, protocol etc.) and that not all medical conduct is regulated by guidelines it seems reasonable to conclude that guidelines play an important role in the work of these tribunals. This further underlines the point that guidelines have normative force in the context of disciplinary tribunals. While healthcare professionals can (and do) explain why they did not follow certain guidelines there is a strong presumption that guidelines reflect the 'professional standard'.

Guidelines can also indirectly influence the organisation of healthcare resources. If reference is made, either directly or indirectly, to level of specialisation required, this might influence the placement of resources. In the Netherlands a development to concentrate care has been taking place, based on quality and volume norms for several specialised forms of cancer treatment.[84] While these norms are themselves not the focus here, they do refer to guidelines as underpinning this decision making.

---

82 Translation from the Dutch by author: 'Het college wijst er allereerst op, dat het bij de tuchtrechtelijke toetsing van professioneel handelen er niet om gaat of dat handelen beter had gekund, maar om het geven van een antwoord op de vraag of de beroepsbeoefenaar bij het beroepsmatig handelen is gebleven binnen de grenzen van een redelijk bekwame beroepsuitoefening, rekening houdend met de stand van de wetenschap ten tijde van het klachtwaardig geachte handelen en met hetgeen toen in de beroepsgroep ter zake als norm of standaard was aanvaard.'

83 By searching for richtlijn (guideline in Dutch) on the website tuchtrecht.nl that publishes judgments by these tribunals.

84 'Zorgverzekeraars Nederland – Nieuwsbericht' <https://www.zn.nl/338067458/Nieuwsbericht?newsitemid=1673035776>; 'De relatie tussen volume en kwaliteit van zorg: tijd voor een brede benadering.' (Consortium Onderzoek Kwaliteit van Zorg 2012).

A final potential influence of guidelines is indirectly as an aspect of the policy that health insurers formulate for contracting healthcare professionals. If a healthcare professional has a contract with a healthcare insurer, they will normally be given a higher payment than a professional without such a contract. Healthcare insurers make contracts conditional upon working according to medical guidelines. An example would be paediatric foot care for diabetes patients where the healthcare insurer De Amersfoortse requires compliance with a protocol for paediatric care based on the diabetic guideline that will be discussed here.[85]

3.4.2. ENGLAND

In England, medical guidelines influence financing and contracting decisions between a CCG and a Healthcare Trust or other healthcare body such as a consortium of GPs. There are +/− 200 CCGs who have made many thousands of procurement contracts (decisions to 'buy' care) a full examination of which falls outside the scope here. A randomly drawn example from these many contracts will hopefully be sufficient to illustrate this argument. The City and Hackney Clinical Commission Group has tendered for end-of-life care to a consortium of GPs in the area; in the (awfully named) contract service specification we find that NICE Guideline (NG31) Care of Dying Adults in the Last Stages of Life has become a service standard, and in that guise the GPs are obliged to follow this guideline.[86]

Just like in the Dutch system, guidelines play a role before disciplinary tribunals. The system is slightly different in the UK where the medical practitioner tribunal[87] is an independent body which adjudicates complaints brought by the General Medical Council. A prime role is played by the GMC's guidance on Good Medical Practice[88] and the 22 other pieces of GMC guidance that overarching guidance document

---

85 De Amersfoortse, 'Protocol Voetonderzoek Bij Diabetes Mellitus 1.3.Pdf' <https://www.amersfoortse.nl/api/pod/getpdf?uri=/POD/r/Pdf/42701.pdf>.

86 City and Hackney CCG, 'End of Life Contract – Service Specification 2017.Pdf' (City and Hackney CCG). Available at: <http://onel.nhs.sitekit.net/ONELCityHackney/Downloads/About%20Us/Tenders%20procurements%20contracts/2017%20contracts/End%20of%20Life%20%20contract%20-%20Service%20Specification%20%202017.pdf>.

87 Or more precisely one of the eight of such tribunals.

88 General Medical Council (n 58).

refer to, as these are employed to establish whether doctors are fit to practice medicine.[89] The focus is, therefore, more on the general conduct of the healthcare professional rather than a forensic examination of a specific medical situation. Nonetheless, in these cases, guidelines do play a role, although they might inform more of the background of a complaint about a doctor's fitness to practice.

The impact of guidelines on the organisation of care in England would work in the same way if, in NICE guidance, explicit mention is made of a preferred professional for the delivery of care. Before 2014, very limited reference was made to service delivery in the NICE guideline manual which stated that this normally fell outside of the NICE's remit.[90] However, the current version of the manual does include an explicit methodology for addressing this issue.[91] It is likely that there will be increasing room in NICE guidelines to address aspects of the organisation of care.

The issue of remuneration and the influence of medical guidelines on this can be illustrated using the example of GPs and diabetes care. Part of the payment of GPs depend on their performance in the Quality and Outcomes Framework (QOF):[92] an element of this framework is diabetes care. To evaluate the care GPs provide under the framework, indicators are used; these are drawn from or based on NICE guidelines.[93]

3.5. CONCLUSION

The history of medical practice guidelines has shown that behind the common focus on 'evidence-based' medicine in England and the Netherlands, the guideline process in the Netherlands is more fragmented, with a great variety of organisations being involved in the process without clear coordination. This is in contrast to the centralised approach used in

89 Ibid, endnotes.

90 NICE, 'Developing NICE Guidelines' (Chapter 2, n 81) 56.

91 NICE, 'Developing NICE Guidelines: The Manual' (2018). <https://www.nice.org.uk/process/pmg20/chapter/introduction-and-overview>.

92 NHS Employers, BMA, NHS England, 'General Medical Services (GMS) Contract Quality and Outcomes Framework' 08157 <https://www.nhsemployers.org/-/media/Employers/Documents/Primary-care-contracts/QOF/2018-19/2018-19-QOF-guidance-for-stakeholders.PDF?la=en&hash=6A53571FC0F7A63FA7354951C733B9E6011EC2CD>.

93 NICE, 'The NICE Menu of General Practice and Clinical Commissioning Group Indicators' (2018) <https://www.nice.org.uk/Media/Default/Standards-and-indicators/indicator-menu-update.pdf>.

England through NICE. There is also a clear difference in ownership in the Netherlands, with a process closer to the medical profession, compared to England where the state has more control. When considering the actors in both countries a similar picture emerges. In the Netherlands, a greater number of diverse type of actors and organisations are involved in the guideline production process, while in England, NICE imposes a more rigid model with certain pre-established participants.

Guidelines in both countries can be described as an attempts at professional regulation by medical professionals that play out along a spectrum between self-regulation and state-regulation, with the Netherlands tending towards the former and England the latter. In both countries, these guidelines are made for use in a healthcare system, but it is the regulatory and institutional environment that forms part of the context of guideline development.

Both countries describe their healthcare system, in general terms, as one of managed competition. This involves a great many arm's-length bodies who involve themselves in setting prices for a 'market' of healthcare to function effectively. The effect this has on the development of guidelines differs. In the Netherlands, these arrangements do not impact the room professional associations have to create guidelines. Rather, the environmental factors are positive, in the sense that the government provides (some) subsidies for the development of guidelines and these are widely used in the healthcare system to support decision making. In England, the situation is similar; competition arrangements do not in themselves directly affect guideline development with the notable exception that the state has decided to create NICE. This means that in the guideline development process, cost considerations are more prominent as the government requires NICE to take these into account. In the Netherlands, these decisions are not taken by guideline makers but by the Zorginstituut, which traditionally has had the role of deciding the extent of the insured care package.

Finally, related to these differences in government involvement in guidelines is the way in which the financing works. While in England there is a government budget to fund NICE and the guidelines it produces, in the Netherlands this funding comes from professional associations, subsidies or other sources. This chapter has provided some of the historical background to guidelines, their current institutional and regulatory embedding within healthcare systems and the way they are financed, which we will further explore in the case studies that follow in Chapters 4 and 5.

CHAPTER 4
LOWER BACK PAIN
Guidelines in England and the Netherlands

Lower back pain is a very common condition, around 60–85 per cent of the population will experience a period of lower back pain during their lifetime.[1] Most of these cases are so-called 'non-specific lower back pain', where there is no identifiable physical cause of the pain. This is an area of medicine where a plethora of different treatments exist for this condition, but not all of them are based on solid evidence: an area where one would expect guidelines to fill a gap by providing advice on which treatments to avoid and which treatments to recommend. We will first consider the English guidelines on this topic before considering the Dutch guidelines. Both these guidelines present a path of care for patients and make several choices on which treatments to offer and in which order to provide them.

4.1. THE ENGLISH GUIDELINE ON LOWER BACK PAIN

The focus of our analysis will be the 2009 guideline on persistent non-specific lower back pain (hereafter: back pain) drafted by the NCCP[2] and authorised by NICE.[3] The guideline was drafted by a group of medical professionals from a diverse background including GPs, physiotherapists,

---

1 Ann C Papageorgiou and others, 'Estimating the Prevalence of Low Back Pain in the General Population: Evidence From the South Manchester Back Pain Survey' (1995) 20 *Spine* 1889; BF Walker, 'The Prevalence of Low Back Pain: A Systematic Review of the Literature from 1966 to 1998' (2000) 13 *Journal of Spinal Disorders* 205.

2 National Collaborating Centre for Primary Care.

3 P Savigny and others, 'Low Back Pain: Early Management of Persistent Non-Specific Low Back Pain' (National Collaborating Centre for Primary Care and Royal College of General Practitioners 2009). Available at: <http://www.atencionprimaria.imib.es/docmanager/Low_back_pain_guia_NICE_2009.pdf>.

a spinal surgeon, nurses and patients. They were supported by a technical team provided by the NCCP consisting of a healthcare economist, information specialists and health fellows.

Before the guideline group was established, the chair for the group was recruited to work with a clinical advisor and the technical team in preparing the scope of the guideline. The chair and clinical advisor were approached informally by NICE and agreed to participate. The reason they were approached was because they had done work for NICE in the past on back pain and related areas and were therefore well-known and well-regarded in this medical field.

The scope sets the limits of the medical condition the guideline will provide recommendations on. In this case, the scope only included back pain from six weeks to one year.[4] So acute back pain that lasted less than six weeks was not included, nor was chronic back pain that lasted longer than a year. This decision was made during discussions between the chair and clinical advisor of the guideline group and the technical team at NICE. NICE had recently published a guideline on acute lower back pain and wanted to draft a separate guideline that had a duration longer than a year.

After the scope had been established it was clear what the expertise of the members of the guideline groups should be; they were subsequently approached informally, based on the expertise of the members of NICE; the chair of the guideline group also had a role in this. Some guideline group members had expressed an interest in being included before they were subsequently approached to take part; some cited reasons of professional prestige as motivating them, while others were driven by an interest to see first-hand how guidelines were developed. The final group consisted of a diverse group of participants: a GP, nurse, chiropractor, clinical phycologist, osteopath, acupuncturist, occupational therapist, two lay members and several academics in the field of back pain.

Once the group was formed, they discussed the scope that had been set before by NICE, and agreed that the focus of the guideline would be on looking for evidence that might prevent back pain from becoming chronic pain. As one guideline group member said about this discussion:

> We were then able to re-discuss the scope … But it was decided to go for 6 weeks to twelve months … It was really to look at what literature was

---

4 Ibid, Appendix A.

> available ... the interest was at that stage to improve early treatment ... to look at how to prevent chronicity (...).[5]

However, not everyone was completely happy with this decision, as a guideline group member explained:

> it [the scope] does tend to cause problems. Particularly with the lower back pain guideline ... we were proscribed [by NICE] from including ... return to work as an outcome measure ... we weren't to look at anything but chronic [back pain studies] and it was predefined how chronic would be described, with something like lower back pain it is very difficult to have a clear dividing line between an acute [back pain] and chronic [back pain] presentation. The reason why this happened was because there was already a guideline for acute back pain, but [that guideline] was not going to be reviewed. As for return to work there was a working party looking at vocational rehabilitation, but that is very different from a treatment. There was no dissatisfaction but there was a lot of discussion. ... it [the scope] can be quite restrictive because it is often drawn up without considering the evidence or the clinical problem [at hand] ... I think they [later] realised their mistake doing something that was a little bit too narrow. It served their purpose at the time, they didn't want to cover surgery, acute [back pain]. Now they realised that it has to be broader not to be contradictory.[6]

This guideline group member is clearly not convinced by the justifications about the necessity to make different guidelines provided by NICE for limiting the scope of the guideline. His ideas about integrated treatment for back pain could not fully be accommodated within the scope of the work as it was set. Nonetheless, the scope remained unchanged, as it could not effectively be modified at this stage of the guideline's development.

Once the guideline group had been formed, the process of searching for medical studies could begin. As part of this process *key clinical questions* were formulated to guide the search in the literature. The guideline group was involved in formulating these clinical questions, in that way they could steer the direction of the topic they looked for in medical studies. Based on these questions, the results of the literature search were then considered by the guideline group. The English guideline group decided only to consider RCTs as evidence. If no RCTs came up after a search of the medical databases or the quality of the studies that were found were

5 English back pain guideline group member 4 (Middlesbrough, 16 March 2015).
6 English back pain guideline group member 3 (Interview by phone, 27 March 2015).

deemed insufficient, the consensus of the group would provide the basis of the recommendations.

This early choice in the process is important, as it excludes a great deal of evidence from consideration, namely all studies that are not RCTs and, as a result, gives an important role to consensus. When asked why the choice had been made to only include RCT-evidence one member of the guideline group said:

> There was a huge number of stakeholders who had their favourite treatment they wanted to see in the guideline … We will accept only RCTs evidence … unless they don't find any [RCTs]. We did that really to draw a level playing field between all the stakeholders. If RCT-evidence is present than we will consider it … So, we won't consider a whole volume of papers that weren't RCTs … It has a simplicity that was clearly attractive … When they [other healthcare professionals] later complained … we could stand up and say when we investigated the literature there was no RCT evidence to support your position.[7] … That was really one of the most important decisions [in the guideline drafting process].

This, however, did not mean that the discussion and recommendations did not include reference to other studies. The participants did discuss other studies they found relevant to the issue at hand. A guideline group member explains this as follows:

> It depends on the chair of the group. In our discussion we would also refer to other studies you had heard about. Normally that would be allowed and we would discuss those but we could only refer [in the guideline] to RCTs.[8]

This shows an interesting tension in defining evidence by members of the guideline group. In the text of the guideline, members have agreed that only RCTs will be referred to, so externally only this type of 'high-quality' evidence is presented to the public. Internally, however, a broader definition of what is considered evidence is adhered to, as guideline members are free to discuss other studies they are aware of in arguing for or against advice for treatments on lower back pain. This provides a starting point to consider how evidence is negotiated and constructed through the debates in the guideline group.

---

7 English back pain guideline group member 4 (Middlesbrough, 16 March 2015).

8 English back pain guideline group member 2 (London, 20 February 2015).

A further selection process played a role, which was tied to the decision to limit the scope to patients with lower back pain for longer than six weeks and shorter than one year in duration and to only accept RCTs. A guideline group member comments on this process of searching the literature in the following terms:

> That [the results of a search in the literature] includes all the studies they [the technical team] have selected. My impression is that [tend] to be quite highly selective based on scope. They tend to be more narrow in terms of their selection from what I have seen, then what you might do if you were performing a Cochrane Review [a type of systematic review]. So, in practice it tends to be broader, if you do a systematic review as a research project you tend to be as broad as you can and select all the data in and analyse it. NICE tend to narrow down much more specifically within the scope question. So, they are much more likely to exclude big studies that look like they might be in the area ... They may well exclude those [studies] because they do not fit closely enough in the 6 weeks to one-year bracket [the scope agreed].[9]

These comments are interesting because, at least in the eyes of this guideline group member, the evidence selection process seems to be too narrow. This opinion was not directly confirmed by other members of the group, but some did say that they would discuss studies other than those selected by the technical team.

These developments show how the process of forming a guideline group and defining both the scope and the key clinical questions introduces a process of selection of evidence. To an extent, the selection of questions to ask, in the form of clinical question, steers what answers will be found. How evidence was constructed and used in making choices for treatments in the English guideline will be considered in greater detail by analysing the recommendations for various treatments in turn.

4.2. EVIDENCE BASE FOR ENGLISH LOWER BACK PAIN TREATMENTS

The English guideline group considered several treatments for lower back pain. Together they form a pathway of care for patients who suffer from back pain from six weeks up to one year. The treatments are offered

9 English back pain guideline group member 2 (London, 20 February 2015).

in sequential order and increase from advice and pain relief to surgical intervention. Four treatments for back pain in this pathway are of particular interest: educational advice, exercise, manual therapy and acupuncture. Educational advice is seen as the first choice; the three treatments to be offered after this and are presented as equal, such that the choice of a treatment should be guided by the choice of the patient. Not all aspects of drafting a guideline would necessarily be controversial. The English guideline group was confronted with a couple of issues in establishing the evidence for treatments and interpreting this evidence in light of the goal of the guideline. One of these was the availability of a large amount of (potential) treatments for lower back pain. The guideline would need to establish which to recommend and which to advise against. When this was established, the group then needed to work out the best order in which to provide these treatments. By defining these two elements, a successful pathway of care could be defined for the group of patients who suffered back pain of between six weeks and one year in duration.

4.2.1. EVIDENCE USE FOR EDUCATIONAL ADVICE

The first area the guideline group discussed was educational booklets and whether they help in the treatment of lower back pain. While there are only three RCTs on this topic and these do not show benefit, they concluded, nonetheless, that educational materials may play a role.[10] This shows that only considering RCT evidence might lead to the realisation that this provides insufficient information on which to make a decision. This advice was reached by consensus, which suggests that for areas where good quality studies are rare, it may play a big role in the decision-making process. This recommendation is not worded in very strong terms: 'No evidence of statistically significant benefit was found. However, the GDG [Guideline Development Group] agreed that educational materials may have a role.'[11] However, showing no evidence of benefit is not equal to no benefit seems to be the logic underlying this consensual position. This sentiment is expressed by several guideline members as they explain that a large part of medical practice is not based on actual evidence and an even smaller part on high-quality evidence,

10 Savigny and others (n 3) 67–68.
11 Ibid.

as defined by this guideline group, which comprises RCTs and systematic reviews of RCTs: 'much of what we do is not based on evidence at all, let alone based on RCTs'.[12]

Taken in this light, the advice that educational materials may have a role is not surprising, as it accords with existing practice in treating lower back pain. There is no harm or side-effects associated with its use and, in these circumstances, such a treatment can be advised despite the lack of 'evidence' of effectiveness according to the standard set by the guideline group members.

4.2.2. EVIDENCE USE FOR EXERCISE

Advice and educational tools alone may not be sufficient and the patient may return to the healthcare practitioner still experiencing lower back pain. The next step in the English guideline is to offer exercise therapy. The advice to exercise is mainly based on the UK-BEAM trial,[13] the largest trial of its kind in England.

The trial can be described as follows: a group of 1,334 patients were randomised in five groups. One group received best care by GPs which consisted of active management of the patient through advice on staying active and providing patients with a copy of the *back book*.[14] The other four groups were divided in such a way that one received exercise therapy in NHS practice, one received manual therapy in NHS practice, one received manual therapy in private practice and one received manual therapy followed by exercise therapy. Discussion in the group centred around the question of whether this RCT evidence was sufficient to recommend this treatment. The group was looking at the effect the size of the treatment had in the trial. Even though the effect of exercise was shown to be small in the trial,[15] according to the group there was a big enough basis to recommend exercise as an option.

When asked why this judgement had been made, the general sentiment seemed to be that even though the effects were small, there was no

---

12 English back pain guideline group member 4 (Middlesbrough, 16 March 2015).

13 UK BEAM Trial Team, 'United Kingdom Back Pain Exercise and Manipulation (UK BEAM) Randomised Trial: Effectiveness of Physical Treatments for Back Pain in Primary Care' (2004) 329 *BMJ* 1377.

14 An educational booklet that gives advice on how to deal with back pain.

15 Even though there was shown to be a statistically significant reduction of pain, commentators doubt whether this was also clinically relevant.

alternative, otherwise you would end up not being able to recommend any treatment. A guideline group member explains this conclusion through an explanation of the pragmatic approach taken to the concept of 'meaningful clinical differences':

> It was a big pragmatic trial which was reasonably positive ... Which shows that in practice this [the treatment of manipulation of the back] shows to be effective so on the basis of that he [the chairman] was going to recommend manipulation [of the back]. That was because he took a pragmatic perspective, he wasn't so interested in what NICE has adopted, an insistence on a minimal important clinical difference over placebo. Which I think is wrong because it is not clinically relevant, the difference over placebo.[16]

The reasoning behind this stance seems to be that there exists a tendency (in doing trials with large groups of participants) to have an average towards the mean. Which would mean that, on average, a participant in the trial would show a small effect but that this would obscure the effect that for a group of patients there could be a large effect and for some no effect at all. The group thus decided that, despite a small average effect, exercise is an appropriate treatment because of the large group of patients with lower back pain.

A further reason behind this step lies in the fact that for all treatments for lower back pain the RCT evidence, if it is available, is relatively weak in the sense that the effect sizes are relatively small. For lower back pain there is not one clear treatment that provides a 'cure.' One guideline group member talked about this dilemma in some detail:

> To a certain extent you could end up saying nothing about some of these things [treatments] because of the lack of evidence in certain areas. And that doesn't really help anybody. It is incumbent on the guideline group to give some steer, so have you given it your best shot, even in the absence of very tight evidence. More so than many other conditions. If you look at the effect sizes of the studies that are most often quoted [in the medical literature] they are very small.[17]

For most guideline group members, the fact that the evidence they reviewed in making their decision was not perfect did not move them to refrain from making decisions. Those decisions, they argued, had to be made, as this was the duty of professionals who draft guidelines. So, they

16 English back pain guideline group member 2 (London, 20 February 2015).
17 English back pain guideline group member 3 (Interview by Phone, 27 March 2015).

tried to reflect the uncertainty of their knowledge in the formulation of recommendations that are relatively broad. As the quote above shows, they nonetheless felt compelled to make a decision regardless of a lack of solid evidence.

4.2.3. EVIDENCE USE FOR MANUAL THERAPY

If we compare the evidence on exercise as a treatment option with the evidence used for manual therapy the picture is very similar. The basis of the recommendation is the same UK-BEAM trial. As we have seen the trial established that manual therapy has a beneficial effect. The group therefore decided that a course of manual therapy should be offered as a treatment option. One guideline group member suggested that this might be due to a preference to keep existing treatments and not 'upset' current practice:

> The discussion varies and the level of evidence varies because of necessity. I get a feeling that common practice has a hand in it as well because you have clinicians that represent that around the room ... They want to some degree reflect practice if possible.[18]

Another guideline group member disagreed with that assessment and stressed the importance of treating evidence as an 'equaliser', providing that a level playing field that would limit the importance of any preconceived notions about treatments because of clinical experience:

> My job was to ensure that we were treating the evidence fairly. It was important that we were treating everything equally. Because ... professionals don't read guidelines, they scan guidelines to see where their treatment is, and then kick off if it not there ... We had quite a lot of alternative therapies that were not routinely provided on the NHS, why shouldn't it be available if it works.[19]

This quote illustrates two important points about the factors that influence the decision-making process in a guideline. Firstly, it provides another example of the use of evidence not only to support the group in reaching a decision about which treatments to recommend but also which treatments to drop. Showing the necessity of a minimum of evidence

18 English back pain guideline group member 2 (London, 20 February 2015).
19 English back pain guideline group member 3 (Interview by Phone, 27 March 2015).

before preferences based on clinical knowledge might be taken into account. The earlier decision to only allow RCT evidence led to treatments not being considered because they could not meet this threshold. This meant that if a treatment could be shown to work, according to the definitions adopted within the group, it should be recommended, whether it was an alternative therapy or regular therapy on the NHS. This would limit the influence of any clinical preferences that different members of the guideline group would have.

Secondly, it illustrates the realisation by the group that the guidelines will be used and assessed in a certain way by clinicians and that they should try to accommodate any potential critique the guideline may receive. To that end it was seen as important to ascribe all the decisions in the guideline to evidence and downplay the influence of any other factors as much as possible.

Manual therapy is broadly defined to include spinal manipulation, spinal mobilisation and massage.[20] This way of defining the treatment also has the effect of changing the organisation of care, because spinal mobilisation and manipulation are treatments provided by physiotherapists, osteopaths and chiropractors, who had a smaller role in the previous guideline. In this way, the guideline not only provides a recommendation to help practitioners choose a treatment option, but it also aims to change the organisation of care. However, my analysis suggests that it is not the evidence that forces these outcomes on the group, rather it is the choices that are made in categorisation of the evidence that provide the group with a basis for the recommendation. If manual therapy had been defined differently, this would have changed the frame through which the evidence would have been analysed. It is likely the resulting recommendation would not have been the same, even though the evidence drawn upon to support it would not have changed.

4.2.4. EVIDENCE USE FOR ACUPUNCTURE

The next treatment that is recommended in the English guideline is acupuncture. The evidence base for acupuncture consists of four RCT's and a systematic review. One of those studies[21] is considered to

20 Savigny and others (n 3) 103.

21 Kate J Thomas and others, *Longer Term Clinical and Economic Benefits of Offering Acupuncture Care to Patients with Chronic Low Back Pain* (Gray 2005).

provide the strongest evidence of the beneficial effect on reducing pain and reducing disability, even though the guideline group recognises that this study deviated from its protocol and had a high proportion of participants who did not complete it. The fact that this study did have the correct population of acupuncture patients, people with back pain between six weeks and one year, is considered to be important. One of the guideline members stated that the RCTs conducted outside England provided stronger evidence for acupuncture than the Thomas paper:

> Yes, this paper from York [the Thomas paper] was interesting … in retrospect I am very pleased they did it. But when they did do it, I thought this was an odd trial to do. It looked like this was propaganda for traditional acupuncture. An a+b trial, acupuncture + usual care versus acupuncture. That is only going to show a positive effect, it cannot really show anything negative. Interestingly, when they first wrote the protocol the primary outcome was at one year, when they finally wrote it up it was at two years. They had already started the trial by the time it moved. At 1 year the result was not significant. They had done 12 weeks of treatment at the beginning of that year not more. It became significant at the 2-year mark. Which I have never seen before in an acupuncture study … It looks to me like instead of the acupuncture group improving the control group deteriorated more [and thus causing a significant effect after 2 years].

Clearly this guideline group member has doubts about the validity of the results of this study, in particular, querying the result becoming significant at two years, while it was not at one year. This cannot be a result of the treatment, because it only lasted 12 weeks. This guideline group member was, however, in favour of providing acupuncture based on German studies:

> I wasn't going to raise any issues, there was already good data from Germany that agreed in terms of cost-effectiveness. The GDG was not interested in the German data because it was outside the NHS. I was not going to say anything [about his doubts about the English acupuncture study] because I knew that the German data [was] much bigger. So, I thought that was more reliable … They [the guideline group members] wouldn't have known the details of this [the English] study.[22]

Most of the guideline members preferred the evidence gathered within the NHS to evidence from other healthcare systems, even if this

22 English back pain guideline group member 2 (London, 20 February 2015).

evidence – in their view – was more convincing. This illustrates a tendency for guideline group members to give more weight to evidence from their own country. This is understandable as they might be more familiar with the research – or as in this case have participated in the trials themselves – when this is conducted in their own country. However, this has the effect of further limiting/restricting what is considered as evidence.

4.2.5. EVIDENCE USE FOR SPINAL FUSION

The guideline also addressed spinal fusion, which is a surgical procedure aim to alleviate back pain. The guideline did not recommend spinal fusion directly, because surgical procedures were not within the scope of the guideline. Rather, it advises practitioners to consider a referral when other treatments have failed. There was not a great deal of evidence supporting this treatment, but in this sense the treatment was not very different from exercise or manipulation that also relied on only a handful of studies.[23]

4.3. ACHIEVING CONSENSUS: INTERNAL WORKINGS OF GUIDELINE GROUPS

The English guideline group both considers and debates evidence and many different reasonable opinions can be formed about the same scientific study by different members of the group. The process of arriving at recommendations is therefore more complicated than a simple mechanical application of a given result of a scientific study to a condition or the tallying up of the positive results of studies. The recommendations that are agreed on are the result of debate among the members of the guideline group. This can take the form of questions about the methodological soundness of the scientific research, the clinical relevance of the scientific research, the acceptability of the choices to the outside world, such as government and healthcare practitioners and its effect on the organisation

---

23 For a meta-analysis of three RCT's, see T Ibrahim, IM Tleyjeh and O Gabbar, 'Surgical versus Non-Surgical Treatment of Chronic Low Back Pain: A Meta-Analysis of Randomised Trials' (2008) 32 *International Orthopaedics* 107. For a systematic review of the same studies and one further RCT see Sohail K Mirza and Richard A Deyo, 'Systematic Review of Randomized Trials Comparing Lumbar Fusion Surgery to Nonoperative Care for Treatment of Chronic Back Pain' (2007) 32 *Spine* 816.

of healthcare. This does not mean that guideline groups always invoke all these considerations/factors all the time. Some of the argumentation in the group is concerned with the more general questions of how to approach the medical studies that are used in the discussion in the group and the difficulties in matching results of clinical trials with the clinical practice of treating people with lower back pain:

> That's a standard [chronic back pain at 12 weeks], it's an epidemiological conceit that is put forward. If you look at the natural history of back pain it is a recurrent problem. Nobody is acute and then magically becomes chronic. It's a conceit that is used that causes all sorts of problems it's a convenience … It is very very very rare for someone to present [to a GP] with a first ever case [of acute back pain] But when you are looking at the evidence if people say we only took people who had back pain for less than 12 weeks it is very difficult to appraise whether they actually did because almost by the nature of the condition people have had it before and this is probably the first time they consulted. It often goes from first consultation not from first report … these sorts of things do muddy the water when you are trying to extract the data.[24]

This member of the guideline group presents his particular interpretation of a more general struggle to interpret medical studies within the context of the treatment of lower back pain. He points out how, in the interpretation of medical studies, one cannot be sure that the population of patients treated can really be meaningfully classified as either 'acute' or 'chronic'. This shows how, in interpreting medical studies and attaching values to the results of these studies, the guideline group uses their collective knowledge and understanding of the nature of the disease (almost everyone has repeated episodes of back pain) and knowledge of the current state of treatment to arrive at acceptable recommendations.

Guideline group members also discussed in more general terms, sometimes explicitly, sometimes implicitly, the approach to treating lower back pain and the underlying message they wanted to convey with the guideline:

> We are still very much on to a structural approach to a lower back pain, and now we moved to a cognitive approach, there is a new approach that [shows] it is a neurological condition … It's not physical. The core component of the NICE guideline was self-management with reassurance, taking part in an active lifestyle, but the papers weren't published at the time. So, we would have said

24 English back pain guideline group member 3 (Interview by Phone, 27 March 2015).

> something very different in two years. We would have loved to have said it because that was how we were practising at the time.[25]

This group member, when asked about the underlying purpose of the guideline, spoke at length about the tension between those treatments where evidence could be presented for the 'softer' interventions, based on changes in lifestyle, where there was no evidence yet to consider, although some members of the group felt they were more important. This shows how the absence of evidence can sometimes lead to the result that certain approaches or treatments cannot be included in the guideline. To introduce a new approach without any support from the existing evidence does not fit the NICE approach to developing guidelines.

The discussion moved on to consider the treatments in greater detail. This part of the discussion was structured early on by the decision to only accept RCTs as evidence; this inevitably led to the need for 'consensus' when evidence was lacking, as the group had agreed they would not accept evidence other than RCTs. This also means that when the group needed to decide whether one treatment is better than the other, they needed to restrict this discussion to weighing the available RCT evidence. Seen in this light, the choice to regard manual therapy, exercise and acupuncture as equally valid options and to give patients and doctors a choice in what to prescribe, enabled all parties involved to be content with the guideline. Conflicts based on the place of a treatment in the pathway for treating lower back pain could thus be avoided. Guideline group members placed these choices consistently in the frame of evidence:

> There was a possible choice of physical treatment, we couldn't clearly say that any one of them was better than the other. The only thing that we found there were a few studies suggested that combining them would be better than one by one. You could [not] really separate them out on head to head trials … there was no difference in QALY's. It is not intended to give clinicians freedom, NICE is keen that the patient is involved in care, so this is an area where patient preference is an issue.[26]

Even though these discussions seem to be about evidence, it is plausible that part of the reasoning in the group is aimed at finding a position that as many members as possible can agree with. The fact that the medical studies do not seem to support a large difference between the various

25 Ibid.
26 Ibid.

treatments makes it easy to reach the consensus that a choice between these treatments is appropriate.

The discussion on spinal fusion differed from those about the other treatments. Providing spinal fusion as a treatment was not part of the agreed scope for this guideline, as the scope excluded surgical procedures. The group could advise, however, about referral to spinal fusion and they did so by advising that a referral could be considered for those that had tried all the previous treatments without success.

With the decision to make spinal fusion available for a select group of patients the group made a pragmatic choice. Given the fact that the guideline only deals with back pain that is shorter in duration then one year, the expectation was that very few patients would complete the pathway and be eligible for spinal fusion. This is because the guideline makers have defined the group of patients that could be referred for an opinion on spinal fusion as only those who have unsuccessfully completed the other earlier steps in the guideline. Some members were critical of the inclusion of spinal fusion: 'Despite rather a lack of evidence it did get in the guideline.'[27] However, a majority of the participants supported this decision.

It is likely that part of the motivation for this decision was, although none of the participants said so in as many words, to make sure that those in the group representing the interests of surgeons would agree with the guideline. If the guideline was written for those with chronic back pain, perhaps a different decision would potentially have been made, given the fact that patients with chronic back pain (i.e. for longer than a year) are more likely to be referred for an opinion on spinal fusion than people who have lower back pain for a shorter duration.

What we can take from these various discussions in the guidelines group is that evidence was a guiding factor in making decisions in this guideline: a minimum threshold of evidence has to be passed to be able to include a treatment, but the decision about where to place a treatment in a pathway was based on clinical reasoning and political considerations that existed outside the evidence. This is illustrated by the criticism this guideline received after adoption. The first main criticism of the English guideline was of the decision not to recommend injections for the back.[28] A further criticism was that this guideline only recommended

27 English back pain guideline group member 2 (London, 20 February 2015).

28 Joan B Hester, 'Official Statement from the British Pain Society' BMJ. Available at: <http://www.bmj.com/rapid-response/2011/11/02/official-statement-british-pain-society>.

treatments that one of the members of the guideline group provided.[29] These critics suggest that the guideline group was not basing their decisions solely on evidence but also leaned on achieving consensus in the group, so treatments that were not 'represented' within the group were not recommended because they were not necessary to reach consensus. This criticism highlights the nature of the compromises a guideline group must make and the unenviable and difficult position it finds itself in. The fact that internal consensus is required in the group to develop a guideline, can lead to external critique. If, however, the group decides to prioritise the expected critique of external partners over the need to reach a consensus, drafting a successful guideline will become difficult. A way out of this dilemma can sometimes be found in a very general formulation of recommendations, so general that all relevant parties can agree with (part of) it.[30] In this case, the group responded to the criticism by pointing to the high level of evidence used for the guideline – only RCTs – to support its choices.

Another dimension of this process of development is that it might affect the organisation of care. When evidence is used to recommend treatments, it is unavoidable that something is said about who performs those treatments and where (in which healthcare setting): even if guideline makers do not set out with the intention of reorganising practice. This is one reason why it is difficult to separate evidence-based decision from consensus-based decisions and 'internal decisions' from external effects.

4.4. EXTERNAL RESPONSES: REJECTION OF THE GUIDELINE

So far, we have considered the internal workings of the English guideline group on lower back pain. There are two ways in which external responses to a guideline might potentially influence its development. After the guideline has been drafted, an official period of consultation follows. During this consultation, registered stakeholders can respond to the

29 Christian Egeler, 'NICE Guidline on Backpain Is Misleading' BMJ. Available at: <http://www.bmj.com/rapid-response/2011/11/02/nice-guidline-backpain-misleading>.

30 An example of this approach is the Dutch guideline on lower back pain.

guideline which might lead to changes. A further, less obvious, way that external engagement might influence a guideline is through the *expectation* of critique by members of the group. If members already expect certain decisions to be controversial, they might try to avoid them. In this way, the guideline might be influenced by external parties, without this necessarily being visible in the text.

It is likely that guideline makers might sometimes try to pre-empt critique on the guideline, as this will likely improve its acceptability and implementation. A different way to put this is to assume that if the guideline drafters are correct in their assessment of the reactions of their peers the guideline will be uncontroversial and, importantly, the document could safely be considered technical and thus free of political decisions. The development of the lower back pain guideline shows how both potential paths of influence can play a role.

The experience of the English guideline on lower back pain shows that guideline development is not always perceived as being technical and that the choices that are made are perceived by some as political and can be contested. In this case, these perceived political choices do not lie in the decision to recommend a treatment, but rather in the decision not to recommend a treatment. This was indeed the case when the English guideline group decided there was insufficient evidence to recommend injections in the back. The relevant section of the guideline is as follows:

> Searches were carried out to identify any form of injection for the lower back, however, only data on facet-joint, prolotherapy and intradiscal injections was identified. The GDG agreed that there was a lack of evidence to recommend the use of these treatments and agreed by consensus injections were of no benefit for this population.[31]

Why was this decision so controversial? The treatment that the guideline does not recommend is performed by a variety of healthcare professionals that are represented by the British Pain Society (BPS). As a result of being excluded, the BPS were concerned that they would lose a substantial number of patients and funding because commissioners of healthcare would no longer fund their therapeutic back injections. The BPS claimed that there was sufficient evidence to warrant injections in the back if one takes cohort studies and clinical case studies into account.

31 Savigny and others (n 3) 162–63.

They criticised the exclusion of this evidence in the guideline. A quote from their letter to the *British Medical Journal* (BMJ) illustrates this:

> We cannot agree with the exclusion of all injections for back pain. The BPS provided evidence to support the clinical effectiveness of such procedures. The Guideline Development Group (GDG) did not consider evidence presented from cohort studies and clinical case series in its deliberations on these, or any other, treatments. We think this was misguided. Although NICE has recommended further research into these procedures, we are most concerned that a significant number of patients will be denied this choice of treatment in the interim.[32]

This statement, taken at face value, would be a discussion about evidence. The BPS was proposing to define evidence differently: they assume that a more inclusive definition of evidence will provide more support for their treatment. There is thus a contrast between the guideline group, which has chosen a narrow/strict definition of evidence, only RCTs and the BPS who proposes a wider definition. There is more to this statement then just a complaint about evidence. The society was mainly worried about the redefinition of the pathway for treating people with lower back pain. It is an issue of defining and redefining professional boundaries through guidelines. Wilson and others in their analysis of the 'fall-out' of this guideline also point this out: 'A key discourse emerged that enabled boundary work by doctors in interventional pain medicine – activity designed to protect and expand jurisdiction, assert professional authority, claim resources and protect autonomy.'[33]

Medical guidelines, in this reading by Wilson et al, can thus be seen as a potential tool to reorganise professionals and thus act as an instrument to try to discipline and steer medical professionals. It is not surprising, given the interdisciplinary treatment of guidelines within NICE, that choices within them will inevitably have some inter- and intra-professional effects. The importance of describing the BPS critique in detail lies in the fact that this is not a one-way street. In this case, the guideline did not simply reorganise healthcare and professionals passively accept the change; instead, they resisted and the way they chose to resist provides an example of the limits of guidelines as regulatory tools.

---

32 Hester (n 28).

33 Nicky Wilson and others, 'Governing Healthcare: Finding Meaning in a Clinical Practice Guideline for the Management of Non-Specific Low Back Pain' (2014) 102 *Social Science & Medicine* 138, 144.

The controversy did not end with the letter by the BPS, this proved to be just the starting point. The BPS, at the request of several members, took a vote at an extraordinary general meeting to oust their president. He was a member of the guideline development group, but not himself a pain specialist and had been tasked with providing independent expertise. The BPS members stated that he had not served their interests well by defending the NICE guideline, and the society asked for it to be either modified or withdrawn.[34] NICE reacted angrily to this development; it emphasised that the president of the BPS was not representing the society during his involvement in the guideline development but was expected to act as an independent expert. NICE feared that medical professionals would no longer participate in guideline groups if they felt pressured by outside groups.[35] Nonetheless, NICE did agree that a consultant in pain medicine needed to be included in the guideline group in the future.[36] In fact, a consultant in pain medicine is now the lead on the new lower back pain guideline. The outside pressure on NICE has thus been successful and professional groups who felt excluded from the process are now included. The new 2016 guideline does not recommend therapeutic injections in the back, but does recommend radiofrequency denervation in certain cases. In addition, in contrast to the earlier guideline, it does not recommend acupuncture or spinal fusion.[37]

What do these developments mean for the lower back pain guideline? How did this controversy affect the development of text of the guideline? Despite this controversy, the text of the guideline was not changed. Both the guideline group and NICE rejected these demands for change. So, in this sense, the guideline was not affected by these external forces. The discussions in the guideline do, however, support the view that there might be an indirect influence. The decision by the guideline group only to use RCTs as evidence was partly taken because criticism of the guideline was expected. In their response to the criticism, the guideline

34 Wilson and others, ibid; Zosia Kmietowicz, 'President of British Pain Society is Forced from Office after Refusing to Denounce NICE Guidance on Low Back Pain' (2009) 339 *BMJ* b3049.

35 'NICE Outraged by Ousting of BPS President' *BMJ*. Available at: <http://www.bmj.com/rapid-response/2011/11/02/nice-outraged-ousting-bps-president>.

36 Wilson and others (n 33).

37 See <https://www.nice.org.uk/guidance/NG59/chapter/Recommendations#invasive-treatments-for-low-back-pain-and-sciatica>.

group also used this choice as a defence and justification for maintaining their original position.

All in all, in this case, the engagement of external parties in the development process of guidelines only has a very limited influence on the text of the final guideline discussed. It did clearly affect the text of the 2016 guideline, so, in this sense the British Pain Society was successful in the long run, showing how the struggle to define professional boundaries is a long game.

4.5. CONFLICTS OF INTEREST: LIMITED RELEVANCE

One of the criticisms voiced about guidelines is the potential influence of the pharmaceutical industry on their creation.[38] This literature suggests that because of direct or indirect non-financial benefits (e.g. reputation and paid and unpaid positions) guideline group members might be unduly swayed to favour certain drugs or treatments over others.

One potential avenue to establish if the development of the guideline might potentially be affected by a conflict of interest of one or more of the members of the guideline group is to look at pharmaceutical interventions. The few pharmaceutical interventions that are advised are all off-patent and are no longer actively marketed by pharmaceutical companies. This study has found no evidence that a potential conflict of interest played any role in the decisions on pharmaceutical interventions in this guideline. This does not necessarily mean that the construction of the guideline was free of potential conflicts of interest. Potential conflicts of interest in this guideline could be related to other elements of the guideline development process.

A conflict of interest may exist when the people who conduct the RCTs used as evidence, in the guideline, partly overlap with the people in the guideline group who must critically asses that evidence. The fact that

[38] Goldacre and Heneghan (Chapter 2, n 130); Goldacre (Chapter 2, n 130); Stelfox Henry Thomas, Choudhry Niteesh K and Allen S Detsky, 'Relationships between Authors of Clinical Practice Guidelines and the Pharmaceutical Industry' (2002) 287 JAMA 612; David Healy, *Let Them Eat Prozac: The Unhealthy Relationship Between the Pharmaceutical Industry and Depression* (NYU Press 2006); Hans Melander and others, 'Evidence b(i)Ased Medicine – Selective Reporting from Studies Sponsored by Pharmaceutical Industry: Review of Studies in New Drug Applications' (2003) 326 *BMJ* 1171; Schott and others (Chapter 2, n 131).

the people who conducted studies must decide about including studies as evidence creates a potential conflict of interest, because they must critically evaluate the weight of evidence, they themselves have a vested interest in, being the authors of the work in question. At the same time, their expertise as authors might be necessary and beneficial to correctly interpret the evidence.

An example in this guideline is the BEAM-study, which is cited as important evidence for some of the advised treatments for lower back pain. The fact that one of the guideline members was involved in co-authoring and designing this scientific study might lead to this evidence being favoured over other potentially stronger conflicting evidence. There are several mechanisms to minimise the risk of this happening built in to the guideline process: the fact that all the evidence is first assessed systematically by the technical team and then given ratings prevents someone from relying on evidence that is not of sufficient quality. Furthermore, the fact that a large group of people debate this evidence also reduces the risk of undue influence by one person on the evidence base. If we consider the declarations made by the guideline group[39] they also list the authorship of articles on various aspects of lower back pain as potential conflicts of interest, so that the kind of scrutiny applied in this analysis is indeed possible.

This potential 'cognitive bias' by members of the guideline has not been supported in the interviews with guideline group members, or analysis of the guideline document. The fact that some studies are (co)authored by those that use them as evidence has not influenced the guideline. In sum, no support has been found for the assumption that conflicts of interest have influenced the development of the lower back pain guideline.

4.6. GUIDELINE DRAFTING IN INSTITUTIONS: SUCCESS WITHIN CONSTRAINTS

Through the study of the institutional context of guideline making we can more fully understand potential limitations and culturally dependent restrictions on the process of guideline development that are the are the result of influences from the government, healthcare professionals or the guideline making institution itself.

---

39 Savigny and others (n 3) Appendix F.

4.6.1. TOP-DOWN GOVERNMENT PRESSURES

If we consider the top-down pressures first, the remit that the UK Department of Health and Social Care sets for NICE seems to be a form of direct government intervention in guideline making. In theory, by setting the remit, the government can control the topics on which NICE has to make guidelines. In practice, this is not the case as NICE itself has identified/ established a large library of guidelines they want to produce. So, the remits in reality are set by NICE and no active intervention by the government takes place.[40] A senior official in NICE explained this in more detail: 'No those remits are discussed with the department, but [now] we have so many topics that we want to make guidelines on. We have put them in a library and NICE decides through its work plans how to prioritise the topics in the library.'[41]

While there is no direct government intervention in guidelines, there is an expectation that care will be provided according to NICE guidelines, although strictly, this is not a legally binding requirement. Clinical Commission Groups (CCG's) must take technology appraisals into account and provide funding for those technologies recommended, but not for treatments recommended in guidelines.[42] Given this background it is not surprising NICE guidelines make extensive use of cost–benefit analysis using detailed breakdowns of Quality Adjusted Life-Years (QALY's) to be able to recommend certain treatments. Given the expectation (but as noted not a legally binding requirement) that recommending a treatment will lead to funding of a treatment, the guideline groups have a duty to analyse the likely costs for the NHS of their recommendations. In the case of the English lower back pain guideline there is no evidence that this has had any effect on the recommendations as all advised treatments have a QALY that is below the threshold identified by NICE.[43]

4.6.2. BOTTOM-UP STAKEHOLDER PRESSURES

What influence, if any, did pressures from healthcare professionals have on the development of the guidelines? In those produced by NICE, comments

40 The exception are the recent safe staffing guidelines, however they do not form part of this book.

41 Senior NICE official (London, 22 May 2015).

42 The National Institute for Health and Care Excellence (Constitution and Functions) and the Health and Social Care Information Centre (Functions) Regulations 2013.

43 Apart from spinal fusion if a decision was made for immediate surgery. This, however, was not recommended in the guideline.

on draft guidelines can only be given by registered stakeholders.[44] Those registered stakeholders are NHS trusts, pharmaceutical companies and scientific and professional associations of healthcare professionals. For the English guideline on lower back pain, in addition to these opportunities for influence, the professional associations were also directly involved in selecting the chair and the members of the guideline group. Since then, the procedures have changed and NICE advertises these positions through open competition. Through these channels, healthcare professionals can try to influence the content of guidelines.

We have already seen that, throughout this process, the British Pain Society was very vocal in its opposition to the guideline. Despite all its protests however, the text of the guideline did not change.

4.6.3. THE INSTITUTIONAL CONTEXT OF THE GUIDELINE

An important element of the development of guidelines, which came to the fore in this case study is the specific institutional environment within a guideline-making institution. Although this guideline was written for NICE, the guideline group was nominally independent from NICE control and had complete freedom to decide on the text. There is nothing to suggest NICE did not respect this independence in practice. In fact, the opposite seems true, they maintained scrupulous barriers between the guideline-making process and their internal procedures.

However, the institutional culture and procedures of NICE does influence and restrict the actions of the lower back pain guideline group. Two aspects of this institutional environment are particularly relevant. Firstly, NICE has developed a guideline manual which describes in detail how to consider evidence and what elements to consider in drafting guidelines and it employs a technical team that applies this manual. This has had a direct effect on the how the group functions and the development of the guideline. Due to these procedural rules, NICE could control the scope of the guideline. We have seen that some members of the guideline group complained about this scope, or at least afterwards expressed regret that they did not get the opportunity to make an 'integrated' guideline that fully covered lower back pain.

It is not surprising that NICE wanted to control the scope of the guideline; it has a vested interest in making sure that its guidelines are

44 See <https://www.nice.org.uk/get-involved/Stakeholder-Registration>.

consistent and it has only limited resources. These choices did affect guideline-making groups as, despite their independence being preserved, they are given a task within set boundaries. The influence of NICE is not restricted to the scope of the guideline; it also influences who the members of the guideline group will be. The scope identifies in which areas the guideline group will need expertise and members of the guideline group who have this expertise are subsequently sought out. This means that NICE can include certain experts, but can also exclude them and could be criticised for those decisions. This was the case here as the discussion in section 4.4 on the exclusion of a dedicated pain specialist from the guideline group shows.

Second, in addition to these elements of influence of the institutional rules of NICE, another element is the operation of the technical team within and with a guideline group. The technical team searches the medical literature looking for studies that are then classified as counting as evidence or not. Constructing what counts as evidence is therefore an interplay between the guideline group and the technical team. While the guideline group applies a 'broad brush' by asking for only RCTs to be included, the technical team fills in the details and decides which studies should be classified in that way and whether they fulfil the inclusion criteria. In this way, the institutional rules and procedures of NICE prescribes and circumscribes what counts as 'evidence' for its guidelines.

NICE procedures are explicitly aimed at ensuring that guidelines are based on the highest quality of evidence available and they invest a great deal of money in enabling the systematic search and appraisal of a large amount of scientific evidence. The paradoxical result is that because of the diligent and high-quality appraisal process carried out by the technical team, the evidence base used for the recommendations is often small, as only a few studies make it through this rigorous process (at least as far as back pain is concerned).

4.6.4. INSTITUTIONAL INFLUENCES CONSIDERED

When considering the various institutional factors affecting the development of guidelines, it is noteworthy that their most prominent factors of influence are those *within* the guideline-making institution. The development of guidelines is only marginally affected by pressures from government or external critique from professionals. In contrast, internal cultural norms and procedures, through their influence on the medical studies used to make decisions, appear to directly shape the framing and selection of evidence used in the development of the guidelines.

4.6.5. COSTS: A COMPLICATING FACTOR FOR THE ENGLISH GUIDELINES

Guidelines drafted by NICE include an assessment of the cost-effectiveness of the treatments proposed. In the NICE guidelines the cost of treatment is expressed in QALY's (quality-adjusted life years).[45] Without providing a great amount of technical detail as to the calculation of these QALY's, for our purposes it is important to note that NICE has defined a threshold of £20,000 below which a treatment would be considered cost effective. It is important to consider cost effectiveness, as it does feature in the guideline group's discussions and so could potentially lead to decisions being changed because of these considerations.

Given the fact that the cost of most treatments in the guideline are well below the threshold of £20,000 per life year gained, a treatment below the threshold could be recommended without having to balance the evidence on clinical effectiveness with that of cost-effectiveness. This was summed up by one of the group members: 'Most of the treatments are relatively cheap so you not going to break the bank if you recommend it. And patients expect some sort of treatment.'[46]

The only treatment for which the guideline group did have to consider the cost-effectiveness was spinal fusion because the economic modelling showed that if this treatment was given to all patients, the treatment would be more expensive than £20,000 per QALY.[47] The guideline did not have to confront this issue directly as its scope did not include the power to recommend surgical procedures. Instead, the recommendation was one on referral. This was only deemed appropriate when a patient would have followed all the previous steps in the guideline without success. Given these constraints on access there was no reason to exclude spinal fusion, given the expectation that the uptake – in the confines of the given guideline scope – would be marginal, therefore the costs of this option would not be too high.

45 For more details on QALY's see: NICE, 'Guide to the Methods of Technology Appraisal 2013' (Chapter 2, n 92).

46 English back pain guideline group member 2 (London, 20 February 2015).

47 Savigny and others (n 3) 217.

There is strong interplay between cost considerations as expressed in the economic models used by NICE and the consideration of clinical relevance or quality considerations. In every assessment of evidence, a reference is made to the cost of treatment. For the reasons given, it did not materially change the recommendation in the case of the lower back guidelines. It is, however, a factor that potentially influences the development of other guidelines.

4.7. THE DUTCH GUIDELINE ON LOWER BACK PAIN

The Dutch guideline on lower back pain that is the focus of this study is that made by the NHG in 2005.[48] This guideline was made by a group of GPs, epidemiologists and healthcare researchers. The members were approached informally by the NHG, based on their knowledge of the topic and preference was given to those GPs with a doctorate. At least one of the guideline group members put himself forward, as he explains, 'because this was a GP guideline [I would not normally be approached] so I decided to put myself forward, when I knew that a new guideline update was being considered.'[49] The final group consisted of several GPs, a back-pain specialist, an epidemiologist and a healthcare researcher. The guideline process was supported by a scientific editor from the NHG who was responsible for drafting the guideline, or versions of it, for discussion among the group members.

The guideline group members all read and appraised the evidence literature themselves, with no predefined restrictions on the type of literature they could consider. Several group members committed on how this process was conducted:

> We had to search literature ourselves, and provide a summary for the group. Everyone did a specific task. We ranked [the evidence] using common sense. We followed the evidence-based ranking, with meta-analysis having the highest weight and the lowest when there is no evidence. We [would] discuss the statement about the evidence. And then given the evidence [we would discuss] what is the recommendation.[50]

48 NHG, 'NHG-Standaard Aspecifieke Lagerugpijn'. Available at: <https://www.nhg.org/standaarden/volledig/nhg-standaard-aspecifieke-lagerugpijn>.

49 Dutch back pain guideline group member 3 (Rotterdam, 5 December 2014).

50 Ibid.

This group member explained how the group had set out a plan, which involved guideline group members, based on their own preferences, setting out to find literature on specific aspects of the guideline (diagnostic, treatments etc.) and then turning the evidence found into a summary for the group to discuss. This group member suggested that, in general, the evidence-based pyramid would be the starting point in undertaking such a search. Another guideline group member confirmed this, describing the process in the following way:

> They [the NHG] have a guideline on how to make guidelines, it was based on the EBRO. The stress was to define a question, and to search according to the well-known evidence-based pyramid. This was the starting point. So, we tried to develop a couple of questions, and that's why the [NHG] invite people in those fields, and they also rely on those people, not on their decisions, but their knowledge of the medical field.[51]

The fact that the guideline group members were asked to do searches in the literature themselves led the NHG to the decision to also invite back pain specialists from other medical disciplines. These members could then be trusted to know the relevant literature in their field well and support the group in finding and selecting it.

The guideline includes both acute, sub-acute as well as chronic back pain in its remit. It is restricted to the treatment of back pain by GPs and referrals made by them. This restriction is seen as self-evident by all participants: 'The common interventions that were in the field of GP-care, that's what you focus on';[52] 'It [the guideline] is really for the support of the GP, that's the bottom line.'[53]

The reason for initiating this update of the original NHG back pain guideline was part of the NHG's regular process of updating guidelines. Guidelines are reviewed every three to five years to see if they need updating.

The Dutch guidelines on lower back pain will be assessed using the analytical questions used in the assessment of the English guideline: focusing on evidence, consensus, external responses, conflicts of interest and institutional factors.

---

51 Dutch back pain guideline group member 2 (Amsterdam, 5 December 2014).
52 Dutch back pain guideline group member 3 (Rotterdam, 5 December 2014).
53 Dutch back pain guideline group member 2 (Amsterdam, 5 December 2014).

4.8. EVIDENCE BASE FOR DUTCH LOWER BACK PAIN TREATMENTS

The Dutch guideline presents several pharmacological and non-pharmacological treatment options for lower back pain. If we survey the options that the Dutch guideline presents under the heading of sub-acute and chronic back pain, the following treatment options: education, exercise therapy, cognitive behavioural therapy and, for chronic pain, referral to a specialised multidisciplinary centre and pharmacological treatments with paracetamol, NSAIDs and weak opioids. At first look, the treatments presented in this guideline are in some points similar to English treatments, while other aspects of the regime are different. Behind these similarities and differences there is a difference in the use and treatment of evidence; this is highlighted by the use of 'narrative footnotes' that are part of the guideline that contain the assessment of evidence underlying the different treatment options.

4.8.1. EVIDENCE USE FOR EDUCATIONAL ADVICE

In the Dutch guideline the first step after diagnosing a patient with back pain should be providing education on how to deal with it. The guideline refers to a study with the English 'Back Book'[54] that shows – in their words – 'that use of this material led to an improved understanding of the condition, and less physical limitations'.[55] They recommend providing patients with a Dutch translation of the 'Back Book'. The fact that the study they cite to support this recommendation does not show *statistically significant* improvements in pain or disability is not mentioned. This contrasts with the focus in the English guideline on the fact that this study showed no statistically significant benefits on pain and disability but, *nonetheless*, educational materials (like the 'Back Book') could be recommended.

This example helps to understand the importance of the use of evidence in guideline making. Here, we have two groups using the same

54 A Kim Burton and others, 'Information and Advice to Patients with Back Pain Can Have a Positive Effect: A Randomized Controlled Trial of a Novel Educational Booklet in Primary Care' (1999) 24 *Spine* 2484.

55 NHG, 'NHG-Standaard Aspecifieke Lagerugpijn' (n 48).

evidence[56] to reach the same conclusion: the recommendation to use educational materials. They base this on two very different readings of that evidence, which provides support for the contention that it is not the evidence, or the medical study itself that presents a finding. Rather, it is in according meaning to some aspects of the study, to the exclusion of others, that the Dutch guideline group draws a specific conclusion from the available material.

It is important to stress here once again that this study does not suggest that any of the interpretations of the evidence are better or worse: they are simply different. They are also necessarily different because both the context and the questions are different. If you ask different clinical questions when reading the same medical study, you will likely draw different conclusions.

In this case, the final recommendation in the two countries is, for all intents and purposes, the same, but the Dutch conclusion is 'evidence-based', the other is consensus-based. The paradox is that the English guideline group could suggest the Dutch group was wrong to use this study as evidence because it provided no statistically significant conclusions, while the Dutch group could suggest the use of consensus was unnecessary because the study provided clinically relevant results. This, in a small way, shows how evidence in itself only acquires meaning through a process of interpretation, it is not evidence of anything until it is deemed to fit within a frame of understanding created by guideline groups.

4.8.2. EVIDENCE USE FOR THERAPY

The next treatment that can be offered in the Dutch system, if education is not successful and the pain remains, is therapy. Therapy is described broadly as including exercise therapy, cognitive behavioural therapy and manual therapy. A preference is expressed for therapies that activate the patient – massage and other passive therapies are discouraged.[57] The guideline group states that it is unclear which specific exercise or cognitive therapy is effective so suggests that the wishes and choices of the patient should play a role and a varied exercise programme should

56 This is, strictly speaking, not completely correct as both groups cited two other studies (that differ from each other) to support their conclusions, but their assessment of those studies is not analysed here.

57 NHG, 'NHG-Standaard Aspecifieke Lagerugpijn' (n 48).

be chosen.[58] The guideline group feels it cannot make any specific recommendations about therapies to provide. Partly, this choice might be due to the limited evidence the guideline has to rely on. It cites four systematic reviews on the topic that can all give only quite generic recommendations on appropriate treatments.[59]

A guideline group member remarked on their use of Cochrane reviews[60] on those therapies in relation to evidence-based medicine:

> Cochrane reviews were considered the best evidence available … [they have a] transparent methodology, other reviews had lower weight … We then discuss the conclusion of the review, it often showed a small effect, and we then took this finding to be true.[61]

This use of systematic reviews was adopted as a good starting pointing for the group as they lacked the time and resources to review individual studies, so reading a systematic review of groups of studies would reduce time. In addition, Cochrane Reviews had (and have) a good name and are a trustworthy source of medical data.

Nothing would stop the group from making more specific recommendations, based on consensus among them, if they felt the evidence was lacking. That they did not choose to do so was because it was not possible to reach consensus on specific forms of treatment. One of the guideline group members summarised the difficulty of recommending a specific therapy for back pain in the following terms: 'doing something is better than doing nothing. If you want to give a succinct summary of the literature that is about the shortest summary you could give.'[62]

Another group member also pointed to the importance of existing practice in the field of back pain, to say that there was no sufficient evidence to exclude any treatments:

> We also looked what is common in the Netherlands: to refer to the physiotherapist or exercise therapist Mensendick.[63] If locally a GP works

58 Ibid.

59 Ibid.

60 Cochrane Reviews are a specific form of systematic review, provided by the Cochrane collaboration which is perceived as an independent and authoritative provider of systematic reviews in medicine.

61 Dutch back pain guideline group member 3 (Rotterdam, 5 December 2014).

62 Dutch back pain guideline group member 2 (Amsterdam, 5 December 2014).

63 A physiotherapist who uses this specific type of exercise therapy.

with a Mensendick therapist that is fine, because the evidence doesn't really discriminate [between different forms of exercise therapy].[64]

In reality, there were big disagreements between the members in the group about the best therapy/treatment. So much so that two members decided to leave the group during the guideline formation process. One of the guideline members commented as follows: 'the discussions in the beginning were very animated. Everyone defending his own favourite treatment. At some point two of the members decided for themselves they didn't want to continue and left the group.'[65]

Eventually the group found a common consensus by presenting treatments in a generic way and not prescribing that one treatment was preferable over another. In this way, all members of the group could agree with the choices made. A guideline group member explains that taking a more high-level view of treatments could solve some of the disagreements: 'we just need to know do we have to refer or not, and what the physiotherapist does [does not matter because] he has his own guideline for that.'[66]

Giving the GP and the patient a free hand as to what type of exercise they prefer diminishes the level of 'guidance' the guideline provides. This was necessary to reach consensus in this group and it reflected the fact that the available medical studies did not provide a sufficient basis to recommend more *concrete* therapies, in the opinion of the members of the guideline group.

4.8.3. EVIDENCE USE FOR CHRONIC BACK PAIN

A similar choice was made in the recommendations for chronic pain. The guideline group recommended referral to a specialised multidisciplinary centre if other interventions are not successful.[67] That choice is also a pragmatic one based on consensus in the group. The evidence for the treatments given in those centres was considered unconvincing and no recommendation could be made for either corsets, injections in the back or spinal fusion. The fact that this guideline was drawn up by GPs to be used by GPs, helps them avoid the controversy of having to define

64 Dutch back pain guideline group member 3 (Rotterdam, 5 December 2014).
65 Dutch back pain guideline group member 1 (Utrecht, 28 November 2014).
66 Dutch back pain guideline group member 2 (Amsterdam, 5 December 2014).
67 NHG, 'NHG-Standaard Aspecifieke Lagerugpijn' (n 48).

the pathway after referral. The fact that the evidence for the treatments to which they refer patients is not convincing does not directly affect those groups of healthcare professionals. So, spinal surgeons, people specialising in pain medicine etc., are not affected by this guideline. When asked why the group choose 'multidisciplinary interventions' and referral to a multidisciplinary team as treatment options for chronic back pain, it became clear that this choice allowed enough flexibility for all parties to interpret multidisciplinary in their own way. One of the group members explained this as follows:

> yes, you could say these words were deliberately vague. That was because we had different treatments then, a centre in the west would do it different from one in the south. We had to cover them all with this recommendation.[68]

Another group member added: 'because of the diversity of forms [of treatment], and the lack of hard evidence you have to let it go, so people can find their solution locally.'[69] The need to choose this wording was thus not a factor of a decision based on evidence, as the guideline discussed and detailed that no judgement can be made about the evidence for these treatments, it was rather a clinical necessity to give GPs this choice, as otherwise there would be no treatment for chronic lower back pain (and implicitly that was seen as a bad thing).

4.8.4. EVIDENCE USE FOR ACUPUNCTURE

Apart from the treatments the guideline recommended we must also talk about the treatments the guideline did not mention. In contrast to the English guideline, the Dutch guideline does not mention acupuncture as a potential treatment. There are broadly two reasons for this: evidence for acupuncture was not included in the search for evidence and nobody with expertise in acupuncture was part of the guideline group. The search strategy used to find the evidence for this[70] and the updated guideline has been published:[71] acupuncture was not included as a potential

---

68 Dutch back pain guideline group member 1 (Utrecht, 28 November 2014).

69 Dutch back pain guideline group member 2 (Amsterdam, 5 December 2014).

70 The search strategy is no longer available online but on file with the author. Both strategies do not reference acupuncture.

71 NHG, 'Zoekstrategieen Lage Rugpijn'. Available at: <https://www.nhg.org/sites/default/files/content/uploads/standaard/totstandkoming/totstandkoming_en_methoden_aspecifieke_lagerugpijn_web.def_.pdf>.

treatment and was not searched for. The guideline group members denied this was a deliberate choice, but some did point out that acupuncture is an 'alternative treatment' and not something 'regular medicine' should promote. One of the members said:

> [it is] alternative medicine, so we won't do it. It is never expressed in those stark terms, I think, but it is an implicit starting point ... it is funny that you should ask [this] because it reminds me that you start a guideline making process with unspoken assumptions that are often not very clear ... we only talk about regular medicine.[72]

This shows that one could say that there was an implicit choice not to include any reference to it, based on a mutual implicit understanding that only regular medicine would be discussed and that acupuncture is not regular medicine. It also highlights how, through a process of selection, one can (deliberately or not) exclude certain aspects and therefore conclude there is no 'evidence' to support certain treatments.

4.9. INTERNAL CONSENSUS BUILDING: HOW RESULTS WERE REACHED

According to my interviewees, there were heated discussions within the guideline group, at least in the early phase of constructing the guideline:

> It was quite chaotic [the development of the guideline] There was a lot of argument, people left the group new people joined, I never experienced that before ... The first meeting was called to study the existing standard and formulate criticism ... In this first meeting people set out their red lines, this person had a PhD on this treatment, another had a PhD on that treatment, ... that immediately caused a lot of friction so at the third meeting people left because they could just not work together.[73]

The discussions centred mainly on the best treatment for lower back pain, with various participants defending different treatments related to their varied background in treating lower back pain. As these differences were fundamental and the group was unable to bridge the differences of

72 Dutch back pain guideline group member 2 (Amsterdam, 5 December 2014).
73 Dutch back pain guideline group member 1 (Utrecht, 28 November 2014).

opinion, two members decided to leave at this stage.[74] This decision did not, however, lead to the guideline being abandoned. Instead, two new members were recruited and in the end the group was successful in achieving consensus. A guideline group member commented on this:

> We ended up with a lot of consensus points in the guideline that we had to discuss. And we discussed about it all and formulated a position [as a group].[75]

Asked how such 'consensus' was achieved I was told: 'At the end of a long discussion one guideline group member would summarize the discussion and we will come back to it next time.'[76] So the method employed was to have long discussions, where debates would be summarised and fed back to participants in a subsequent session until it was decided that everyone could agree on the formulation of a recommendation.

One of the reasons the new group of guideline group members were able to work out a consensus on the treatments for lower back pain was because they abandoned the option of declaring one treatment to be superior to another. One of the guideline group members links this to debates about clashing ideas about the model of back pain, specifically applying this to the weighing of medical studies: 'When there is no hard evidence, you see that you see a different weighing from different believers. So, you see then if you believe it, you will weigh this [study] highly.'[77] Another guideline group member also related this to discussions about different ideas about the condition:

> Yes, that is [about] our vision on what you should do with this condition, sometimes even stronger than evidence that points in a different direction. Eventually it has to fit with the model that you have in your head about the disease.[78]

It was through establishing a shared vision of the disease that the group could accommodate different perspectives. As noted earlier, the fact that the treatment options were described in relatively open terms made it

---

74 Regretfully, this author has not been able to identify those participants, and thus has not been able to hear their side of the story. It is important to note that in describing these events, this author does not wish to give any value judgement.

75 Dutch back pain guideline group member 1 (Utrecht, 28 November 2014).

76 Ibid.

77 Dutch back pain guideline group member 2 (Amsterdam, 5 December 2014).

78 Dutch back pain guideline group member 3 (Rotterdam, 5 December 2014).

possible for everyone to agree. In this way a statement on whether one treatment was better than another was avoided. A specific example of how this was achieved was through the description of the possibility of referral to an interdisciplinary centre. This decision was purposefully drafted in an ambiguous way, no explanation was provided in the guideline as to what would constitute an interdisciplinary centre. This ambiguity was a useful tool for the guideline group because of the differences in the treatment of lower back pain in various parts of the country, where a choice for a specific centre or specific method would risk the exclusion of many current providers of treatment for those with chronic back pain. One guideline group member was quite frank in explaining with reference to international studies on back pain that: 'We don't have a clear definition of what a multidisciplinary centre is.'[79] In the case of this multidisciplinary intervention, this ambiguity was thus a tool to help achieve consensus and make sure the guideline would accommodate for regional diversity in treatments within the Netherlands at the time.

In sum, the guideline group thus used different overlapping methods to achieve an acceptable result. Evidence was used at a starting point in discussion, but this was complemented with knowledge of clinical practice, an understanding of the condition and a desire to compromise on the specificity of recommendations to allow everyone to agree. The fact that to reach this consensus that guideline in some areas became less specific was seen as a necessary trade-off.

4.10. EXTERNAL RESPONSES TO THE GUIDELINE: A DEAFENING SILENCE

The Dutch response to the guideline was limited. One critical response came in the form of a letter to *Huisarts en Wetenschap*,[80] in which the authors conclude the guideline did not conform to daily practice and gives a false sense of security. The letter argued that a further classification of non-specific lower back pain patients before providing them with treatment would provide higher quality treatment and lower costs,[81]

79 Dutch back pain guideline group member 2 (Amsterdam, 5 December 2014).

80 One of the most important academic journals on care in general practice in the Netherlands published by the NHG.

81 'NHG-Standaard Aspecifieke Lagerugpijn, Een Herziening?' 2005 Huisarts en Wetenschap 526.

referring to an RCT to support their position.[82] In a response in the same journal, the guideline drafters dismissed the complaints as unfounded, based on a misreading of the literature.[83] We can conclude that the Dutch guideline was not as controversial as the English guideline turned out to be. There are several reasons why this might be the case.

Firstly, this Dutch guideline was able to neatly sidestep the more controversial aspects of the treatment of lower back pain, such as injections in the back and spinal fusion as these elements of the treatments are not covered by GPs. Secondly, this guideline was potentially not as ambitious as the English guideline: the treatments it prescribed are relatively openly formulated and provide little in the form of guidance other than stating that 'passive' treatments should be avoided. Thirdly, this guideline was made by the NHG, which as the professional association of GPs, ensures in several ways that it was supported by its members. For example, 50 randomly selected GPs were sent the guideline and were invited to make comments. An authorisation committee, consisting of professors of general practice, must authorise the guideline before it becomes final. In this way, the chance of a guideline being controversial are limited.

Moreover, this article appeared after the guideline was published. As it did not result in any changes to the text of the guideline, the impact of these external commentaries was minimal.

4.11. CONFLICTS OF INTEREST: A LIMITED ROLE

A direct or indirect influence by the pharmaceutical industry has not been established in the research into this guideline. Pharmaceutical influence would in any case have been unlikely given the fact that the only medication that forms part of the guideline is no longer under patent, so it is no longer profitable for the companies who hold those patents to pursue aggressive marketing. As these drugs are now generic, anyone can produce them, the costs of these medications are low and so are the profit margins. Pharmaceutical companies direct their marketing towards

---

82 Julie M Fritz, Anthony Delitto and Richard E Erhard, 'Comparison of Classification-Based Physical Therapy with Therapy Based on Clinical Practice Guidelines for Patients with Acute Low Back Pain: A Randomized Clinical Trial' (2003) 28 *Spine* 1363.

83 'NHG-Standaard Aspecifieke Lagerugpijn, Een Herziening?' (n 81).

drugs that are patented as, during this period, they can make a profit, aimed at recouping the costs of developing the medication. In addition, the potential for guideline group members to influence the pharmaceutical choices in the guideline was limited given the decision to follow a different generic NHG guideline on pain relief and apply this to lower back pain. For other medication that fell outside of the remit of the NHG pain relief guideline, the group decided not to recommend any (this concerned muscle relaxants and antidepressants). It is unlikely this aspect of the guideline was in anyway unduly influenced.

This is not the only potential influence on the guideline as the result of a potential conflict of interest, it is worth looking at the financial and non-financial interests of the group members. One of them has a financial interest in a clinic that provides a certain type of injection for the back. This member's position was scrutinised by the head of the division for guideline development of the NHG and he was accepted as a member of the group. His potential influence on group decisions was clear from the outset. However, the group members interviewed all stated that they felt there was no undue influence on their decision making. Given the fact that the group discourages referral to monodisciplinary specialists who provide injections in the back,[84] and in general observe that there is limited evidence to support this treatment, any influence this specific guideline group member may have had to service his personal interests was absent.

The only potential influence or conflict of interest that affects this guideline is the fact that some guideline members have also (co-)authored publications they cite as evidence. This potential for a 'cognitive bias' is thus a possibility where, through the preferences of the members of the group for using and citing work they have authored themselves, the 'evidence' on which they base their decisions may be distorted. Some of the guideline group members are co-authors of several of the Cochrane Reviews used in the guideline. Given the extensive vetting process that is adopted for making Cochrane reviews, it is unlikely that the fact that guideline members have worked on the evidence they cite will unduly 'corrupt' the evidence used. What is likely, however, is that the guideline group chooses to cite documents with which they are familiar. In this way, a conflict of interest, having co-authored a medical study, might lead to a bias in the process of selecting evidence. Even though such a bias cannot be excluded, a large part of the Cochrane reviews they rely on

---

84 NHG, 'NHG-Standaard Aspecifieke Lagerugpijn' (n 48) 768.

are all co-authored by one high-profile person, who is one of the most prominent epidemiologists in the field of back pain and a well-known figure to the members of the guideline group. So, even if these guideline group members had not been involved in this study, those studies would nonetheless have been selected, because of the prominence they have in the field of back pain. So, in this way, these 'cognitive biases' have not materially affected the text of the guideline. We can conclude that potential conflicts of interests have not played a role in influencing the Dutch guideline on lower back pain.

4.12. INSTITUTIONAL FACTORS: PRESSURES TO CONFORM

When analysing the Dutch guideline on lower back pain in its broader regulatory context we should take into account two interrelated viewpoints: how is the guideline positioned from a top-down perspective from government to profession and how is the guideline positioned in a bottom-up perspective from individual healthcare practitioner vis-à-vis the guideline. We can also examine the meso-level question of how guidelines are positioned within the institutions that produce them.

4.12.1. TOP-DOWN GOVERNMENT PRESSURES

If we consider the top-down perspective, it is important to clarify the relations between the various organisations involved in aspects of guideline making in the Netherlands. The government is involved in controlling certain aspects of guidelines. The most important organisation in this regard is the Zorginstituut Nederland that, as explained in Chapter 2, regulates what is insured under the private insurance policies Dutch citizens are required to have. So, the fact that the guideline on lower back pain recommends several treatments does not mean that this is part of the package for which people are mandatorily insured.

This is can be illustrated by looking at physiotherapy: the guideline recommends this as a possible treatment for lower back pain, but it is not covered by insurance as patients must pay for this treatment themselves. This also explains why there no explicit cost–benefit analyses to be found in Dutch guidelines, as these do not in any way create rights for patients to receive reimbursement for a certain treatment. In this sense there is a greater distance between government bodies and guideline-making organisations. It is the government (in the form of the Zorginstituut) and elected politicians who have the final say on what is covered by health care insurance, but they use guidelines to help them decide instead of influencing those guidelines themselves.

For the lower back pain guidelines this means there was no government involvement in making the guideline, nor does the guideline refer to government rules in any way. It seems that, at least for the Dutch guideline, the profession was independent in formulating the optimal treatment strategy. These efforts were, however, embedded within the broad legislative guidance provided in the Law on the Medical Treatment Contract[85] that care of a good standard conforming to the norms of the profession should be provided. It is this legislative backdrop which indirectly steers the profession towards developing its own professional standard; guidelines are one instrument used to do this.

There are other ways, however, for the government to exercise control and secure a high quality of care. Medical tribunals can discipline doctors and they often use medical guidelines to establish what care of a good standard is. These medical tribunals consist of a mix of judges and medical professionals so that control of the quality of the profession is not completely in the hands of the profession itself. Nonetheless, to a large extent, having medical guidelines to back up what the profession considers a good standard of care results in the profession effectively controlling what good care is. In essence, the profession creates, to a large extent, the norms with which they then have to comply. Medical tribunals follow guidelines to enable them to formulate the expected course of action of a medical professional so they can assess whether deviations from that standard can be tolerated.[86] The claim that guidelines diminish the professional autonomy of medical professionals is not something that would be argued for here, but it is correct to say that by making their procedures more explicit, the profession gives part of their knowledge monopoly away and enables forms of control and accountability. Van Everdingen predicted this almost 30 years ago in his book on consensus-based guidelines when he said:

> So far consensus-guidelines have not been used in legal procedures. That they will be used in the future seems quite likely. Through a correct formulation

[85] Wet op de geneeskundige behandelovereenkomst.
[86] van Everdingen (Chapter 1, n 2).

of the guideline text this will more likely strengthen the legal position of the doctor rather than weaken it.[87]

Guidelines have grown to be instruments of accountability that can be used against doctors, but as Everdingen predicted correctly, they can also strengthen the position of a doctor by giving him an argument to support his actions when they are controversial. So, what exactly is the position of guidelines as a form of regulation and how should we characterise this form of regulation precisely? I would suggest that the Dutch guidelines are a specific form of mandated self-regulation, somewhere on the spectrum between 'pure' self-regulation and fully delegated rule-making: this is self-regulation in name, but not in substance.

Guidelines in the Netherlands are a result of a symbiotic relationship between professional bodies like the NHG and the government. The government needs guidelines, as they break the information asymmetry between those inside and outside the profession. The government gets an insight into what healthcare professionals define as good care. As a result, they can regulate the profession through various mechanisms. But guidelines are positive for the professional organisations as well. It gives them a way of trying to control their members, in case of the NHG GPs and steer them in the direction of better care. Whether they are always successful in that aim is not part of this study: research suggests results are mixed, but in general the acceptance of NHG guidelines is high.[88] Some guidelines, of course, are more directive than others. The lower back pain guideline provides relatively few directives apart from the statements that MRIs should not be used for lower back pain unless a specific cause of back pain is suspected. As we have seen, the external response to this guideline was muted. There was little in the way of professional steering from the NHG in this guideline. It seems the main reason to revise the previous guideline was the general policy that guidelines should be updated after five years. In the Netherlands, GPs try to influence their professional association and look for guidelines that are helpful in their daily work, solving practical dilemmas they face in providing treatments for their patients.

---

87 Ibid, 56–57.

88 Richard Grol and others, 'Implementatie van NHG-Standaarden: Succes of Probleem?' (2010) 53 *Huisarts en wetenschap* 42.

4.12.2. THE INSTITUTIONAL CONTEXT OF THE DUTCH GUIDELINE

An important element in the regulatory context that easily is overlooked is the position of guidelines within the guideline-making body. A part of this institutional context is the larger culture and values of the NHG. More specifically, of particular relevance to the development of guidelines are the *perceptions* that guideline group members hold (whether true or not) about the culture of the NHG. The decision for example that acupuncture would not be considered was not an explicit decision made by the group, partly as a result of the values of the NHG as one guideline group member explained:

> The NHG doesn't want to promote this [acupuncture] or homeopathy, as long as it is not evidence-based effective it will not be put in the guideline.[89]

This guideline group member described a generally held view that perhaps reflects a broader norm in Dutch healthcare that acupuncture does not belong in the category of 'regular medicine'.

There are further institutional mechanisms within the NHG that limit and steer to an extent the room a guideline group has in drafting a guideline. The NHG has installed an advisory committee of GPs that are (or strive to be) representative of GPs in the Netherlands that suggests topics for medical guidelines to be developed by the NHG.[90] Furthermore all guidelines are sent to a sample of 50 GPs and their comments are incorporated in the final guideline. This might have some moderating effect because guideline groups will only be able to produce guidelines on topics that this advisory committee recommends being addressed or are otherwise put on the agenda by the NHG. Furthermore, this round of commentary by 50 GPs will have a moderating effect on the guideline, where larger deviations from current practice might lead to more comments being made. More important in practice is the so-called 'authorisation committee'.

This committee consists of professors of GP-care in the Netherlands and it has the final say over whether a guideline will be authorised and thus be published as an official NHG guideline. This process consists of one

---

89 Dutch back pain guideline group member 1 (Utrecht, 28 November 2014).

90 The NHG adviesraad standaarden. Available at: <https://www.nhg.org/nhg-adviesraad-standaarden-nas> [The NHG advisory board for medical guidelines].

or several meetings where the whole guideline group must appear before the committee to defend the guideline and fully justify all the choices it has made. More ambitious guidelines that drastically want to change existing practice will have a harder time convincing this committee that the guideline should be adopted. One of the guideline group members summarises the position of several members of the group in explaining the process:

> A guideline has to be supported by the profession. The authorisation committee looks [at the guideline to see] if everything was thought through properly. There are always discussion points where we go through the arguments again for taking a position. And then they agree. But if they say you have to think about these points we would have to go back and look at it.[91]

This is clearly more than just a simple rubber-stamping exercise; the group members must all be present to be able to talk in detail about all the aspects of the guideline. In this way, the NHG retains institutional control over the guidelines it publishes.

One of the ways this manifests itself in general is the more risk-averse strategy adopted by the NHG. The *NHG-standaarden*, I would argue are reluctant to adopt new treatments and require a relatively higher threshold before adopting new treatments because of the moderating influence of the authorisation committee that moderates large changes in guidelines and so acts as a brake on guideline groups. In general, GPs in the Netherlands are seen as being conservative; they provide lifelong care and are reluctant to adopt new treatments because if they find out the treatments are unsafe a couple of years later, they will still be responsible for the affected patient. A Dutch guideline group member said: 'Yes I guess you could say that we [GPs] are conservative. In most cases it is something like, oh there is something new what should I do? Let's wait and see what happens before we try it ourselves.'[92]

4.13. COMPARISON OF GUIDELINES: DIFFERENCE OR SIMILARITY?

This chapter has so far reviewed both the English and Dutch guideline on lower back pain. As we shall see, the guidelines present a complicated

---

91 Dutch back pain guideline group member 3 (Rotterdam, 5 December 2014).
92 Dutch back pain guideline group member 1 (Utrecht, 28 November 2014).

picture of similarity in recommendations despite differences in procedure, context, evidence and interest. At the same time, we can observe differences in recommendations where evidence is very similar.

4.13.1. EVIDENCE INTERPRETED

If we take the findings from both our guidelines together it becomes clear that evidence is used in different ways. In the Dutch guideline the authors are interested in illness behaviour, so they stress the findings of the study with the 'Back Book' that the subjective perceptions of disability decrease, especially for those who are risk averse. The English guideline is more interested in the results on pain and disability, the objective results as it were, so they report those (less favourable) results of the study.[93] This is a good example to show that it takes a lot of effort to disentangle the evidence in 'pure form' and the clinical consideration of that evidence. Only by looking at the selections and omissions made in using, or not using, particular results, do we see the selection process that is an integral part of the adjustment process to make a guideline fit into a clinical context.

If we return to the various treatment decisions taken in the English guideline, the repertoire of science plays an important role. In the description of the decisions taken it is clear the guideline group carefully describes the various strengths and weaknesses of the studies used. This is especially the case when acupuncture is discussed. The controversy surrounding this treatment is greater than for treatments that have been recommended in previous guidelines. This might explain the greater stress that is put on the robustness of the scientific evidence base in this case.[94] From the interviews with the guideline group we could learn that great stress was also placed on the robustness of the evidence considered and the attempts that were made to account for evidence that might have contained methodological flaws or shown only small benefits.

93 In the case of the English guideline this seems to be a result of the following clinical question that was used to search the literature: What is the effectiveness of prepared patient information material compared to no information or alternative information on pain, functional disability or psychological distress? In reporting the results, however, the element physiological distress is not reported and to focus is on pain and disability.

94 This decision has indeed attracted criticism which was discussed under external politics.

The technical team and the definition of the research questions they used in their search through the literature have a marked influence on the repertoire of science as Moreira defines it.

As we have seen, the fact that research questions are defined narrowly, may lead to search terms that only turn up a part of the literature and this literature then undergoes a further filtering: examples include the exclusion of reviews due to the heterogeneity of the studies involved, a sample size that is too small, etcetera. It is only after this filtering process has been completed that the *remainder* of studies are discussed and the process of considering their robustness takes place.

If we compare the English case with the way the Dutch guideline group treats evidence, we see that there are some important differences in the way evidence is handled. The Dutch guideline group adopts a less strict definition of evidence and does not restrict itself to considering RCTs, nor does it employ the GRADE-methodology, nor can it rely on technical assistance from a team of methodologists. The potential evidence the Dutch guideline group could have considered is therefore broader and one might expect that more low-quality evidence would be used. This, however, was not the case as the guideline group relied heavily on Cochrane reviews, which are systematic reviews, seen as the highest possible quality of evidence.[95] This is logical if one considers that the Dutch guideline group had to read and appraise *all* evidence themselves, there was not enough time to consider separate randomised control trials, other than for those areas where no systematic review was available.

The differences in the treatment of evidence between the two guideline groups lies not in the decision of what evidence to select, but on how to appraise it. The Dutch guideline group was more strictly focused on the clinical relevance of certain evidence for GPs and paid less attention to the strict requirements of evidence-based medicine. An example of this is provided in the treatment of the same evidence for educational materials: whereas the Dutch group stressed the clinically relevant results, the English group stressed the statistically relevant results. It is easier for the Dutch guideline group to stress clinical relevance because they had to write a guideline from the perspective of only one profession, whereas the English guideline group had to incorporate the perspective of several different professionals. Early in the guideline-drafting process, members of the Dutch group left, the subsequent decision to see

95 They are at the top of the evidence-based medicine pyramid discussed in Chapter 2.

back-pain treatments as interchangeable helped achieve consensus. This means that the Dutch eventually found it easier to reach a compromise and found it easier to tailor their message to their specific audience: the Dutch GP.

If evidence is not the reason the guidelines are so similar what is? The fact that the guidelines are so similar is due to the fact that they are drafted in quite general terms to make sure that they confirm to a great extent to the current practice in the treatment of lower back pain in and the evidence is fitted to this reality.[96] The route towards this result differs: the use of consensus when high quality evidence is lacking in England, compared with a pragmatic interpretation of evidence based on clinical preferences in the Netherlands – but this did not lead to very different outcomes. The areas where we see a clear difference support this: the inclusion of acupuncture in the guideline and a greater role for forms of manual therapy in the English guideline, are also the areas where there is greater difference in the practice of treatment of lower back pain between the two countries and where the NICE guidelines are perceived to be the most controversial.

4.13.2. INTERNAL CONSENSUS BUILDING: A CAREFUL PROCESS OF CREATING ACCEPTABILITY

The discussions in guidelines groups can be passionate and heated but, in the end, both groups, reached a consensus. Guideline members have different opinions about the clinical relevance and context of guideline decisions. They can differ passionately about the relevance of results from clinical trials. Is a small treatment effect enough if the finding applies to a large population of patients? Are certain therapies more effective than others and, if so, should we discourage doctors from referring to those therapies that are less effective? The answers to those questions are complex and the evidence derived from scientific articles cannot provide simple answers to those questions.

In reality, guideline groups adopt a pragmatic approach to these questions and strike compromises. Differences in guideline texts appear because those compromises work out in different ways. The Dutch guideline group has chosen to give relatively general recommendations or,

96 The areas where the two guidelines differ (acupuncture) is also where a deviation from current practice is recommended.

in the case of multidisciplinary treatment, use deliberately vague terms to reach their consensus. In the English guideline, the group introduced the choice of the patient as a factor in choosing a treatment and so neutralised any differences of opinion over which of the several treatment options where more effective. Here, both guideline groups managed to achieve consensus and incorporate evidence in a balanced way.

Words have no fixed meaning in and of themselves. They are, in these careful processes of consensus building, imbued with specific meanings that help to bridge differences in understanding between the various parties around the table.

4.13.3. EXTERNAL RESPONSES: FROM SILENCE TO UPHEAVAL

The external responses to the two guidelines have been very different. The English guideline led to a storm of criticism from various professional bodies, but the Dutch guideline did not. This seems to be related to the perceived controversial nature of the recommendations adopted in the respective guidelines. There were those who complained about the exclusion of certain injections in the back as a treatment for lower back pain, while others complained about the inclusion of acupuncture as a treatment option in England. The guideline group is in a difficult position as the different 'worlds of a guideline',[97] as Moreira defines them, inevitably will clash. If the guideline group is determined to present an ambitious guideline which actively changes service delivery, it is inevitable that this will cause a measure of resistance. But if the guideline group chooses to present a conservative guideline that just duplicates existing practice, what is the rationale for making it in the first place? Is there any need for a guideline if practice already conforms perfectly to evidence-based recommendations? The guideline group will always have to navigate between those two extremes different diseases have different profiles in this regard. Lower back pain is an area where our knowledge in the last 20 years has not dramatically changed; for diabetes we shall see that this is completely different. The extent to which a guideline is willing to adopt positions that might be seen as political is not only related to its level of ambition but also premised on consensus within

[97] Moreira (Chapter 2, n 21) 1976.

the group. This is an important reason the Dutch guideline was less controversial: there was no consensus to adopt very specific treatment recommendations.

4.13.4. CONFLICTS OF INTEREST: NONE ESTABLISHED

As we have seen, the fear that guideline groups have conflicts of interests that negatively influence their recommendations has not been borne out in this case. This study has found no evidence that the pharmaceutical industry had any influence on either of these guidelines. Personal or financial conflicts of interest were adequately dealt with.

The only remaining potential conflict of interest lies in the fact the guideline group members are sometimes involved in the trials they use as evidence. Group members are invited to participate in guideline drafting precisely because they are experts in the field at hand or have other methodological expertise that is of use. It is therefore unavoidable that members will be confronted with studies that they have conducted themselves. As long as there are sufficient safeguards in the form of a balanced representation of members in the group, this is unlikely to influence guidelines in any negative way. This shows that not all guidelines are equally prone to influence and corrupting conflicts of interest: in the case of the lower back pain guidelines no evidence was found to support this.

4.13.5. INSTITUTIONAL AND REGULATORY FACTORS: COMPETING PRESSURES

We have so far analysed extensively how guidelines are drafted by looking at the use of evidence, analysing the internal politics of guideline groups and gauging the direct reactions to a guideline. It remains necessary to place guidelines in a broader regulatory context.

Considering the top-down regulatory pressures, one would expect to see a rift between the two countries as, on paper, their healthcare systems are based on two different models. The Dutch system is based on insurance with private hospitals and elements of market competition, so one would expect limited government interference with guidelines, compared to the NHS with a system of nationalised hospitals and funded care, where one would expect more government interference. In practice, however, the differences are not as stark for lower back pain guidelines.

In the Netherlands, as expected, direct government control of lower back pain guideline production is almost completely absent, but the government does have influence on how guidelines are used *after* they are produced. Through rules on remuneration, medical tribunals and rules about contracts between healthcare insurers and healthcare professionals the government uses guidelines outside of the context in which they were originally drafted and for other purposes then originally intended. The Dutch government does not directly influence guideline drafting, but through these other mechanisms does informally require the profession to satisfy a standard of good care, which guidelines help deliver.

The English guidelines are drafted under the auspices of NICE and their remit is set by the Department of Health and Social Care. As we have seen, this is just a formality and does not mean that the government is actively involved in setting topics for guidelines. Arguably, using NICE is a good way for the government to distance itself from the guideline-making process. One element the government does provide guidelines for is the cost-effectiveness of treatments. NICE operationalises this through the use of Quality-Adjusted Life Years so, in this respect, the government has control over guidelines. The necessity to include a form of cost–benefit analysis in guidelines also has the potential to change the choices the guideline group makes. This is a way to avoid politically controversial decisions on (pathways of) medical treatments for the government.

For bottom-up pressures, the expectations would be different. There is no reason to expect differences in pressures from healthcare professionals on guideline makers in the two countries as their interest and composition are very much the same. Here, however, we do observe a difference because of the different institutions making the guidelines.

For the lower back pain guideline, the issue came to the fore in the criticisms expressed by the British Pain Society. This seemed to be based on a lack of a feeling of ownership (and thus support) for this particular guideline. Despite the fact that their President was involved in drafting the guideline, they felt their interests were not represented. Whereas other healthcare professionals involved in the delivery of care for patients with lower back pain were part of the guideline group, they felt excluded. Such issues of ownership were less of a problem in the case of the NHG, where only the profession itself, the GPs, needed to feel ownership of the guideline recommendations.

If a guideline changes in a major way, this is a good opportunity to explore what has driven this change and on what evidence this change is based on. On this basis, we can conclude that the Dutch guideline group has a low risk appetite with only minor changes to the lower back pain guideline and a view that the evidence for lower back pain is not of a high quality.

Given these constraints, it seems surprising that both countries have drafted lower back pain guidelines that are so similar. A closer look reveals that while the results only differ in certain respects, the way in which the result was reached was different. In summary, evidence used in the Dutch and English guidelines was based on the perceived importance of clinical knowledge, the relevant regulatory environment and the relative difficulty in obtaining consensus in the guideline group.

CHAPTER 5
TYPE II DIABETES
Guidelines in England and the Netherlands

Type II diabetes is a serious chronic condition that can have debilitating complications and affect patient's quality of life severely. Simply put it is characterised by a heightened level of blood glucose, because of the body's inability to process sugar or glucose[1] sufficiently. This has several consequences as it increases the risk that (severe) complications will ensue such as stroke, heart attack, blindness, kidney failure, neuropathic pain[2] and amputation. Diabetes treatment is not (yet) aimed at curing diabetes, but the aim of treatment is to normalise the blood glucose and lipid levels in the blood as much as possible so that the risks of developing these complications is reduced. Successful treatment would find the optimal point between reducing the risks of the disease and the harm from the side effects of the treatment.[3]

Type II diabetes is distinct from type I diabetes: type I is a condition with a predominantly auto-immune component where the patients are not able to produce any insulin and are dependent on external injections of insulin. Type I diabetes will not be covered in this book. For patients with type II diabetes, the treatment is evolving fast and new medication is coming onto the market every year. The challenge in drafting medical guidelines is to provide up-to-date advice while being mindful of the cost of new treatments versus the health benefits gained.

The treatment of diabetes recommended in guidelines is variable but often involves one or more of the following steps: providing patients with information/advice to lose weight; a diet; a drug to lower blood glucose, moving on to two or even three drugs lowering blood glucose and, finally, insulin by injection possibly in combination with medication

1 Throughout this chapter blood sugar and blood glucose will be used interchangeably.
2 Pain as a result of nerve damage, a complication of the disease.
3 An important development here is the recognition that this optimum differs between patients.

to lower blood glucose. This treatment pathway is thus one that increases in severity to help control the blood sugar levels of a diabetes patient. The treatment of diabetes is, however, related to how long a person has had diabetes, the age of the patient and the other healthcare conditions a patient might suffer from. In designing diabetes guidelines, the group members must decide when to intensify treatment and which combination of drugs should be provided at the different stages of treatment.

In researching the drafting of type II diabetes guidelines, the focus is on medication to lower blood glucose. This means other aspects of diabetes care will not be covered in detail. This choice has been made for two reasons. Firstly, there is not enough space to cover all aspects of diabetes care: as diabetes is a chronic condition with a great many side effects its medical treatment reaches over many medical disciplines. A further reason for picking out only a few aspects of diabetes care is the fact that the scope of the Dutch and English guidelines varies considerably. It is helpful to only discuss those aspects of diabetes care that the English and Dutch guidelines pay attention to and formulate recommendations on. This means that most of the complications of diabetes care that are treated in hospitals and other second-line services (such as diabetic foot care and eye care) will not be covered.

5.1. THE ENGLISH GUIDELINE ON TYPE II DIABETES

In this section we will discuss two diabetes guidelines developed by NICE: the 2008 guideline developed by the National Collaborating Centre for Chronic Conditions and authorised by NICE[4] and the update of this guideline by a so-called short guideline produced by NICE in 2009.[5] The focus is placed on the 2008 guideline and reference is made to the short guideline, when relevant, for parts of the original guideline that have been updated.

---

4 National Collaborating Centre for Chronic Conditions (Great Britain) and Royal College of Physicians of London, *Type 2 Diabetes National Clinical Guideline for Management in Primary and Secondary Care (Update)* (Royal College of Physicians 2008) <http://www.ncbi.nlm.nih.gov/books/NBK53885/>.

5 NICE, 'Type 2 Diabetes: Newer Agents' <http://www.nice.org.uk/guidance/cg87/resources/cg87-type-2-diabetes-newer-agents-a-partial-update-of-cg66-short-guideline2>.

5.2. EVIDENCE BASE FOR ENGLISH TREATMENTS FOR TYPE II DIABETES

The 2008 guideline provides guidelines on the treatments for the whole trajectory of the type II diabetes patient. The elements that will be discussed under this heading are: education and lifestyle advice, drugs that lower blood glucose and blood sugar target levels.[6] As discussed above, other elements of diabetes care will not be covered.

The 2008 guideline as the first element of treatment outlines lifestyle advice and education for diabetes patients. This is significant as it involves non-pharmacological interventions that have the potential to stop people from having to use medication. Paradoxically, this is the area in the guideline where there is only a small amount of evidence to base decisions on. The guideline group based its decision on a health technology assessment report[7] that reviewed 14 studies but concluded that they were of a poor quality and it was hard to draw firm conclusions from them. A similar picture emerges when it comes to lifestyle advice: only four studies are included; all of them have a different design, which only allows for the drawing of tentative conclusions. As a result, the recommendations formulated in the guideline in this area are of a general nature such as: 'Provide dietary advice in a form sensitive to the individual's needs, culture and beliefs being sensitive to their willingness to change, and the effects on their quality of life.'[8] These general recommendations by the guideline group are understandable given the fact that it is unclear which type of education and/or lifestyle advice is most effective.

5.2.1. MEDICATION FOR LOWERING BLOOD GLUCOSE

Drugs for lowering blood glucose form the second step in the guideline: if education and lifestyle advice does not control the blood sugar levels of the diabetes patients to a sufficient degree, medication is required to

---

6 Technically we would need to speak about levels of HbA1c, as this is the measure used to express the average blood sugar (or better blood glucose levels) over a period of time. For the sake of clarity blood sugar is used as the preferred term.

7 Loveman and others (Chapter 2, n 88).

8 National Collaborating Centre for Chronic Conditions (Great Britain) and Royal College of Physicians of London (n 4) 38.

reduce the chance of the micro- and macro-vascular complications of type II diabetes. The central question facing the guideline makers was to advise which medications to prescribe and in which order, because if blood glucose is not sufficiently lowered using one drug, one or more drugs are added to the treatment regime. Diabetes management is complicated; there are a multitude of choices to be made in prescribing medication. This creates a dilemma as, on the one hand, one could argue that every patient is unique and diabetes management should thus be the ultimate tailored treatment but, on the other hand, there is the idea that diabetes care should be protocol driven to achieve consistent results in a large population and to ensure everyone receives the best quality of care for the lowest societal cost. In analysing the use of evidence and how the guideline group appraised and used evidence in the two guidelines, this tension emerges consistently. The guideline group had to make decisions that fall within this spectrum, where sometimes a uniform approach might be prominent and other times more tailored advice is given. Group members might not describe their reasoning in these terms, but this clearly played a role in their deliberations.

In systematically discussing the evidence used and the choices made, the guideline refers to several classes of medication for type II diabetes. In this study no mention will be made of the brand names of these medications, but they will be referred to by their generic name, which is the name for the active substance in the drug.[9]

It goes too far for our purposes to explain in detail all the differences between these drugs but in a general sense one can say that each class of drugs employs a different mechanism to lower blood sugar levels and insulin as a treatment eventually completely replaces the insulin produced by the body to help lower blood sugars. Prescribing medication from a different class is therefore a choice that makes a difference, even though all these drugs are employed for the same purpose of blood glucose control. Within these broad classes of drugs there are individual drugs, complicating the choices that a clinician has even further, depending on whether one views the drugs within the classes as interchangeable or not.

---

9 The classes are: Biguanides, Sulfonylurea, Meglitinide, Thiazolidinediones, Alpha-Glucosidase inhibitors, GLP-1 mimetics, DPP-4 inhibitors, HPV-insulin, Biphasic Analogues and Long-Acting Insulin Analogues. This leaves out the Sodium-glucose-co-transporter-2-inhibitors that are discussed in the Dutch guideline but not included in their treatment plan, as these earlier English guidelines do not include these newest drugs.

In describing the various drugs and their relative worth, the focus will be placed on the reasons for preferring one drug over another or the reasons for making exceptions for specific groups of diabetes patients. There are 18 diabetic drugs, of which some belong to the same class of drugs that will be discussed in this case study. There are many different ways in which they can be combined in providing diabetes treatment, which underscores the complexity of this area of medicine.[10] In describing the evidence base for the choices in the treatment of diabetes reference will be made to these drugs to explain the options available to the guideline group in making their decisions.

5.2.2. DRUGS TO LOWER BLOOD GLUCOSE

In choosing the first treatment offered to patients who require drugs to lower blood glucose, the guideline group makes reference to studies that show that Metformin lowers morbidity and mortality and has a cardio protective effect.[11] The choice for Metformin is largely a result of the UKPDS study, the largest available study of diabetes patients.[12] In this study, the use of Metformin/Sulfonylurea/insulin was compared with diet alone. It showed that Metformin was superior to the other drugs in reducing both mortality and morbidity. There was little discussion in the guideline group on this issue and the evidence for Metformin. The primacy of Metformin was uncontroversial as the UKPDS results were seen as convincing evidence. Added to its proven effectiveness was the fact that the drug was safe and also highly cost-effective.

There was a limited role in the guideline for Sulfonylurea as a first line treatment for diabetes in three very specific clinical circumstances: for diabetes patients who are not obese, if metformin is not tolerated, or in

10 And even this is a simplification as most of these drugs can also be taken in combination form (e.g. Metformin and Pioglitazone) and/or are presented in several different formats (different strengths as well as different forms of 'release' of the active substance over the day, so-called modified release drugs). Which brings the total amount of drugs that can be prescribed up to around 30 at the time of this guideline and this has grown continually since.

11 National Collaborating Centre for Chronic Conditions (Great Britain) and Royal College of Physicians of London (n 4) 85.

12 Irene M Stratton and others, 'Association of Glycaemia with Macrovascular and Microvascular Complications of Type 2 Diabetes (UKPDS 35): Prospective Observational Study' (2000) 321 *BMJ* 405.

cases of severe hyperglycaemia.[13] These were all quite specific clinical circumstances that confirmed that, in specific cases, if Metformin really was not an option Sulfonylurea could be prescribed. This did not alter the overall picture the guideline group draw from the evidence that metformin was its preferred drug.

In deciding which drug to recommend as the second step, adding a further blood glucose drug to that already prescribed, the group had a wide array of choices and evidence to rely on. In an 'ideal' world, the group would be able to compare studies using metformin as a first treatment (or Sulfonylurea) and compare this within an RCT with patients who are using metformin and the four different classes of drugs the group considered as a second-step treatment: Sulfonylurea, Meglitinide, Thiazolidinediones and Acarbose.

The reality is that this level of evidence was not available to the guideline group. Not all these comparisons between various drugs are covered in RCTs as they mostly compare a particular drug with a placebo or with another drug in the same class (for example, comparing Glimepiride with Gliclazide, both drugs in the Sulfonylurea class). One of the guideline group members explained limits in the evidence considered:

> Every study that was put in front of us [contained] people who did not do dreadful [did not have severe complications], so say 8.5%Hb1Ac [blood sugar level], ... people with Hb1Ac >11 might have responded differently [to the drug] ... The studies were not set-up to support guideline development ... but to satisfy the FDA [Food and Drug Administration] and EMA [European Medicines Agency].[14]

This point is an important one and a specific factor that affects the evidence-base of the diabetes guideline as a whole. As one group member explained, more extensively, 'the pharmaceutical companies who produce the drugs used to treat diabetes don't have to show that their drugs are superior to those already on the market, they merely have to show that they are safe, so their comparator group in a medical trial is very often a placebo'. The information that can thus be gained from these studies is that the drug is safe and indirectly its effectiveness can be compared by looking at other RCTs comparing different drugs to placebos. But – and this is the central point – this does not answer the question of whether

13 National Collaborating Centre for Chronic Conditions (Great Britain) and Royal College of Physicians of London (n 4) 87.

14 English Diabetes guideline group member 3 (Leeds, 20 May 2015).

one drug is superior or inferior when prescribed with other drugs. It is precisely this question that guideline groups had to answer.

The group used the evidence that was available to compare the different classes of drugs on several characteristics: glucose levels, weight, lipid profile[15] and adverse events. In making the decision on the preferred second-line treatment, these measures of effectiveness were taken into account, as well as the cost of the drug and its clinical profile. This multi-layered decision-making process did not point to uniform solutions for all diabetes patients, several examples from the guideline can illuminate how this complicated weighing exercise was carried out. The guideline text gives an indication of the approach the guideline group endorsed in this area:

> Because such people vary in attributes (such as body weight and insulin sensitivity) which can affect choice of medication, and because some medication side effects can have consequences for aspects of daily living (such as driving motor vehicles), blanket recommendations cannot be made for everyone with Type 2 diabetes.[16]

In weighing the position of the various drugs, specific elements of the evidence stood out that tipped the analysis of the medical studies in a certain direction depending on the particular position of this drug in the treatment regime for diabetes.

For Sulfonylurea, an important question was whether its side-effects might restrict their use. The GDG group decided that the side-effects would be a problem for specific occupations such as bus drivers. Here, one sees an example of an attempt by the guideline group to bridge the gap between providing one type of advice for everyone and medicine tailored to the individual. The concerns about side-effects were not enough to say that Sulfonylurea should not be used at all: so, by distinguishing sub-groups of diabetes patients for which the drug is not suitable, a balance was struck between the benefits and side-effects of the drug. Distinguishing these sub-groups was an important tool to establish a tailoring of treatment, making sure that patients who differ on relevant characteristics receive the diabetes care best suited to them.

The guideline group than compared the Meglitinide class of drugs to the Sulfonylurea class of drugs as their working mechanisms are similar.

---

15 Not further explored in this book.

16 National Collaborating Centre for Chronic Conditions (Great Britain) and Royal College of Physicians of London (n 4) 53.

It considered that Repaglinide[17] is not superior to Sulfonylurea because it must be taken three times a day and is more expensive. This led the guideline group to conclude that it should not be recommended for the general population of diabetes patients. One factor that presented challenges for the guideline group was that there was only one RCT directly comparing Meglitinide with Sulfonylurea.[18] It seems that the fact that the drug had to be taken three times a day was a major barrier.[19] From a clinical point of view, it was difficult to endorse Repaglinide over Sulfonylurea as the uptake in clinical practice was very low and there was limited experience among GPs and other diabetes experts in using the drug.

In this case it was not the evidence that drove a recommendation because, by all accounts the difference between Repaglinide and Sulfonylurea is marginal, it was the added complexity of administering the medication in clinical practice. It is interesting to note how the guideline group framed the evidence for Meglitinides: they focused on the fact that they were not superior to Sulfonylurea and concluded that there was no reason to change the recommendation in an earlier guideline. This shows that not all evidence is equal. If a drug such as Sulfonylurea has already been recommended, then the superiority of the alternative drug presented must be demonstrated before recommendations are changed.

A third class of drugs for which evidence was compared were the Thiazolidinediones. There are two drugs in this class: Rosiglitazon and Pioglitazon. The discussion around these two drugs was heavily predicated on an evaluation of the adverse effects emerging from ongoing trials and the consequential worry about their safety. This mainly involved evaluating the potential increased risk of myocardial infarction and death from cardiovascular causes. The discussion concentrated on a meta-analysis[20] which showed a 43 per cent increased relative risk of myocardial infarction, which in absolute terms meant that 14 more people had a myocardial infarction compared to the control group.[21] The same

17 One of the specific drugs in this class of medication.

18 National Collaborating Centre for Chronic Conditions (Great Britain) and Royal College of Physicians of London (n 4) 66.

19 For fear that the therapy adherence by patients would be low. Frequent visits to the GP would be necessary to adjust the doses of the medication.

20 Steven E Nissen and Kathy Wolski, 'Effect of Rosiglitazone on the Risk of Myocardial Infarction and Death from Cardiovascular Causes' (2007) 356 *New England Journal of Medicine* 2457.

21 86/14371 in the pioglitazone group and 72/11634 in the control group.

study concluded that there was a 'borderline significant'[22] increased risk of death from cardiovascular causes. For Pioglitazone, the main risk discussed was that of serious heart failure.[23]

This data was emerging at the time the guideline group was deliberating. The studies were not seen as robust enough as to warrant a complete rejection of the drugs, but the eventual recommendation suggested it was only to be used when other drugs were unacceptable, as in the case of insulin, or not tolerated, as in the case of Metformin and Sulfonylurea.[24] Again, the group was here working towards establishing sub-groups of people who might benefit from these drugs. However, the therapeutic room here, seems particularly small as the drugs cannot be prescribed to people with evidence of heart failure or who are of increased risk for fracture.[25] These drugs provide an interesting case as they show the difficult balancing act required. The emerging safety evidence had to be weighed in deciding whether to advice against medications that were used frequently in clinical practice. In this case, the potential side-effects were the preponderant consideration in evaluating the correct position of these drugs in the treatment pathway.

The final drug considered as a second-step treatment was Acarbose. Acarbose was not favoured by the guideline group because it has a high number of side-effects. The most important one being flatulence. It also noted its higher cost and the fact it lowers blood sugar slightly less compared to Metformin and Sulfonylurea. Here again the guideline group stated that it would not change its earlier recommendation. Even though Acarbose as a mono-therapy has the advantage of not causing hypoglycaemia, it was not preferred over any other drug.[26]

The way the various diabetic drugs are treated therefore differs depending on the availability of evidence, their clinical and safety profile and their historical role in treating diabetes. The same compromise must be struck between the various elements of cost, side effects, efficacy and clinical role; which element is decisive differs. In this way,

22 National Collaborating Centre for Chronic Conditions (Great Britain) and Royal College of Physicians of London (n 4) 93.

23 A Lincoff and others, 'Pioglitazone and Risk of Cardiovascular Events in Patients with Type 2 Diabetes Mellitus: A Meta-Analysis of Randomized Trials' (2007) 298 *JAMA* 1180.

24 National Collaborating Centre for Chronic Conditions (Great Britain) and Royal College of Physicians of London (n 4) 123.

25 Ibid.

26 Ibid, 86.

a guideline is built up using several layers of decisions that in themselves are compromises between the various interests. In advising the use of Sulfonylurea, the guideline group did not make a blanket recommendation; it carefully crafted alternative clinical scenarios where other drugs could be used, thereby retaining clinical autonomy and choice for patients.

If the second-step treatment 'fails' and the blood sugar is not yet sufficiently controlled, it is possible for a third drug to be added. Three classes of medication could be considered at this stage: DPP-4, GLP-1 and the Thiazolidinediones. The 2009 guideline update mainly discussed the position of the DPP-4 and GLP-1 drugs in the treatment of diabetes.

DPP-4 inhibitors were a new (in 2008/2009) class of drugs. The 2008 guideline group did not consider these drugs as it was decided that they would be covered in a 'rapid update' provided by NICE, which became the 2009 short guideline.[27] These new drugs were thus evaluated separately. The group that drafted the 2008 guideline was unhappy with this arrangement as it prevented them from considering all the relevant drugs in one guideline.[28] The 2009 guideline was based on a health technology assessment report reproduced in its annex.[29] In the Cochrane systematic review of RCTs used as the main evidence to make decisions on the DPP-4 drug, only four turned out to be relevant. They fit with the licenced use of the drugs, are all sponsored by the manufacturers and are short studies (one year or less in duration).[30]

The 2009 guideline group recommended the use of DPP-4 as second-line therapy if either Metformin or Sulfonylurea was not suitable or as third-line therapy as an alternative for Pio- or Rosiglitazone. An interesting addition to these recommendations is the formulation of a 'stop rule' where the use of a DPP-4 inhibitor should only be continued after a beneficial metabolic response. This is interesting for various reasons: it is clear that this rule is not based on evidence but is a result of consensus within the group. A substantial decrease in blood sugar was seen as clinically meaningful, it would make sure that people did not stay on medication that was not beneficial and would ensure blood sugar did

27 NICE, 'Type 2 Diabetes: Newer Agents' (n 5).

28 National Collaborating Centre for Chronic Conditions (Great Britain) and Royal College of Physicians of London (n 4) Foreword.

29 NICE, 'Type 2 Diabetes: Newer Agents' (n 5) Annex 2.

30 Ibid, Annex 2 87.

not remain uncontrolled for too long.[31] In this way the guideline group fulfilled two goals. They gave sufficient heed to the fact that there was no long-term safety data for these drugs, as they only recently entered the market. They also – and this is a continuation of the 2008 guideline group – strove to define smaller sub-groups of patients who benefitted from, in this case, DPP-4.

Glucagon-Like Peptide-1 mimetics were the newest class of drugs available at the time and their appropriate place in the pathway of care was part of the discussion in both the 2008 and 2009 guideline groups. The only drug in this class licensed at the time was Exenatide. Exenatide was considered by the 2008 guideline group as a drug that might help prolong the period a patient with diabetes could postpone using insulin. The main debate was around the fact that Exenatide led to weight loss and a lowering of blood sugar comparable to other drugs (either insulin of Glitazones). It is important to note that glucose-lowering drugs are not prescribed for their weight loss properties, although this effect could be seen as a positive as weight loss helps to maintain blood sugar control.

The question facing the guideline group was how to weigh this evidence. Did the potential for weight loss justify the extra cost associated with this new treatment? The detailed cost–benefit model used to answer this question will be dealt with when dealing with costs in the construction of these guidelines: however, both guideline groups suggested the benefits outweighed the costs. Exenatide had clinical benefits as a guideline group member discussed:

> This was a dilemma because we were back at cost … we were now at 69 pounds a month, what we didn't want [is] people using GLP-1 it is not appropriate for, the more obese you are the more insulin resistance is the issue instead of beta-cell failure. The large amount of insulin … can cause weight gain. We didn't want it [GLP-1] to be a weight-loss treatment, but the GLP-1 could help people change their diet and so reduce their weight.[32]

For people who are obese, specifically for those with a BMI higher than 35, Exenatide could be an option.[33] Here, again, the guideline group defines a specific sub-group of diabetes patients who they expect to benefit

---

31 Ibid, 64.

32 English Diabetes guideline group member 3 (Leeds, 20 May 2015).

33 Or in the 2009 guideline also for those with a BMI <35 if 'therapy with insulin would have significant occupational implications or weight loss would benefit other significant obesity-related comorbidities'.

most from this treatment. It is interesting to note that both guideline groups went to great lengths to interpret the limited evidence[34] in such a way that Exenatide could gain a place in the pathway. The main basis for its desirability as a treatment was not blood sugar reduction but the potential for weight loss, combined with the high cost of very large doses of insulin for people who are obese. Only in this scenario could Exenatide be prescribed. The reason that both the 2008 and 2009 guideline groups were keen to afford Exenatide a place can partly be explained by their willingness to accommodate those with anxieties about their weight and to prescribe medication that has a beneficial effect on weight: because this would benefit the whole of diabetes care in an integrated way (even if cost-effectiveness could not be established by looking at the effect of the drug in a more isolated fashion). In this case, the limited evidence was used to support the clinical reasons to favour Exenatide as it provided an extra option for clinicians to treat people with diabetes. This clinical need provided sufficient reason to include the drug, while the 'stopping rule' invented by the group was aimed at assuaging fears that the cost of the drug would be too great. One guideline group member summarised the issue succinctly: 'the justification for Exenatide is that it should lead to weight loss.'[35]

If we compare the new diabetic drugs to the 'old' ones, there does not seem to be a fundamental difference in how they are treated in the guideline development process. The necessity to strike a balance between the various elements of cost, side effects, efficacy and clinical role remains. For the new diabetic drugs, however, the costs are higher; efficacy is not yet clearly established so the focus of the discussion is placed on the proposed clinical role and the judgement of the group is focused on whether the drugs are likely to cause fewer side-effects. DPP-4 was included because it provided an alternative to the Thiazolidinediones class of drugs, which suffered from safety issues. Exenatide was welcomed because it could prolong the period a patient could remain without insulin and allow further tailoring of treatment. The uncertainty surrounding the long-term safety of the drugs is addressed by the guideline groups through consensus-based 'stop rules' which enabled them to strike a balance between the lack of evidence on long-term safety issues and the clinical wish to employ these drugs.

---

34 The 2008 group relied on eight RCTs and the 2009 group on five.

35 English Diabetes guideline group member 2 (Cambridge, 6 May 2015).

5.2.3. THERAPEUTIC TARGET FOR LOWERING BLOOD SUGAR

In addition to formulating the best therapeutic pathway for a patient by defining first, second- and third-line therapies, the guideline also provides guidance on blood glucose levels. This advice has two functions: it advises on a target level for blood glucose for people with diabetes in general and it provides thresholds above which intensification of treatment should commence. These targets are based on an analysis of the UKPDS study.[36] The achievement of these targets levels by patients should lead to a decrease in all microvascular and microvascular complications of diabetes and mortality correlated with a decrease in blood sugar. The guideline describes this as follows:

> The risk of each of the microvascular and macrovascular complications of Type 2 diabetes ... was strongly associated with hyperglycaemia as measured by updated mean HbA1c [blood sugar level]. There was no indication of a threshold for any complication below which risk no longer decreased, nor a level above which risk no longer increased.[37]

Given this data, the blood sugar target level should be set as stringently as possible. The group balanced the need for tight blood sugar control with the cost of very intensive treatment and decided to maintain the level of 6.5% HbA1c [blood sugar level] set in an earlier guideline:

> However, expensive therapies or very intensive interventions are required to achieve glucose control in the normal range in most people with diabetes. Consequently, a population target should not be any tighter than the HbA1c [blood sugar level] of 6.5% previously chosen for those at macrovascular risk. Nearly all people with Type 2 diabetes are of high CV [cardiovascular] risk, usually in association with insulin insensitivity, but if not with age. Additionally, there has been very recent concern (no evidence yet to review) about pursuing very intensive glucose control (target <6.0%) in people with higher CV [cardiovascular] risk and longer duration of diabetes, mostly on multiple insulin injection therapy.[38]

---

36 Stratton and others (n 12).

37 National Collaborating Centre for Chronic Conditions (Great Britain) and Royal College of Physicians of London (n 4) 42.

38 Ibid, 45.

The very recent concern the group refers to is the ACCORD[39] trial, which was not yet published at the time this guideline was drafted. This trial had to be stopped early as it later transpired that people in the intensive blood-sugar-lowering group had a 22% relative and 1% absolute increased mortality after a 3.5 year follow-up period.[40] This established for the first time that a glucose target that is too low can also do harm through increasing death from cardiovascular causes. A member of the guideline group remarked on this choice of target level: 'It's all clinical judgement, the clinical view around the table. All the other guidelines seemed to have 6.5% at that moment, I can tell you the 6.5 [target] came out of thin air. There is the whole issue of goal-setting, which is necessarily an evidence-free area.'[41] What this member is explaining is that all the studies the group could rely on to set these target levels discussed people who have achieved certain levels, which does not necessarily translate into goals for the patient population as a whole. So, it was the clinical consensus of the group that drove this recommendation.

The English diabetes guideline group went through each step in the treatment of diabetes in a systematic fashion. Every treatment/drug was considered separately drawing upon existing medical studies, clinical knowledge and cost-effectiveness studies. The way for the group to find a balance between these various types of knowledge was to define sub-groups of patients for which a particular drug was suitable. In this way costs could be presented as being justified, clinical choice could be preserved and differences in opinion could be bridged.

5.3. ACHIEVING CONSENSUS: INTERNAL WORKINGS OF THE ENGLISH GUIDELINE GROUP

The English guideline group consists of a wider variety of medical professionals: GPs, practice nurses, endocrinologists and academic medical professionals with a specialisation in diabetes care. The impetus

39 The Action to Control Cardiovascular Risk in Diabetes Study Group, 'Effects of Intensive Glucose Lowering in Type 2 Diabetes' (2008) 358 *New England Journal of Medicine* 2545.

40 Ibid, 2553.

41 English Diabetes guideline group member 1 (Warwick, 26 May 2015).

for producing this guideline was the regular process of updating the existing diabetes guidelines produced by NICE.

In analysing how the English guideline group achieved consensus we will take their discussion of evidence as a starting point because it illuminates the process that they followed. Their discussions about evidence shows how the guideline group worked their way through the various medications and made a series of compromises to achieve a result which everyone could be happy with. This process differed depending on the type of medication that was under discussion. For the older and more established medications, the question was not whether they should have a role in the treatment of diabetes, but only to what extent their existing position should be modified. For the newer drugs, the question was more fundamental: should their use be recommended? Only after it was decided that newer drugs could be recommended, could their place in the therapeutic pathway be established.

The discussion therefore varied with each drug, depending on which aspect of its profile as a treatment was the most controversial. An example would be the discussion about the inclusion of Exenatide, 'the new diabetic drug', in the guideline. This decision was a difficult one for the guideline group in the sense that it pitted several forms of knowledge against each other and a resolution of this conflict required making a definite choice. Exenatide was considered to be too expensive for the NHS, the original cost-effectiveness modelling performed for the drug showed that it had an incremental cost-effectiveness ratio far above £40,000 per year. A guideline group member discusses this cost-effectiveness model in the following terms:

> We were very challenging about the cost-effectiveness studies … they did not include enough on the cost of hypoglycaemia. So, the cost-effectiveness [study] was redone … The general consensus was that we weren't quite sure we come up with a good enough number [of quality adjust life-years] but we have done the best we could.[42]

Subsequently, the modelling was changed to more closely reflect the situation of a patient who the guideline group thought could profit from Exenatide. This clearly showed how the clinical wish to employ Exenatide was a motivating force to make sure patients would benefit from this new drug and that considerations of cost were of secondary importance.

42 English Diabetes guideline group member 3 (Leeds, 20 May 2015).

This same guideline group member expresses clearly the direction of thinking in the guideline group: 'What we did … Exenatide came out as we cannot recommend it, the clinicians around the table said: you cannot say that, this is a new clinical area, a new drug, we must not allow the NICE guidelines to say a blanket no. So, we wrote this slightly strange recommendation … those additions were written by the clinicians … as a sop to the health economics data, you cannot say no … because it is new.'[43]

The choice to recommend Exenatide was thus a combination of several factors that worked together to create a space it in the guideline. The potential for weight loss was an important factor and something older medication could not provide (as it would lead to weight gain). Especially in a group of obese diabetes patients, to postpone the decision to start insulin therapy was positive for patients. However, arguments against Exenatide were its high cost and unknown safety profile.

In this case, the guideline group thought the arguments for inclusion outweighed the arguments against. They approached the issue of cost by casting doubt upon the cost-effectiveness data. The relevant section of the guideline clearly showed this approach:

> Exenatide therapy is expensive, and the health economic modelling suggested it was not cost-effective for an unselected population as compared to commencing human insulin therapy. However, the GDG did not consider comparison with an unselected population to be applicable (…) The GDG was uncertain that these agents (including Exenatide) would be found to be not cost-effective if the model fully reflected the negative quality of life issues of insulin, … Furthermore, the more obese require much higher insulin doses, such that insulin costs alone can easily exceed those of Exenatide … In these circumstances a confident judgment of costs and benefits to be gained from HbA1c and weight change, and side effects, could not be made. However, the GDG's judgment was that costs of insulin and Exenatide by the end of the first year would be equivalent on average for people with a starting BMI (before these medications) of approximately >33 kg/m2, while in this obese group the small metabolic advantage to insulin on HbA1c would easily be outweighed by the metabolic advantage of 4 kg weight loss on Exenatide. In this restricted circumstance, and particularly at higher BMI's, the cost-effectiveness of Exenatide would then be at least as good as that of insulin.'[44]

43 English Diabetes guideline group member 1 (Warwick, 26 May 2015).

44 National Collaborating Centre for Chronic Conditions (Great Britain) and Royal College of Physicians of London (n 4) 122.

It is clear the guideline group considered the cost-effectiveness data from various angles. The first step was to create a sub-set of diabetes patients, corresponding to the clinical views of the group of patients for which the group thought this treatment would be beneficial. The next step was to identify several factors not captured in the economic model to underpin the fact that the conclusion the drug is not cost-effective cannot be supported. A key point is the fact that insulin is seen to be linked to negative quality-of-life issues and that the weight loss related to the use of Exenatide is a way of addressing these issues, in contrast to insulin which would lead to an increase in weight for most patients. When framed in this way, the argument carried less weight because the drug could be shown to be as cost-effective as insulin if one adopted a broader view of costs (and benefits) than the model provides. At the same time, as observed earlier, the guideline group did not disregard cost entirely and devised a 'stop-rule' to limit the use of Exenatide to a specific sub-group:

> Consider exenatide as an option only if all the following apply for the individual: a body mass index over 35.0 kg/m2 in those of European descent, with appropriate adjustment in tailoring this advice for other ethnic groups [,] specific problems of a psychological, biochemical or physical nature arising from high body weight inadequate blood glucose control (HbA1c ≥7.5%) with conventional oral agents after a trial of metformin and sulfonylurea [,] other high-cost medication, such as a thiazolidinedione or insulin injection therapy, would otherwise be started. Continue exenatide therapy only if a beneficial metabolic response (at least 1.0% HbA1c reduction in 6 months and a weight loss of at least 5% at 1 year) occurs and is maintained.[45]

It is interesting to note that the BMI cut-off point in this 'stop-rule' is 35, while the narrative text cited before mentions 33. One of the members of the guideline group members confirmed that this was an editing mistake and the number in the narrative should have been changed to 35. He said: 'You make these changes to quite a tight schedule; it should have been updated [in the evidence statement].'[46] While this might seem a trivial error, on closer inspection it shows that the guideline was extensively debated and that several proposals for cut-off points were considered before that of BMI greater than 35 was adopted. Several guideline group members describe how this cut-off point was debated, as well as whether patients should fulfil both the weight loss and

45 Ibid, 124.

46 English Diabetes guideline group member 2 (Cambridge, 6 May 2015).

blood sugar level decrease requirement or only one of them. As one group member recalls: 'The weight cut-off was a major major bone of contention … we weren't giving it [Exenatide] as a weight loss treatment, if someone has significant improvement in their HbA1c even if they had no weight loss … this is what we want.'[47] The safety concerns around Exenatide are no different than for any of the new medication, so did not feature prominently in the reasoning of the guideline group.

Exenatide provides us with an example of the consideration of a new drug that changes the pathway of care and how the reasoning of the guideline group is an interplay between evidence, cost, clinical knowledge, patient wishes and institutional constraints. The option to consider Exenatide was based on evidence, searched for through a process of clinical questions and careful assessment of the weight and strength of evidence fully in keeping with evidence-based medicine. But the appraisal of what this evidence means for clinical practice and whether the drug should be seen as a positive addition to the arsenal of options available for treating diabetes, is one informed by clinical knowledge from people who have the experience of using the drug. These considerations were then pitted against cost-effectiveness data that has a different purpose, to find the optimal medication within given cost constraints, to enable a compromise that could satisfy the conflicting demands of those two types of knowledge.

Not all medication is treated in the same way. Exenatide was particularly controversial and required extensive debate. Other medications were less controversial: Metformin is an example. The fact that Metformin is cheap, safe and effective and well tested in practice meant that the guideline group did not have to debate its position in the guideline as extensively. This underscores the fact that the guideline drafters do not start with a *tabula rasa* but instead build upon earlier guidelines in a layered way, in which the only aspects that were changed were those where new evidence, or other reasons, forced a change. An example of the other reasons forcing a change is the consideration of Rosiglitazone and Pioglitazone in this guideline.

Rosiglitazone was highlighted in guideline discussions, not in relation to its effectiveness or costs, but in relation to its safety. The safety data which we have discussed in the evidence section of this case study provided the guideline group with a difficult dilemma. The crucial decision to be discussed was the precise weight that should be attached

[47] English Diabetes guideline group member 3 (Leeds, 20 May 2015).

to the emerging findings about negative side-effects, especially of Rosiglitazone. Would this mean the drug should no longer be prescribed at all? The group decided that the safety data did not warrant this far-reaching conclusion. One of the members described their reasoning thus: 'we weren't clear at the time whether the signal on heart attacks was genuine or not.'[48]

While another put it in this way:

> The Glitazone water was seriously muddied in the middle of doing this guideline ... the Glitazone I think are a group of drugs that have split the diabetes fraternity ... some people already have concerns in the group ... I think as a result of the meta-analysis people wanted to be more conservative ... I thought it was a really poor study ... the fact that studies had been excluded ... that didn't have any cardiac events didn't make sense.[49]

Another member said:

> We put in some sort of weasel phrase ... be aware of current safety concerns. ... There was no evidence to do that [not recommend the drug] if you actually look at Stephens analysis ... the absolute numbers where 72 versus 88 events, which was an increased risk of 44%, the relative risk looks huge, the reason why it was significant, was that Rosiglitazone was introduced on the basis ... that we deal with insulin resistance, therefore we are bound to reduce cardiovascular events [heart attacks] as soon as ... the fact that Rosiglitazone ... increases [cardiovascular events] you have [a] ship pulled below the water line.[50]

This shows how the guideline group has weighed this evidence, which suggested risk and reasons to be vigilant, but this did not present enough risk to advice against using the medication. With the reference to the advice of the European Medicines Agency and the Medicines and Healthcare Products Regulatory Agency,[51] the guideline group underscored the need for clinicians to stay up-to-date about the developments regarding Pio- and Rosiglitazone.[52] The example of Rosiglitazone, illustrates how the

---

48 English Diabetes guideline group member 2 (Cambridge, 6 May 2015).

49 English Diabetes guideline group member 3 (Leeds, 20 May 2015).

50 English Diabetes guideline group member 1 (Warwick, 26 May 2015).

51 National Collaborating Centre for Chronic Conditions (Great Britain) and Royal College of Physicians of London (n 4) 123.

52 The market authorisation of Rosiglitazone was suspended (which means the drugs had to be taken off the market) in March 2010 by the European Medicines Agency

guideline group dealt with the question of the potential non-inclusion of a treatment in the guideline. Just like the inclusion of a treatment, the potential exclusion of a treatment requires that a certain threshold be met before the group decides to include or exclude a drug. In this case, the guideline group felt the evidence did not warrant an exclusion of Rosiglitazone.

The decisions taken in the guideline group are tailored attempts at reaching a consensus among a varied group of healthcare professionals. While discussions were always presented as those about evidence, they were complemented by knowledge of clinical practice and acceptable compromises were reached between the members of the group as to how clinical practice could deal with the choices on diabetes treatment. Sometimes this pitted economic knowledge on cost-effectiveness against clinical knowledge about the use of medication; at other times, safety concerns were prominent. An important tool for the group in reaching a common position after a long process of deliberation was the possibility of separating distinct sub-groups of diabetes patients all with a separate treatment regime; this allowed for the disparate views to be reconciled.

5.4. EXTERNAL RESPONSES: CONFRONTATIONS OVER CLINICAL CHOICES

The response to the guideline was muted. There was an article in response to the 2008 guideline that outlined the need for an update because of the new safety data for Pioglitazone and the emerging data for the new diabetic drugs.[53] The new guidelines from NICE did not seem to cause much of a stir. So, in this case, any external responses did not cause any changes to the text, but it might have influenced the decision to quickly update the 2008 diabetes guideline.

This was very different when the draft of what became the 2015 NICE type II diabetes guideline was published.[54] In the draft 2015 diabetes

because of the increased risk of myocardial infarction. EMA, 'European Medicines Agency Recommends Suspension of Avandia, Avandamet and Avaglim. Anti-Diabetes Medication to Be Taken off the Market.' Available at: <http://www.ema.europa.eu/docs/en_GB/document_library/Press_release/2010/09/WC500096996.pdf>.

53 Stephen Atkin and Christopher Walton, 'Commentary: Controversies in NICE Guidance on Management of Type 2 Diabetes' (2008) 336 *BMJ* 1308.

54 NICE, 'Type 2 Diabetes in Adults: Management | Guidance and Guidelines'. Available at: <https://www.nice.org.uk/guidance/ng28>.

guideline, Repaglinide was given a prominent place in treating diabetes but many healthcare professionals thought this was the wrong move. Among the criticism levelled was the fact that the guideline group had only considered the cost of the medication, ignoring the fact that the drug was not often prescribed in clinical practice, had no licensed combination other than with Metformin so would have to be stopped if another drug had to be added and required frequent visits to GP practices to deal with adjusting of the dosage of the drug because of its variable effects.[55] The final guideline dropped Repaglinide, only mentioning it in a footnote, after a second consultation was held.

This episode shows that, in some cases, where a guideline directly contradicts clinical practice, NICE can face difficulty in only providing cost-effectiveness arguments as justification and was often forced to weaken or change recommendations to accommodate criticism by clinicians.

5.5. CONFLICTS OF INTEREST: POTENTIAL INFLUENCES

Several members of the guideline group reported a potential conflict of interest: Annex E of the guideline provides details of these.[56] This includes being paid for lectures, sitting on advisory boards of pharmaceutical companies and involvement in educational and charitable organisations sponsored by pharmaceutical companies. The question is whether these involvements have had any influence on the guideline.

In all the interviews conducted, guideline drafters were asked about whether they felt that they had a conflict of interest and whether this influenced their recommendations. Perhaps unsurprisingly, none of the members felt that the conflict of interest had any influence on their recommendations.

---

55 Anthony H Barnett, 'NICE Draft Type 2 Diabetes Guidelines: A Cause for Concern' (2015) 3 *The Lancet Diabetes & Endocrinology* 403; Jo Stephenson, 'Nurses Claim NICE Diabetes Guidance Will Put Patients at Risk' *Nursing Times* (15 September 2015). Available at: <https://www.nursingtimes.net/clinical-archive/diabetes/nurses-claim-nice-diabetes-guidance-will-put-patients-at-risk/5090329.article>; Price (Chapter 2, n 132).

56 National Collaborating Centre for Chronic Conditions (Great Britain) and Royal College of Physicians of London (n 4) Annex E.

Some members of the guideline group stated that they feel a conflict of interest did not influence their recommendations in the guideline group because they work with all diabetes-related pharmaceutical companies, so do not favour one over the other. One member formulated this argument: 'you work for everyone therefore you are beholden to no one'.[57] While another guideline group member echoed this: 'Everybody had every company, as a potential conflict of interest.'[58]

This argument is not wholly convincing as it neglects the potential bias that an association with pharmaceutical companies brings to the assessment of medications that are off patent where there is no campaign to promote these drugs by pharmaceutical companies. So even if guideline makers feel that in this way they favour one company over another, there still might be a selection bias when it comes to deciding which drugs should be prescribed for the treatment of diabetes.

Despite this potential for selection bias, it is difficult to establish a causal link between the fact that a certain treatment has been recommended and a potential conflict of interest for one or more of the guideline group members. There is, however, a link between the consideration of the evidence on Exenatide in the guideline group and conflicts of interest that provide some support for the argument that the group was (in)directly influenced by conflicts of interest.

The stress the group places on the weight loss achieved by patients on Exenatide and the reduced risk of hypoglycaemia for the newer diabetic drugs could be driven by the campaigning of the pharmaceutical industry to promote these aspects of the new drugs. The problem, however, is that we do not know whether the group favours those drugs because they believe in their superiority, based on their own independent reasoning, or because they are influenced by the conflicts of interest they have. It is quite likely that the practitioners themselves do not know this either. We rarely ever question the source of our beliefs.

So, this study is restricted to arguing that it is plausible that the existence of conflicts of interests made the group look more favourably upon the newer diabetic medication. Existing literature in this field also points in this direction, showing a correlation between conflicts of interests and recommendations for drugs in guidelines, without being able to discern any direct causal relationship.[59]

---

57 English Diabetes guideline group member 1 (Warwick, 26 May 2015).
58 English Diabetes guideline group member 3 (Leeds, 20 May 2015).
59 George, Vesely and Woolf (Chapter 2, n 131).

5.6. INSTITUTIONAL FACTORS IMPACTING ON GUIDELINE DRAFTING

In the development process of these two diabetes guidelines the institutional structure and processes of NICE played an important role. The drafting of two diabetes guidelines, the 2008 guideline and the 2009 short update guideline was the result of a decision by NICE to divide the assessment of diabetes care into two guidelines: one to assess the older medications and the first licensed GLP-1: Exenatide and a second to include DPP-4 and GLP-1. Originally, NICE had intended to perform a health technology assessment to include the newer diabetic drugs, but later decided to 'upgrade' the treatment to a short guideline. As one guideline group member explained:

> NICE did not want to include this [the new medication] in the scope because they thought it would subject to a separate technology appraisal ... In hindsight we should have a broader scope that included those drugs.[60]

This disjointed treatment of the guideline process led to some frustration for the members of the guideline group, which was expressed in the foreword to the 2008 guideline.[61] The result of this institutional set-up was that the 2008 guideline was out of date almost as soon as it was published. Even during the drafting process of the 2008 guideline it became clear there would be an update, which duly followed in 2009. Furthermore, the extensive drafting of the 2008 guideline took around two years to complete and only appraised one of the new drugs, while the short guideline was produced in four two-day meetings and covered more of them. This disparate treatment was a direct result of the particular institutional choices made at the time and might plausibly have been related to the fact that NICE only had limited resources and put a limit on the amount of clinical questions that can be set within the scope of one guideline: for the 2008 guideline, 32 clinical questions were identified.[62]

This shows one of the inherent difficulties in producing guidelines: they take time to develop, by which time the medical field might have changed substantially.

---

60 English Diabetes guideline group member 2 (Cambridge, 6 May 2015).

61 National Collaborating Centre for Chronic Conditions (Great Britain) and Royal College of Physicians of London (n 4) Foreword.

62 Ibid, Annex A.

5.7. COST-EFFECTIVENESS MODELLING AND CLINICAL CHOICES

The cost-effectiveness of treatments for diabetes is an integral part of the NICE guideline. For all the treatments provided, the guideline group searches for economic evidence in the form of a cost-effectiveness analysis of the treatment (compared to one or more other treatments). If existing literature is available, this is used to estimate the ICER (incremental cost-effectiveness ratio) per QALY (quality-adjusted life-year) gained. Examples of this approach are the cost-effectiveness of Metformin, Sulfonylurea and Rosiglitazone as second-line therapy. The guideline group also commissioned a new cost-effectiveness study done to compare various third-line treatments for diabetes.[63] This new analysis is especially relevant for this study as it informed the choice of the guideline group to give Exenatide a place in the guideline together with Rosi- and Pioglitazone and NPH-Insulin. The following results, given in table C20 in the cost-effectiveness report, provide the starting point for their discussions.

Table 1. Costs and QALYs of Diabetes Drugs[64]

	Total QALYs	Total costs (£)	ICER
Human insulin	8.05	19,527	[First choice]
Pioglitazone	8.03	19,828	Dominated
Glargine	8.00	21,467	Dominated
Biphasic analogue	8.05	23,033	Extended dominance
Rosiglitazone	7.94	24,978	Dominated
Exenatide	8.08	29,001	£280,495

From this table it becomes clear the least costly option is Human Insulin and the option with the highest quality-adjusted life years is Exenatide. Pio- and Rosiglitazone, as well as Glargine, are less effective than human insulin, have lower quality-adjusted life-years and thus are 'dominated' by human insulin in the terminology of the model. Biphasic analogues are as effective as human insulin (both 'score' 8.05)

63 Ibid, Appendix C.
64 Ibid, Appenix C table C20.

but the costs are higher, in the terminology of this model, termed 'extended dominance'. The ICER (incremental cost-effectiveness ratio) is a way of expressing what the cost would be if the NHS would pay for one quality-adjusted life year. In this case, because an extra 0.03 quality-adjusted life year on Exenatide cost around £9,000 pounds to 'buy', a whole quality-adjusted life year would cost £280,495. This is far above the £30,000 threshold NICE has defined as their willingness to pay to gain one quality-adjusted life year. These results stay the same in several sensitivity analyses[65] and are consistent throughout. Human insulin is thus presented as the most cost-effective option for third-line treatment of diabetes. There is, however, one scenario in the model where Exenatide can be considered cost-effective, with an incremental cost-effectiveness ratio of £29,865 just below the threshold defined by NICE.[66] This is when Exenatide is compared with the other drugs under specific circumstances detailed in table C37 of the cost-effectiveness report.[67] In this analysis, it is assumed that Exenatide is successful in achieving a 5 per cent weight loss over two years, while the other treatments cause weight gain. To express this difference the Exenatide patients are given a BMI of 27 in the model compared to a BMI of 33 for the other patients. It is further assumed Exenatide does not cause nausea. In these limited circumstances Exenatide can be seen as cost-effective, mainly because weight loss is assigned an added utility gain. The utilities in this scenario were based on a poster presentation by the (former) manufacturer of Exenatide.[68] It is this particular scenario, weight loss of 5 per cent versus weight gain on insulin, which plays a big role in the clinical consideration of this economic evidence, as we have seen in the analysis of the discussions of the guideline group, particularly in the following section from the guideline:

> However, the GDG's judgment was that costs of insulin and Exenatide by the end of the first year would be equivalent on average for people with a starting BMI (before these medications) of approximately >33 kg/m2, while in this obese group the small metabolic advantage to insulin on HbA1c would easily be outweighed by the metabolic advantage of 4 kg weight loss on Exenatide. In this restricted circumstance, and particularly at higher BMI's,

---

65 Appendix C, Table C23–C31.

66 Ibid, Table C37.

67 Ibid.

68 'Contributed Poster Presentations' (2006) 9 *Value in Health* A24, A42.

> the cost-effectiveness of Exenatide would then be at least as good as that of insulin.[69]

A striking fact is that all the treatments, when assessed, are so close to each other, with differences in QALY in the range of only 0.05 or slightly more in some of the sensitivity analysis. With such small differences, which all fall well within the margin of error for a model of this complexity, some of the underlying assumptions of the model require further scrutiny. This is clearly what the guideline group members have done as the above quote illustrates.

One of the main reasons behind the very similar results for all the drugs is that the model used to calculate the cost-utilities only models the relationship between decreasing blood sugar and the complications of diabetes. As the drugs are very similar in the extent to which they lower blood sugar, the model provides these results. This also explains why cost-effectiveness modelling could not provide a definite answer in the eyes of the guideline group, because the modelling did not include weight loss, the fear of and cost of hypoglycaemia and the costs of continuous blood glucose monitoring. The last two points could be addressed by adding these to the model, but the effect of weight loss could only be indirectly assessed, through modification of the parameters to mimic the effect of the drug. In this way the guideline group could square the circle by both accommodating the cost-effectiveness considerations, through the careful construction of a clinical scenario in which the drug could meet the formal requirements of cost-effectiveness and clinical need in having an opportunity to use the drug. Eventually, with the passage of time, the restrictions on the use of this treatment could be further relaxed, once the initial decision to give it a place in the treatment regime for diabetes patients had been taken.

The way the guideline group framed the cost-effectiveness evidence is very revealing: it shows how it was able to reconcile to conflicting sources of knowledge and different interests. The cost-effectiveness data pointed towards the conclusion the drug Exenatide could not be recommended for the treatment of diabetes. However, because one specific clinical circumstance could be found where the drug, within the parameters of NICE policies, was cost-effective, it could be recommended, by tailoring the guideline.

---

69 National Collaborating Centre for Chronic Conditions (Great Britain) and Royal College of Physicians of London (n 4) 122.

5.8. THE DUTCH GUIDELINE ON TYPE II DIABETES

The Dutch guideline for diabetes was drafted by a guideline group supported by a member of the NHG and completed in 2013.[70] This was the third revision of the original diabetes guideline, drafted by the NHG in 1988.[71] The guideline groups consisted of GPs with a specialisation in diabetes care, endocrinologists and a professor of diabetes treatment in primary care settings.

5.9. EVIDENCE BASE FOR DUTCH TREATMENTS FOR TYPE II DIABETES

The treatment options presented in the Dutch guideline on type II diabetes are wide-ranging. The first step consists of education on the disease and lifestyle advice. Losing weight and stopping smoking are important in controlling the blood glucose levels of diabetes patients. This aspect does not require any 'medication' however, it is nonetheless considered by doctors to be a very important element of the treatment of diabetes. One of the GPs in the guideline group even provides running classes for his diabetic patients where he takes them running through a local village every fortnight. It is important to draw attention to this element of diabetes care because it precedes all the further steps to be taken. As diabetes is a progressive disease, most people will, at some point, require medication to lower blood glucose. The various types of blood-glucose medication and the choices surrounding this treatment will be our primary focus.

5.9.1. MEDICATION FOR LOWERING BLOOD GLUCOSE

When medication for lowering blood glucose is required, the Dutch guideline presents as the first medical treatment option, the drug Metformin. If this does not reduce the blood-glucose levels sufficiently, one of the class of Sulfonylurea can be added with a preference

70 GEHM Rutten and others, 'NHG-Standaard Diabetes Mellitus Type 2 (Derde Herziening)' (2013) 56 *Huisarts en Wetenschap* 512.

71 JD Mulder and others, 'NHG Standaard Diabetes Mellitus Type II' (1989) 32 *Huisarts en Wetenschap* 509.

for Gliclazide as the first choice. If both of those medications are insufficient, the patient should be given insulin with a preference for HPV insulin. This list of options seems to be relatively straightforward; three types of medication are to be given consecutively. The list is noteworthy, however, for what it omits. In the list, the 'new' diabetes drugs that have been developed in the last ten years do not feature.[72] The guideline does mention those drugs but it also states that they should only be used after the preferential drugs are used and have found not to be tolerated or ineffective.[73] This implicit choice against the new diabetic drugs warrants attention and explanation, to understand the main drivers and arguments for this choice.

The evidence base used in this decision is derived from a systematic review published in the *British Medical Journal* clinical evidence section which was co-authored by some members of the guideline group.[74] This systematic review was adopted by the members of the guideline group as the basis of their decisions on drug treatments for diabetes. Several group members explained that it was not necessary to do additional searching for evidence[75] on this topic as the systematic review was very extensive and doing additional or different searches would unnecessarily duplicate results.

The fact that the systematic review was adopted was not surprising given the overlap between the members of the guideline group and the authors of the review. This, however, did not mean that the systematic review itself could determine in which order to prescribe the medication, or which medication to prioritise. Guideline group members offered several different reasons for making the choice for the older diabetic drugs. One group of arguments revolved around concerns of safety and effectiveness. Put in the following terms:

> And we had an opinion about DPP-4 and GLP-1 because there was and is little literature on [it]. But we did have reviews of the total effect of those drugs, and that was very modest. We agree with each other very quickly if you don't

[72] This includes DPP-4, GLPT-1, SLDG-2 and newer forms of insulin.

[73] Rutten and others (n 70) 2.

[74] Kees J Gorter and others, 'Diabetes: Glycaemic Control in Type 2 (Drug Treatments)' (2012) *BMJ* Clinical Evidence 0609.

[75] With the exception of a small update for papers between the end of the search conducted in the systematic review (Feb 10) and the start of the deliberations of the guideline group.

> know long-term effects and safety than we have to adopt a very conservative stance.[76]

A selected and related reason brought forward is the cost of the new medication. This was stated in more general terms such as 'the drugs are relatively expensive and the guideline group members feel they don't know enough about their effectiveness and safety profile so we didn't choose them'. While another guideline group member highlighted that the main reason was in the nature of the algorithm, the guideline group wanted to provide to GPs:

> We talked about the nature of the algorithm we wanted to use. Would it be one where we set out extensively if this happens you do that, but we said it would become so complex, a horns nest, but we didn't want that. We did want nuanced targets for blood glucose … So we arrived at metformin, sulfonylurea and Insulin, and if you want another medication use your own judgement.[77]

The guideline also provides a list of 'other medication' that can be given if the preferred medication is not suitable. The list is, in order of preference so the medication mentioned first is preferred over that mentioned second and so on. The second drug[78] on this list is Acarbose, which, in contrast to the guideline in England, is seen as a good and safe and cheap alternative to Gliclazide. The choice for Acarbose is interesting, the gastro-intestinal side-effects (flatulence) are not seen as sufficient to warrant a rejection of this drug. One of the guideline group members who did have a PhD on this drug (under the supervision of one of the other members of group), when asked about the inclusion of Acarbose, explained the choice as follows:

> I have not prescribed a single patient with Acarbose [in my career], I have nothing special with this drug. But that might happen now, because if I look at the evidence calmly and the safety, it is the least bad … It is interesting to see that the small chance someone will die from a drug [with Pioglitazon] will be taken more easily [by prescribing GPs] then the small change of flatulence and diarrhoea, very remarkable, people think it is an embarrassing drug or something. But we know if you start the drug gently and up the dose

---

76 Dutch Diabetes guideline group member 4 (Amsterdam, 11 June 2015).
77 Dutch Diabetes guideline group member 3 (Nijmegen, 17 June 2015).
78 After Repaglinide.

> carefully this is not much of a concern, and you can always stop giving it … Especially if you compare it with the new drugs, the long-term effectiveness is unknown (…), as a patient I would never take it.[79]

While another member of the guideline group when asked about Acarbose remarked:

> It did not feature in the previous guideline. It also said do not prescribe. What has changed, it is a very funny finding: Acarbose was never really advertised in the Netherlands, so there isn't a group of doctors that is enthusiastic about Acarbose … But after the new drugs arrived, we asked ourselves what to do with Acarbose? … When we analysed it [it looked good].[80]

This shows a certain pragmatic attitude to this drug: while none of the interviewed members of the guideline group were particularly enthusiastic about it, they did see it as a cheap and safe alternative for a small group of patients who would not be able to use Metformin. Whereas they felt that side-effects could be managed through careful incremental increasing of the dose of the medication.

5.9.2. 'OTHER' DIABETIC DRUGS

Only if none of these drugs establish a satisfactory control of blood glucose levels the guideline suggests other drugs can be prescribed. The additional drugs that are mentioned in the guideline are Pioglitazone, DPP-4 and GLP-1.

The decision to list Pioglitazone as the last option deserves further scrutiny as it contrasts with the decision by the English group to give Pioglitazone a place as second- or third-line treatment for diabetes. Pioglitazone is evaluated very unfavourably by the group; some members even wanted to exclude it from the guideline and to state explicitly that it was not recommended for the treatment of diabetes. A guideline group member took a strong view and said:

> I felt we should throw TZDs [Pioglitazone] out, but X [different guideline group member] remarked I do not know why … I thought he was the least reliable, I found it difficult to work with him, he said TZDs should be in there,

---

79 Dutch Diabetes guideline group member 3 (Nijmegen, 17 June 2015).

80 Dutch Diabetes guideline group member 1 (de Bilt, 9 June 2015).

> but I disagreed. We don't even know how they [TZDs] work, the guy who invented them spoke on a conference, in a back room … to explain it was actually … a different receptor … altogether. This is a drug where we do not know how it works, and it has caused harm![81]

Other members of the group thought that Pioglitazone could have a role and therefore wanted it included in the guideline. The eventual compromise struck in the group was that if Pioglitazone would be mentioned, then all drugs with a market authorisation in the Netherlands should be included in the guideline as one of the guideline group members explains: 'It is sold in the Netherlands so we should give advice on it. But then we said we should also say something about Acarbose and Repaglinide.'[82] The guideline group had a negative view of Pioglitazone because it was not superior to other drugs such as Metformin and Sulfonylurea and because it was not suitable for large numbers of patients. The therapeutic range of the drug was so small that they felt it should be a last resort.

The conclusion of the group was that DPP-4 and GLP-1 should only have a minor role in the treatment of diabetes; a combination of the lack of long-term safety data, no clear evidence of superiority and high costs led to this decision. One of the guideline group members was very sceptical about the pharmaceutical industry's claims about the superiority of the drug because of a lower incidence of hypoglycaemia: 'The TECOS[83] trial came out, no extra cardiovascular deaths, yeah that's great that's the minimal you can expect that you don't die from the drug. But where is the good news? Hypoglycaemia? But 90% of patients don't have hypoglycaemia, what are we talking about.'[84] In contrast to the English group, the Dutch group did not define smaller sub-groups of patients for which these drugs would be suitable, it also did not spend a lot of time and resources on establishing whether a DPP-4 was superior to a GLP-1; by putting all drugs in one table they shelved that problem.

The discussions in the Dutch guideline group were interesting in the approach to 'evidence' they developed. While discussions started from a close reading of medical studies relevant to the particular drug that was

81 Dutch Diabetes guideline group member 2 (Amsterdam, 10 June 2015).

82 Ibid.

83 Darren K McGuire and others, 'Association Between Sitagliptin Use and Heart Failure Hospitalization and Related Outcomes in Type 2 Diabetes Mellitus: Secondary Analysis of a Randomized Clinical Trial' (2016) 1 *JAMA Cardiology* 126.

84 Dutch Diabetes guideline group member 2 (Amsterdam, 10 June 2015).

being considered, evidence was seen as a broad category that should include considerations of side-effects as well as safety.

5.9.3. TARGET LEVELS OF BLOOD SUGAR

The second topic of discussion in the guideline group was the appropriate target levels for blood glucose. Put simply, this is the decision in cooperation between patient and health care professional to decide on the levels of blood glucose that are 'normal' for the patient concerned. This decision is important as a low level of blood-glucose reduces the risk of micro- and probably also macro-vascular complications of diabetes and increases quality of life, but if the level is too low, mortality might increase. A balance must be struck between these two options to approach an optimal solution for a patient. Ideally, the blood sugar targets of every patient would be personally tailored to personal circumstances. However, this does not always happen and a guideline could never exhaustively describe all the circumstances that should be taken into account. So, the Dutch guideline chooses to give target levels for blood sugar.

In the most recent guideline, the guideline group has chosen to differentiate the target levels for the first time. The background for these changes are three new trials: ACCORD, VAADT and ADVANCE.[85] One of the members explains why they decided to differentiate the blood sugar targets: 'For older people it has advantages to have slightly higher target levels, it prevents harm, whilst for newly diagnosed diabetics you go for a strict target and that's reflected in the guideline.'[86] The scientific evidence was robust enough to recommend the change. But it was not that the group followed the change in evidence and therefore changed the guideline on this point: the process took place in reverse. The clinical conviction among the members of the group, that glucose targets for the elderly have a different meaning compared to those for newly diagnosed

85 The ACCORD Study Group, 'Long-Term Effects of Intensive Glucose Lowering on Cardiovascular Outcomes' (2011) 364 *New England Journal of Medicine* 818; William Duckworth and others, 'Glucose Control and Vascular Complications in Veterans with Type 2 Diabetes' (2009) 360 *New England Journal of Medicine* 129; The ADVANCE Collaborative Group, 'Intensive Blood Glucose Control and Vascular Outcomes in Patients with Type 2 Diabetes' (2008) 358 *New England Journal of Medicine* 2560.

86 Dutch Diabetes guideline group member 3 (Nijmegen, 17 June 2015).

people with diabetes, led them to search for evidence to back this up, as this quote reveals:

> three or even four meetings, so much discussion about this. We searched a lot of literature and why: nobody excepted, everyone was deeply convinced that a blood sugar treatment of someone who is older than seventy has a completely different meaning than for younger people. And ... we had some data from one of those big intervention trials that had just come out. And from the ZODIAC study ... and we had some data from our own cohort. We had an idea that it [the evidence] is not so hard but so many indications that it increases mortality in the elderly, we have to do something with this fact ... This [the target levels] is not so evidence-based but this is the best we have ... The guideline is a compromise based on what we knew from the literature.[87]

This shows how the idealised depiction of searching for evidence leading to changes in guidelines must be nuanced. Recommendations in guidelines changed without the evidence changing, as with Acarbose. Or clinical convictions changed and the recommendations were updated and evidence is presented as justification for this change after the fact.

The guideline group members quickly agreed on the need to differentiate the target levels but talked for a long time about the best way to present this new information in the guideline. One guideline group member noted: 'We went through more than five different flowcharts because we wanted to give the clinician an aid [to help them decide].'[88] And another remarked: 'We knew that if this flow-chart wouldn't work, people wouldn't understand it, they would throw the whole guideline away, so we had to get it right.'[89] The discussion centred on the most accessible way of presenting the new options. Several diagrams were trialled to help the group decide the best way of conveying the information to GPs and diabetic nurses. This is an illustration of the fact that the guideline group was actively engaging with the implementation of their guidance and this was facilitated by the lack of conflict or uncertainty about the assessment of the evidence. Particularly relevant in this regard is that this guideline was developed in conjunction with other 'products' by the NHG that facilitate 'protocol-driven' care by diabetic nurses; this was a part of a movement to organise diabetic care in so-called

87 Dutch Diabetes guideline group member 4 (Amsterdam, 11 June 2015).
88 Dutch Diabetes guideline group member 1 (de Bilt, 9 June 2015).
89 Dutch Diabetes guideline group member 3 (Nijmegen, 17 June 2015).

'care-chains',[90] to aid (further) substitution of hospital care (second-line care) by GP-led care (first-line care). Eventually, the group was happy with the ordering of this part of the guideline and endorsed the diversification of blood sugar targets.

A detailed consideration of two key themes that emerged in the guideline group's use of evidence shows how the Dutch guideline group defined their task. Their approach was steered towards producing a clear-cut guideline for use by GPs. The decision on the target levels for blood glucose shows how evidence is used as a justification for a clinical belief – both approaches are complementing each other in this case; whereas for medication for lowering blood glucose, prior assumptions about the importance of safety led to a specific interpretation of existing medical studies.

5.10. ACHIEVING CONSENSUS: INTERNAL WORKINGS OF THE DUTCH GUIDELINE GROUP

The Dutch guideline group consists of several GPs with expertise in diabetes care and several specialists who treat diabetes patients in hospitals. The group knew each other well as they worked together on academic articles, some members also had academic and professional relationships with each other while others were involved in drafting earlier guidelines by the NHG on diabetes. All in all, one can say that this group was clearly socially close-knit: given that diabetes experts among GPs are thin on the ground in a small country like the Netherlands this is not wholly surprising. The closed character of the group is relevant, however, for our consideration of how the group reached consensus on key elements of the guideline. The members of the group shared a view of diabetes medication that was informed by a one vital assumption: that long-term safety is very important. One of the guideline group members put it in these words: 'You know the NHG has the principle that new has to be better than old, and safe in the long-term. We want to prescribe things that are safe, so we are very conservative in recommending new treatments if we don't know whether they are safe.'[91] This sentiment was shared by the majority of the group, which steered their consensus on certain issues. This meant that in the treatment for the evidence of the new diabetic drugs, the absence of

[90] Dutch: Ketenzorg.

[91] Dutch Diabetes guideline group member 1 (de Bilt, 9 June 2015).

long-term safety data was presented as a critical factor. Another guideline group member reinforced this view:

> The critical points were safety and price, and you know it is not difficult to change gear, it is just like driving a car, you start in gear one if you reach a certain amount of revolutions of the motor you move up a gear. You start with the drugs that are cheap and safe and work, if they don't work you move up a gear. That's the philosophy … I still stand behind it.[92]

The consensus on this issue shaped the decision to only recommend the old diabetic drugs: 'I think is a guideline group we were quite rigid, we don't want to give them [the pharmaceutical companies] that because it is too expensive for the healthcare system.'[93]

A further concern in their discussions was the potential for the pharmaceutical industry to use the guideline to say that the new drugs were now recommended by the NHG: 'We were very afraid that there would be too much room for the new drugs, but we also didn't want to deny GPs the room to deviate and give new drugs.'[94] Another said: 'I know from my colleagues that they were approached by the pharmaceutical industry, which they discussed in the guideline group … We were afraid the pharmaceutical industry would [mis]use the standard, which did happen.'[95] This misuse of the standard that this guideline group member referred to was an advertisement by a pharmaceutical company that claimed their drug was in the guideline, which was a misleading statement because the drug was mentioned in the guideline, but not in their recommended algorithm, which is what the advertisement suggested. The company retracted the advertisement after a complaint by the NHG.[96]

In addition, the group recommended Gliclazide, driven by their earlier systematic review, which showed a positive safety profile for the drug and its cardio-protective properties. A guideline group member remarked on this systematic review and the choice for Gliclazide:

> If you analyse the RCT that have been done that compare DPP-4 with a su[lfonylurea], that look at the risk of hypoglycaemia you see that those studies

---

92 Dutch Diabetes guideline group member 2 (Amsterdam, 10 June 2015).

93 Ibid.

94 Ibid.

95 Dutch Diabetes guideline group member 3 (Nijmegen, 17 June 2015).

96 NHG, 'Klacht NHG Tegen MSD Gegrond Verklaard' (Herziene NHG-Standaard Diabetes Mellitus Type 2). Available at: <https://www.nhg.org/actueel/nieuws/klacht-nhg-tegen-msd-gegrond-verklaard>.

> are mainly done with su[lfonylurea] that give a lot of hypo[glycaemia] Then you can observe an advantage for DPP-4. But if you take Gliclazide, that gives the least hypo[glycimae], there are only two studies! In those studies, you observe a difference that is hardly clinically relevant.[97]

The group stood behind the conclusion that was drawn in this systematic review and adopted Gliclazide as the preferred Sulfonylurea. There was not a lot of doubt about the nature and robustness of the evidence, but this decision was extensively debated because it would mean quite a substantial change in clinical practice – as this guideline group member discusses:

> we talked much longer, not that we didn't agree with each other, but because it was quite a decision, because we now put in the guideline: you should use Gliclazide. That was quite a decision, because you say other drugs are less good or you shouldn't use them at all … Glimepiride you could use, but we would rather you do not. That was quite something. We didn't really talk about the evidence [but about the clinical consequences].[98]

This decision was (relatively) unique, because most other guidelines treat Sulfonylurea as a class, implying there are no (clinically) relevant differences between the drugs in this class. There was a sense of pride among the members of the group in making this choice; they felt this continued a (valued) tradition of cautious prescribing by GPs, with an eye on minimising the side-effects of drugs. One of the guideline group members placed this decision in a wider 'tradition' in NHG diabetic guidelines to critically assess Sulfonylurea for safety concerns and how this squared with the logic of the hierarchy of evidence in evidence-based medicine:

> As a guideline group you are looking at the best of what the pharmaceutical industry wants us to see. The waste [negative studies[99]] we don't see … And those studies are designed to achieve that [positive] results … So, if you want to look at safety, which is important to us, … you have to turn to population studies, where the drugs have been used long-term in clinical practice, where you have a yearly follow-up to see what happens with those people that takes those drugs. But strangely in the evidence-based hierarchy this

97 Dutch Diabetes guideline group member 1 (de Bilt, 9 June 2015).
98 Dutch Diabetes guideline group member 4 (Amsterdam, 11 June 2015).
99 Meaning here studies showing results where drugs are not effective.

> [those studies] have a lower value, even though if you look at safety it has much more value.[100]

The fact that the group decided to single out Gliclazide was therefore based on evidence of its superiority from the perspective of the lower incidence of hypoglycaemia and better cardiovascular profile. From the perspective of the hierarchy of evidence it is interesting to note that, as the guideline group members indicated, cohort studies and other lower rated studies play an important role in the evidence base in this guideline, moving beyond a focus on pure RCTs.

A third change the group reached consensus on was the differentiation of targets for lowering blood glucose. This debate in the group centred on the exact relevance of the various large RCTs conducted in this area and best way to interpret the findings of the ADVANCE, VADT and ACCORD RCTs, an English retrospective cohort study,[101] as well as the Dutch[102] and American[103] observational studies. The RCTs provided the main impetus for the conclusion that very intensive targets can be harmful. It is the observational data that provides the knowledge about the optimal window for blood sugar levels. In this instance we can see how a combination of trial and observational evidence provides a solid foundation for a differentiation of targets. In this instance, such combinations of evidence were the guiding force behind the decision to differentiate targets for blood sugar levels. The group debated the differentiation of the targets but was convinced by the need for a higher target for the elderly and those who have diabetes for over 10 years. The UKPDS data, based on a younger cohort of people who had newly diagnosed diabetes, supported the positive effect of a stricter target in that stage of the disease because this would be achievable without many side effects. In this way, the evidence allowed the identification of several sub-groups of diabetes patients and the guideline was further tailored towards those groups of patients than had happened in the past.

The best way to communicate this decision was the subject of intense debate in the group. This element was unrelated to the medical evidence

---

100 Dutch Diabetes guideline group member 1 (de Bilt, 9 June 2015).

101 Craig J Currie and others, 'Survival as a Function of HbA1c in People with Type 2 Diabetes: A Retrospective Cohort Study' (2010) 375 *The Lancet* 481.

102 Gijs W Landman and others, 'The Relationship between Glycaemic Control and Mortality in Patients with Type 2 Diabetes in General Practice (ZODIAC-11)' (2010) 60 *The British Journal of General Practice* 172.

103 Elbert S Huang and others, 'Glycemic Control, Complications, and Death in Older Diabetic Patients: The Diabetes and Aging Study' (2011) 34 *Diabetes Care* 1329.

but was more a form of 'psychology' where the group tried to imagine the user of the guideline and the easiest way to read it. In ordering the diagram in a clear way, the group aimed to make the choices as intuitive as possible. In this sense, the drafting of the actual diagram (as well as the words in a guideline) extends beyond the 'evidence' into an effective tool for communication of complex knowledge.

The use of consensus regarding the three key decisions in this guideline show the interrelated and complicated way 'evidence', clinical knowledge and preferences interact to produce answers. The differentiation of blood-glucose targets came about through a close analysis of the specificity of the various clinical trials and the reliability of observational data; in this way it comes closest to a pure application of evidence. But in this case, it is still clinical expertise that drives the question of whether the reported results are robust enough to warrant a change in practice and recommendation.

5.11. EXTERNAL RESPONSES: ACCEPTANCE AND RESISTANCE

The response to the guideline was muted. Several organisations welcomed it, such as Farma Magazine, which provides information to pharmacists,[104] as well as the website of Medicijnbalans, an organisation subsidised by the Ministry of Health to provide objective information about drugs, where a video appeared outlining the various changes in the new guideline.[105] These comments showed that several parties appreciated the simpler algorithm to follow and were supportive of the choice to limit the use of the new diabetic drugs. Among GPs the guideline was well received, which was shown by the fact the drugs that the guideline recommends (Gliclazide, Acarbose, Repaglinide) showed an increase in prescriptions and the new diabetic drugs (GLP-1, DPP-4) show a decrease.[106]

As noted, one of the pharmaceutical companies claimed their drug was now mentioned in the guideline, which is true, but misleading,

104 Farma Magazine, 'Herziene NHG-Standaard Diabetes Mellitus' (2015). Available at: <http://farma-magazine.nl/nhg-standaard-diabetes-mellitus-type-2/>.

105 Medicijnbalans, 'NHG-Standaard Diabetes Mellitus Type 2, December 2013'. Available at: <http://medicijnbalans.nl/video/40243>.

106 GIP Databank, 'Databank'. Available at: <https://www.gipdatabank.nl/databank#/g//85_dia/ddd/bijlage>.

as the drug was not recommended: they later retracted this claim.[107] In addition, one of the pharmaceutical companies published a 'contra-guideline' consisting of a folder detailing the NHG guideline and the position statement by the EASD,[108] suggesting these two were of equal weight. While the EASD is financed by the pharmaceutical industry, their position statement cannot be seen as a guideline. Rather it is a statement of all the different available medication so it does not provide guidance in the way a guideline does.[109]

There are several reasons that can explain why this guideline was well received and followed by Dutch GPs. The recommendations that the guideline makes do not ask GPs to do something extra, such as providing a new treatment, but instead ask them not to do something: prescribe the new diabetes medication. Such advice is much easier to follow as it doesn't require any change of practice or the investment of many resources. In accordance with the study of Burgers and colleagues[110] these are the circumstances that are conducive for guideline effectiveness.

In conclusion external comments on the guideline did not alter its content and the guideline seems to work well in practice.

5.12. CONFLICTS OF INTEREST: AN ANTI-INDUSTRY BIAS?

Three of the seven members of the guideline group reported a conflict of interest. Two had received research funding from pharmaceutical companies, one had joined several advisory boards of pharmaceutical companies. On first sight one would expect that this might steer the group into favouring newer diabetes medication and the newer generation of insulin drugs. The group also consisted of several people who had more of an anti-industry bias, who were very active in providing diabetes information to GPs without sponsorship by industry. These people were dominant in the discussions in the group and

107 NHG, 'Klacht NHG Tegen MSD Gegrond Verklaard' (n 96).

108 European Association for the study of Diabetes.

109 'Hoe de Farmaceutische Marketingmachine Medische Richtlijnen Manipuleert' *De Correspondent* <https://decorrespondent.nl/467/Hoe-de-farmaceutische-marketing machine-medische-richtlijnen-manipuleert/14363052-1f180d9f>.

110 Jako S Burgers and others, 'Characteristics of Effective Clinical Guidelines for General Practice' (2003) 53 *The British Journal of General Practice* 15.

the recommendations closely reflect their view of the evidence. Several members were approached by the NHG to take part in the guideline group, because they had participated in guideline making for them before. These individuals then suggested further names and approached other people they knew to take part in the guideline group. In this selection process people who were seen as 'independent' (from industry) were favoured. One of the group members explains this in detail: 'there was a fixed core and several other people where asked every time to take part.'[111] Another commented: 'I was surprised, because I am no opinion leader … I asked my boss have you given this to me? But it turned out [guideline group member X] had suggested me, because he thought I would be independent.'[112] While another said: 'yes, I got a call from the chair, and I suggested some further names … it's very inner circle but that happens in this country'.[113]

The result of this selection process was that a majority of the members of the group shared common assumptions about the role of the GP in diabetes care, the value of new diabetic drugs and the relevance of blood glucose targets, which were rooted in a critical view of the pharmaceutical industry and a strong insistence on safety data. A guideline group member explains that in the run-up to making the guideline he and another member became convinced they should break ties with industry completely:

> around the time the guideline was made X and I had the idea, we should have no ties with the pharmaceutical industry, I feel we were the most outspoken on this point. I had 2.5 year ago contact with X who said, if you are a guideline committee you should break with industry. And I replied but then I would amputate a part of my research? And he replied: that's making choices. And he had done it, not an unimportant man, gosh! I decided to break with them [industry] and spent the last half year sending letters to all of them, telling them I would no longer do research with them. At that time the guideline was ready, but I think it helped the discussions.[114]

The members of the guideline group realise that the way the group was composed favoured certain outcomes, given the fact that the Netherlands is so small all of them knew of colleagues with different views on the new

---

111 Dutch Diabetes guideline group member 3 (Nijmegen, 17 June 2015).
112 Dutch Diabetes guideline group member 2 (Amsterdam, 10 June 2015).
113 Dutch Diabetes guideline group member 4 (Amsterdam, 11 June 2015).
114 Ibid.

diabetes medication. A guideline group member put it thus: 'I certainly know colleagues who give talks where they are very positive about new drugs ... Whether they are just more into new drugs than I am or [they are biased].'[115] The group members talked extensively about the various ways in which outsiders tried to influence them:

> I felt that the endocrinologists that were asked [to take part] were asked for their independent view on the pharmaceutical industry. We also get commentary from other specialists, where we could clearly see, oh this person always tells this story. Those people are used by the pharmaceutical industry to push their drugs. There was an acute awareness about how to judge these comments. Those are people who go completely for the newest drugs and are always able to find the best available evidence for it.[116]

While another expresses his surprise at the fact that his participation in the group had leaked to the pharmaceutical industry: 'I was asked [by the NHG] to sign a confidentiality agreement, ... I do so on Friday and on Tuesday I was speaking to someone who works for [pharmaceutical company X] who knew [expletive] I was part of the guideline group! ... One of the other guideline group members must have done that ...' And I told the group X already knew it.[117] And he goes further to detail how the company then went to try to 'help' him not to miss any trials: 'so I found a whole package of trials on my doorstep, so at least I wouldn't miss anything. With me it only happened with company X.'[118] He decided that because of a potential conflict of interest, he would not write part of the guideline that made recommendations on the drugs he was familiar with.

There was also a strong institutional dimension to the way the guideline group dealt with conflicts of interest, namely the view that the NHG valued independence very highly: 'I think if we had given a more prominent place to drugs were there was a conflict of interest that in that case there would have been more discussions [with the NHG].'[119] The guideline group members took this into account when they had their discussions. This was an institutional element of their conception of conflict of interest that influenced everyone in the group.

115 Dutch Diabetes guideline group member 2 (Amsterdam, 10 June 2015).
116 Dutch Diabetes guideline group member 3 (Nijmegen, 17 June 2015).
117 Dutch Diabetes guideline group member 2 (Amsterdam, 10 June 2015).
118 Ibid.
119 Dutch Diabetes guideline group member 1 (de Bilt, 9 June 2015).

Another interviewee remarked on the potential tension between the wish to employ the foremost experts and wanting to have independent experts:

> I don't buy the argument that there are no independent people. It is true that people in the front of their field … will more often have conflicts of interest. We have tried to address [at hospital X] this through giving everything we get for talking to the pharmaceutical industry to a foundation we set up, and we use this to fund our own research.[120]

The effects of the industry through medical journals on the prescribing of doctors was seen as a problem by another member of the group: 'the latest issue of Diabetes Care was filled only with articles about diabetic drug treatments, DPP-4 and SGL-2, you read it, and you think this looks suspect, that's my worry, that's industry … You trigger people and doctors are going to read it, and the average doctor will not read this critically, the industry clearly plays a role.'[121]

The discussions about conflict of interest with members of the guideline group were surprisingly candid: they openly talked about attempts at being influenced by the pharmaceutical industry and, for some of them, the decision to really make a radical break and no longer conduct any research funded by industry, even to the detriment of the research groups they were a part of. In many of their stories scepticism shone through about the efforts of the pharmaceutical industry to promote their new drugs. The vehicle to express this scepticism was a strong focus on safety and safety evidence. In almost every question put to them about the new diabetic drugs, the answer included a reference to the lack of knowledge of the long-term effects and missing safety data.

The way the guideline group members dealt with the potential conflict of interest in this case shows more of an anti-industry bias than a pro-industry stance. This outlook influenced strongly how they read the evidence, by consistently insisting that safety was the overriding concern they came to different conclusions than the guideline group in England did. It also led them not following the strict hierarchy of evidence, as proposed by evidence-based medicine, where RCTs trump other evidence, but instead relied on cohort studies and anecdotal evidence when it came to the safety of the drugs.

---

120 Dutch Diabetes guideline group member 2 (Amsterdam, 10 June 2015).

121 Dutch Diabetes guideline group member 4 (Amsterdam, 11 June 2015).

A further important element is the institutional environment in which the guideline drafting was conducted. Several guideline group members spoke spontaneously about the critical view of the pharmaceutical industry within the NHG and their expectation that they had to live up to those ideas, otherwise their guideline might be needed to be revised when they presented it to the authorisation committee. The committee is comprised of advisers who must accept a guideline before it can be published as an official NHG guideline. This culture of a critical stance towards industry, which the guideline group members felt a part of, was conducive for them to reach a consensus on not recommending the new diabetic drugs.

The combination of a small homogenous group and an institutional environment which was favourable, worked together to steer the guideline towards a conservative course when it came to prescribing blood-sugar lowering medication.

5.13. INSTITUTIONAL FACTORS: TOO MUCH INDEPENDENCE?

The guideline on diabetes is a slightly atypical guideline for the NHG. It was the first one made by the organisation and is the most developed. It went through several revisions in such a way that a new guideline group only changed those elements that warrant it. In this sense it is very different from guidelines that are designed from scratch in areas where there was no guideline before. A guideline group member explains the process:

> It is guideline in which much has already been done I decided to do the systematic search myself and write the justification. The NHG was in a process of making the process of selecting and analysis more systematic. I already had several search strings that I had used, that I could employ.[122]

Another remarked: 'We did proposals for chapters, based on our research … I felt I had a complete picture.'[123]

The way the Dutch guideline group approached the guideline process was materially different to the approach taken in England. Instead of a

[122] Dutch Diabetes guideline group member 3 (Nijmegen, 17 June 2015).
[123] Dutch Diabetes guideline group member 4 (Amsterdam, 11 June 2015).

research question being set, literature being searched systematically and presented by the NHG, the Dutch group took a different approach. They divided the different sections of the guideline between themselves, based on their own expertise on those aspects of diabetes care. They conducted a literature search based on a search string they made themselves and produced a summary for the group to discuss. In this way the group independently searched for and appraised the evidence, with limited added assistance from the NHG. The fact that searches might be less systematic, as every group member employed their own way of searching for evidence, was accepted. The fact that there were already several systematic reviews, written by members of the guideline group that could underpin parts of the guideline might have played a role in this approach to the organisation of the group: there was less of a need for assistance by the NHG in developing research questions and search strategies.

This process provides a nuance to the more mechanical view of how guidelines ought to be produced: as this study shows that these processes do not always follow a regimented course but depend on the specific institutional history and group specific approach to evidence-based medicine.

5.14. COSTS: INCLUSION BY OMISSION

The Dutch guideline does not include any cost or cost-effectiveness modelling. The prices of the drugs are not mentioned in the guideline nor is a formal assessment of costs and benefits of the choices in the guideline performed. Guideline group members when asked were consistent in stating that cost did not influence the choices they made, it also did not lead them to change their preferences as the following quote illustrates: 'yes cost played a role, but a small one. Yes, we were aware that we have a duty to make sure healthcare is delivered efficiently, and that includes cost-efficiency. But it was never a reason to make a choice'.[124] While another remarked on the absence of cost-effectiveness data: 'We haven't looked for cost-effectiveness research, this is not part of the NHG remit, so we didn't consider QALY's.'[125] That does not mean costs were completely neglected in the guideline but they were used in a different way.

---

124 Ibid.

125 Dutch Diabetes guideline group member 3 (Nijmegen, 17 June 2015).

The approach the guideline group took to those two new drug classes was summed up by the following anecdote from a guideline group member about advice he had given to other clinicians:

> During a case report evening, we evaluated a patient [where a GP had asked questions about the best strategy for the patient] … and if we feel that this a patient that should get a DPP-4 or GLP-1 he gets it. I feel this is how it should be, everyone who really needs it gets the new drugs, but no one who doesn't need it get the best drug. My data shows that less than 10% gets hypo[glycaemia] so 90% you can treat for sixty cents and for the 10% you spend €400.[126]

Guideline group members referred to cost for the healthcare systems as a whole so, in that sense, had an incentive to avoid drugs that are too expensive, but this was secondary to safety concerns about the new drugs. The way costs were expressed was simply through calling drugs cheap or expensive. Because the new diabetic drugs were expensive and the 'old' ones cheap, this could count as an extra reason to be restrictive in prescribing them. A recent report by the Institute for Rational Medicine Use calculated that the decision to be restrictive with prescribing new diabetic drugs had saved the healthcare insurers and patients €335 million over a period of four years, compared to healthcare policies and prescribing decisions in Germany.[127]

The reason cost did not feature as prominently in the guideline has to do with the fact that decisions about treatments which belong in the package of care in the Netherlands and which treatments should be funded by health insurers through their health insurance packages is determined by the Zorginstituut. There was no expectation that if care was described in the guideline this would also be funded under the care package healthcare insurers must provide: this decision rests with the government.

This marginal role of cost in the guideline could be seen as positive from NHG's perspective. It is more likely that these guidelines by the NHG will be seen as made *by* healthcare professional *for* healthcare professionals

126 Dutch Diabetes guideline group member 2 (Amsterdam, 10 June 2015).

127 'Huisarts Boycot Dure Diabetespil, Farmaceuten Lopen Geld Mis', *de Volkskrant* (8 April 2016). Available at: <http://www.volkskrant.nl/economie/huisarts-boycot-dure-diabetespil-farmaceuten-lopen-geld-mis~a4351320/>; Insitituut voor Verantwoord Medicijngebruik, 'Kosten Bloedglucoseverlagende Middelen Nederland versus Duitsland'. Available at: <http://www.medicijnbalans.nl/content/userfiles/files/Kosten%20bloedglucoseverlagende%20middelen%20Nederland%20versus%20Duitsland(1).pdf>.

and not as instruments of healthcare rationing. The fact that prescriptions for Gliclazide and Acarbose increased and those for the new diabetes medication decreased after it was published makes it very plausible the guideline was successful in its aim.[128]

5.15. COMPARATIVE ANALYSIS: DIFFERENCES DOMINATE

When comparing the English and Dutch guidelines a picture emerges where differences are predominant. The reasons for this are multi-layered and go beyond (mere) differences in evidence. In analysing these differences and similarities, the complex nature of the factors that drive them will become apparent.

5.15.1. THE EVIDENCE BASE: THE IMPORTANCE OF FRAMING FOR THE CONSTRUCTION OF EVIDENCE

Diabetes guidelines and the evidence underpinning them throw up some interesting questions. Despite a greater convergence in the number of studies the two guidelines have in common, there is greater divergence in recommendations than in the case of the lower back pain guideline. Why this is the case it is complex: several factors explain this when taken together, including the year in which the guideline was drafted; the process of selection of the evidence; the frame through which the evidence was viewed; and the role of the guideline in the healthcare system studied. While all these factors affect each other and are linked to other aspects of the guideline process, nonetheless here they are presented as analytically distinct to show how they work more clearly.

The English guidelines were published in 2008 and 2009 and the drafting process started in 2006. The Dutch guideline was published in 2013, while drafting started in 2010. While this few years' difference might seem small, they are significant for some aspects of diabetes care. Between 2009 and 2011, the evidence on target levels for blood glucose shifted with the publication of important new trials, Rosiglitazone was taken off the market and more safety data emerged on Pioglitazone and the

[128] GIP Databank (n 106).

GLP-1 and DPP-4 drugs. The different targets for lowering blood glucose could thus potentially be explained by differences in the evidence base. The fact that the new 2015 NICE guideline[129] differentiates between two targets (for those with only diet or Metformin and those with more oral medication) in contrast to the three targets described in the NHG guideline published in 2013, shows that, in addition to evidence, this is an area where clinical interpretation and preferences is an important factor.

A further important structural difference between the two guideline groups lies in the process of selecting evidence. The English guideline group follows a strictly prescribed formal searching of the literature and has an extensive process of eliminating lower-quality evidence, in such a way that RCTs are most important in their evidence. The Dutch group is less systematic in their searching of the evidence, but more importantly they see cohort studies as more important and valuable than RCTs for some of the questions they faced in the guideline. This meant that the English recommendations closely reflected the RCT data, while the Dutch group was steered in a different direction through its reliance on cohort studies.

Following on from these two points is the fact that the two guideline groups use a different frame for analysing their evidence; this is potentially a decisive factor in explaining the observed differences. This frame can be described as a set of principles that were important for the guideline group in evaluating the evidence, which steered the extent to which they let evidence influence their recommendations. The Dutch group cited safety as an overriding concern, in reading the evidence for the new diabetic drugs the lack of safety data was therefore decisive. The English group framed their discussion through the concepts of patient-centred care and choice for clinicians and viewed the new drugs more favourably as a result.

A further factor that clearly influenced the guideline groups in different ways was the position of the guideline in the wider healthcare system. The Dutch guideline was made by GPs for GPs and is a clear expression of the desire to provide practical advice for use in clinical practice, while at the same time providing a counterweight against the pharmaceutical industry. The English guideline is multi-disciplinary and must pay heed to issues of cost and cost-effectiveness; it is therefore more likely to be seen as a tool for healthcare rationing.

---

129 NICE, 'Type 2 Diabetes in Adults' (n 5).

5.15.2. CONSENSUS: HOMOGENEITY IS KEY?

When analysing the way consensus was reached in the guideline groups the homogeneity of the Dutch group is an interesting factor, as this seemed to help the group to reach consensus quickly on important parts of the evidence, while focusing attention on communicating the various messages in the guideline. It is important to note that the Dutch group used consensus not just to supplement the evidence, as is envisaged in normative models of evidence-based guideline making, rather they sometimes used evidence as a rationalisation after the fact. A good example of this is the new targets for blood sugar levels, where the clinical wish to change practice, mainly for the elderly, led to a search for evidence to help support that position. The relative homogeneity of the Dutch guideline group also helps to explain why the positions they took were more radical and clear-cut because they made fewer compromises. This is because they shared a body of knowledge and shared common assumptions about safety, cost and efficacy of diabetes treatment.

The English group was more diverse and less close-knit: more compromises were necessary for a guideline group that had to work with less evidence and more pressure to keep the cost of medication under control. They made compromises that are visible in the text of the guideline through defining smaller sub-groups of patients for which they advise a certain treatment, thereby avoiding excluding treatments altogether while keeping the costs within agreed limits.

5.15.3. PROFESSIONAL PRESSURES TO CONFORM: THE ROLE OF EXTERNAL ACTORS

Neither guideline drew much criticism or commentary after publication. But that does not mean that external actors do not play a role in influencing guideline-making groups. In this case we can infer indirectly that guideline group members are influenced by their perception of 'normal clinical practice.' When a guideline steps outside this norm, as happened with the draft of the 2015 NICE guideline, pressure for various groups will make sure this is 'corrected.' It seems that only with overwhelming evidence is it possible for guideline groups to recommend radical changes, otherwise they will be confronted with resistance in various forms.

5.15.4. CONFLICT OF INTEREST: HOW BIASES SHAPE THE EVALUATION OF KNOWLEDGE

When we analyse the various conflict of interest that guideline group members report it becomes clear that, in both groups, a large minority of participants have one or more conflicts to declare. These written declarations only tell a story on paper: through interviews with various participants it was possible to establish that these conflicts play out in very different ways.

The Dutch group employed an anti-industry bias in its reading of the evidence. Instrumental was the fact that several members of the group worked for a foundation that had a mission to provide objective diabetes information to GPs, without sponsorship by industry. Some members of the guideline group who declared conflict of interest decided (before they joined, or during the process), to end all ties with the pharmaceutical industry. This shared position shaped their reading of the evidence and influenced the way in which the group reached consensus.

A further aspect that so far has been neglected in the literature on this topic is the strong institutional dimension of how the group felt they should approach the evidence and deal with conflicts of interest. There was a strong expectation by the NHG that new drugs should be evaluated critically, so the group felt supported in taking the stance that the new drugs were not recommended for the treatment of diabetes.

The English group leant more towards favouring the pharmaceutical industry in their reading of the evidence. It does not necessarily follow that this was because there were conflicts of interest, but it is plausible that this partly explains their enthusiasm for Exenatide and the successful attempt to keep this drug in the guideline, despite cost-effectiveness evidence which showed an unfavourable picture.

5.15.5. INSTITUTIONAL FACTORS: PRODUCING EVIDENCE (IN)FORMALLY

The fact that one set of guidelines was produced under NICE and another by the NHG, obviously made a difference. Their separate and distinct institutional histories and culture influenced the guideline groups in several ways.

The English guideline group had to follow the NICE manual for producing guidelines,[130] which required the consideration of economic evidence on cost and set out a strict procedure for the definition of research questions, selecting evidence and appraisal. The group was confronted by this process because of NICE's decision to keep some of the new diabetic drugs that were licensed at the time outside the scope of the guideline. This decision caused some disquiet in the group because they feared – and were proved right – that this would necessitate a quick update of their guideline, as it would be out-of-date just after publication.

A further consequence of this institutional regime is exposed in the selection of evidence by the guideline group. The evidence the group relies on is primarily (but not exclusively) RCTs, with a focus on the data of the United Kingdom Prospective Diabetes Study (UKPDS).

The Dutch diabetes guideline group functioned in a more informal institutional environment, where the guideline group members had more control over their search of the relevant literature and where no cost-effectiveness data was included in the deliberations. This made the process of selecting literature less systematic than was the case in the England. However, the guideline group relied on more observational data from Dutch, Danish, English and American studies to underpin their choices, especially with regard to the safety of medication to lower blood sugar.

5.15.6. COST AND COST-EFFECTIVENESS: ECONOMIC EVIDENCE CREATING DIFFERENT PRESSURES

Cost-effectiveness modelling affected the discussions of the English guideline group. They considered economic evidence, especially when it came to the appropriate third-line therapy for diabetes. The negative cost-effectiveness of Exenatide forced the guideline group to devise restrictive conditions for its use, to square the conflicting pressures of costs with the clinical desire to employ the drug. The Dutch guideline group did not employ any cost modelling. They did, however, formulate a more general rule: that their choices should not be costly for the health service as a whole.

This led to the paradoxical result that the English guideline recommends drugs which are costly in more cases than in the Dutch guideline.

130 NICE, 'Developing NICE Guidelines' (Chapter 2, n 81).

This suggests that the threshold defined by NICE to conceptualise cost-effectiveness had the unintended result of the group recommending more expensive medication, because they found an instance where this drug was (just) cost-effective.

5.16. CONCLUSION

The Dutch and English diabetes guidelines were produced to provide guidance in a difficult and fast-moving area of clinical practice: diabetes care. In several critical areas, such as oral medications to lower blood glucose and target levels for blood sugar, the guidelines differ from each other. This chapter has focused on explaining the reasons behind these differences and has presented a multi-layered picture of various interlocking factors that have steered the two groups towards adopting recommendations that differ.

In conclusion, diabetes guidelines show how guidelines are a focal point of many different forces. Patients, medical professionals and governments all exert pressures to achieve the results they would like to see. The guideline groups deal with those pressures in their own way, which explains why their guidelines differ in important respects. The significance of these findings for the theory and practice of evidence-based medicine will be discussed in the next chapter.

CHAPTER 6

GUIDELINES IN A COMPARATIVE SENSE

Chapters 4 and 5 showed that while there are some similarities between guidelines, there are also some important areas of difference between medical practice guidelines in the Netherlands and England. This chapter draws together the findings from the case studies presented in those chapters and considers the implications drawing upon all four different cases. This chapter outlines six key areas for analysis that have emerged from the case studies: evidence, consensus, institutions, external factors, conflicts of interest and cost-effectiveness.

6.1. EVIDENCE: SOCIAL AND INSTITUTIONAL CONSTRUCTION OF OBJECTIVITY

A central aim of this study has been to understand how guideline developers select, use, appraise and understand medical evidence in constructing guidelines that purport to be evidence-based. It has endeavoured to add to a more nuanced understanding of evidence, conceptualising it as a social and institutional construction used in a collaborative and communicative process aimed at creating 'objective facts'. This approach rejects other theories that offer either normative description of how evidence should be used or see evidence as the mechanical application of knowledge to specific medical cases. This section examines the results of the study as they relate to social and institutional choices in evidence selection, appraisal and use in the two case studies and across all four guidelines.

The case studies provide a varied image in how the different groups deal with evidence. The first factor that explains some of the difference between the Netherlands and England is the level of formality employed in searching for medical studies in medical databases. The institutional environment of NICE provides a more formal way of searching evidence, as they have a dedicated team of technical support staff and specialists on searching the medical literature. This results in a more formal selection of evidence in the guidelines in English case studies. A more formal way of searching for evidence in theory should produce more varied evidence to support decision making. However, in England the opposite was observed as guidelines were based on fewer studies and fewer types of studies than the Dutch guidelines. This was caused by the fact that the 'search strings', which are the words that are used to search these medical databases, were themselves based on specific clinical questions that had been formulated. The search strings copied very closely the precise words employed in the specific clinical questions posed by the guideline group. As the search strings were defined narrowly to very closely mimic the clinical question formulated, they turned up fewer results that met the inclusion criteria. This led to the rather paradoxical result that following evidence-based methods, employing a systematic searching methodology, led to less – and less varied – evidence to consider. The specific ways in which in these clinical questions were formulated was heavily influenced by the methodology prescribed in the NICE guideline manual. As will be discussed, the clinical questions and search strings were all institutionally shaped and socially constructed: meaning that the selection of evidence used in English case studies was directly impacted by institutional and social choices.

The Dutch guideline makers had less institutional support and methods for searching for evidence were employed in a more informal way. The drafters of the lower back pain guideline read and appraised every study themselves which forced them to consider only RCTs and systematic reviews that could be managed by the group. They employed an informal process among group members checking with each other whether anyone knew of studies that had not been mentioned, in addition to searches that were done by the NHG. The Dutch diabetes group took a different position: they divided the task of searching for literature among themselves, with everyone designing their own search strings, while also using an existing systematic review members of the group had written for the *British Medical Journal*.[1] This difference in approach meant that the Dutch guideline groups used more varied evidence, included more observational studies and were open to other types of evidence – especially if these were conducted in the Netherlands.

As a result, the Dutch groups did not fully follow the evidence-based approach of searching for medical studies as was done in England – but

1 Gorter and others (Chapter 5, n 74).

their guidelines can be said to be based on more varied evidence than their UK counterparts. This shows how in the selection of evidence, there are more factors at play than a purely mechanical search of medical databases. This searching is the result of a social and institutional process of selection so the outcomes are determined by the questions already set by the group and influenced by the institutional structure surrounding the guideline makers. This gives the various guideline groups different starting points right at the beginning of the guideline process.

As well as selection of evidence, the differences and similarities in recommendations are the result of a more fundamental difference in *framing* between different guideline groups. The various guideline groups all employ different frames in assessing or appraising the evidence, so even if all the evidence they viewed had been exactly the same, they would still have drawn different conclusions from it. This is best illustrated through a comparison of the appraisal of evidence by the diabetes guideline groups in both England and the Netherlands. Appraising the evidence happens after it has been selected and involves the process of attributing meaning to the results drawn from the medical studies selected from the searches. For example, the Dutch guideline group recommended Gliclazide, while the English group did not differentiate between the various Sulphonylurea family of drugs.[2] One could argue this might be due to the fact the Dutch guideline group had different evidence to review, as they based their recommendations on a study conducted in 2012, whereas the English group could have had less evidence to review as their guideline was published in 2008. But this misses the point, as they both refer to studies available before 2008 and made this choice based on those studies. The Dutch guideline groups made their choice based on their assessment that Gliclazide had a positive safety profile. The evidence in this case was guided by the framing that prioritised the safety of diabetes medication over other considerations.

This specific clinical approach, which stressed safety issues, led them to adopt a frame where the appraisal of evidence was geared towards satisfying themselves that the drug chosen was the safest available. So, they framed the clinical question in this way: Which of the Sulphonylurea drugs is the safest? This led them to recommend Gliclazide. This does not mean the English guideline group was wrong not to further differentiate between the different drugs in this example. This normative statement is not supported by this example; rather, it is used to outline a mechanism

2 Neither group recommended Glibenclamide, so this drug is not relevant here.

behind different choices: a different frame leads to a different appraisal of evidence and therefore results in different recommendations. All guideline groups make the claim that the recommendations they make are directly based on evidence, while this set of examples has shown that there is a social and subjective process of framing that mediates the process of evidence choices.

In this way, this book further extends earlier work by Cambrosio et al. on 'coordination regimes'[3] by offering further insight as to how this process of coordination takes place within a guideline group, by offering that a process of framing makes this coordination activity possible. Furthermore, a different question left open by Cambrosio et al. is how the process of creating (socially constructed) facts can be seen as being objective by outsiders. Later in this chapter, the argument will be advanced that the perceived objectivity of these facts lies in the rhetorical power of evidence-based medicine as an approach to generating scientific knowledge.

The process of negotiating a guideline consists of a complicated set of trade-offs and necessary compromises to satisfy all its different audiences. Guideline makers must position themselves in a field of diverging powers: government interest in healthcare rationing, patients looking for the newest treatments, pharmaceutical companies trying to get their product recommended and clinicians who look for usable advice in clinical practice.

The selection and appraisal of evidence is intimately linked to the negotiation and process by which evidence choices are made. A real understanding of the role of 'evidence' starts with the realisation that evidence is always used for a purpose. This purpose is discussed and established during the process of guideline creation. 'Evidence' can therefore not be seen separately from the process of negotiating in a guideline group. Negotiating of evidence is highly dependent on specific cultural and institutional contexts and is embedded in a multi-layered frame of understanding that is created in every guideline group. So, it can be said that it is not the evidence that drives recommendations, but the complicated interrelation between social and institutional forces.

Another example that further illustrates this argument is the contrasting conclusions the English and Dutch guideline groups have drawn from looking at exactly the same evidence on educational materials for lower back pain. While the English guideline group focused on the fact that the results of the medical studies of educational materials were not

[3] Cambrosio and others (Chapter 2, n 24).

statistically significant, the Dutch group focused on the clinical relevance of the results. They adopted different frames, as what they wanted the purpose of the evidence to be differed: the English group was looking for robust knowledge that was methodologically sound, while the Dutch were more interested in practical knowledge that was usable. In this case, these differences in approach and frame led both groups to the same recommendation. They both recommended that educational materials should have a role in treating lower back pain. The English group based this recommendation on consensus between the guideline group members rather than the medical studies. The Dutch group did base their decision on the same medical studies, because they found value in the practical use of the knowledge they provided. It is in the confrontation between evidence and a frame that a reading of the medical studies leads to the construction of social facts.

Examples drawn from all four guidelines show that for all guideline groups, evidence is of central concern. But how exactly the meaning of evidence is constructed is a process of framing that is different and unique for every guideline group. The primary reason for that difference is that evidence can only be understood and applied in a guideline once a guideline group has collectively trashed out what its primary purpose is going to be. In other words, every guideline groups creates its own unique frame through which to view the evidence, one which also exhibits common features.

The relationship between a frame and the evidence is not a static one, as these examples demonstrate. It could be conceptualised as a continuum with, on the one hand, the Dutch diabetes case, where an overarching frame had a large influence on all aspects of evidence selection because of strong preferences of the guideline group. In the English back pain group were participants who were far more neutral about what they wanted to do with the evidence and did not formulate any particular direction so their framing had a less decisive effect on the evidence.

It is argued here that evidence is a tool used by guideline groups in making clinical choices, which are also normative and political. This section has shown that these choices are social in nature and are the result of institutional shaping and social construction. The claim by decision makers that guidelines are evidence-based is not meaningless because this allows guideline groups to suggest that the results of their deliberations are objective. However, guidelines are not entirely evidence-driven choices, in the sense they are subjective, necessarily compromised by a multitude of conflicting pressures and encapsulated in institutional frames. These frames are multi-layered in that they incorporate concerns that go beyond evidence alone. Multi-layered framing includes influences from institutional environments, conflicts of interest, the composition of the guideline group and cost considerations: these aspects will be further explored in the following sections.

6.2. CONSENSUS: DIFFERENT MECHANISMS THROUGHOUT THE PROCESS

To understand how guidelines are made we need to appreciate the various elements that influence how guideline groups reach consensus and how this consensus feeds into the various recommendations in a guideline. Here, the term consensus goes beyond the social negotiations and agreements and understands its role in directing policy making and the wider considerations that made the guideline groups move from the medical evidence base to making recommendations. This section will analyse how the Dutch and English guidelines are influenced by their aims, understanding of disease and considerations of cost, clinical practice and institutional framings surrounding them. This section will then make the argument that these factors all influence the process of reaching consensus and shape the resulting guidelines.

The consensus between various participants in guideline groups is essential for its success. The only way for guideline groups to achieve consensus is to make compromises. This study has detailed various examples of compromises made in various guideline groups and we can draw from these examples to establish two mechanisms that drive guidelines on the same conditions apart and two mechanisms that work to make guidelines on the same disease similar. This study focuses on the importance of the outcome of consensus-based decisions on the text of the guidelines and how this is informed by the purpose of guidelines as a form of professional self-regulation.

6.2.1. PURPOSEFUL GUIDELINES

The way the members Dutch and English guideline groups thought about the purpose of the guideline they were drafting influenced the goals and objectives they adopted during the negotiations and process of creating a guideline. Guidelines will differ depending on the aim of the guideline in the wider healthcare system. The NHG guidelines are drafted by one specific profession (GPs) and are exclusively aimed at providing guidance for the daily clinical practice of GPs. Furthermore, these guidelines provide an important element of training for new GPs and provide a way for the profession to secure it status as a specific and specialist profession among the other medical professionals. For example, for the drafting of the Dutch guideline on diabetes, the focus of the recommendations was specifically on the clinical role of GPs in managing diabetes care and did not consider other diabetes-related healthcare concerns. Importantly, the group drafting the guideline were predominately GPs with clinical experience. As a result, the consensus they reached was informed by their implicit agreement with the consensus already formed on the goals of the guideline.

Guidelines made by NICE have a different purpose and these guidelines are also perceived differently by medical professionals. NICE guidelines are always multidisciplinary; several different groups of medical professionals were represented in the guideline group. In the case of the NICE guideline, the goals of the group were less clearly focused as they had to provide recommendations that would cover the whole span of the delivery of care of diabetes patients. This meant the NICE guideline was not the statement of a specific professional group, as in the case of the Dutch GPs, therefore medical professionals might not feel the same allegiance to them. Due to the necessity of satisfying various medical groups, this guideline was characterised by far more compromises to help secure an agreement on thorny issues. The implication of this social outcome is that guidelines might differ because there was a need to accommodate diverging views on the purpose of the guideline, rather than them being dictated by medical evidence or clinical necessity.

6.2.2. COST MOTIVATIONS

Convergence between English guidelines is driven by cost motivations that play a role in the deliberations in guideline groups there. NICE guidelines are therefore seen to be instruments of healthcare rationing. This aim of healthcare rationing is served through the inclusion of cost-effectiveness as a criterion in the discussions about recommending treatments. An identifiable threshold for cost-effectiveness also provides a yardstick to help parties decide whether they can recommend a treatment. The fact that in practice guideline groups sometimes deviate from this target of £20,000–£30,000 per quality-adjusted life year gained, as the results of the diabetes case study show, does not negate the fact that this requirement gives the guidelines a different position. This translates into different recommendations by guideline groups. Paradoxically, as we have seen in the case of the diabetes guideline the English group recommended more expensive treatment than the Dutch group. It has been shown that issues of cost-effectiveness directly impacted on the recommendations in the English case, as it featured heavily in their discussions resulting in compromises that restricted access to expensive medication.

The Dutch guidelines do not formally include aspects of cost-effectiveness as these are dealt with by the Zorginstituut, a body separate from professional associations like the NHG. This is significant because it changes the way the Dutch guideline group reaches consensus; aspects of cost play a far more marginal role in their discussions. It also reinforces the view by other professionals that the advice given in the guideline is only driven by clinical and evidence driven considerations, so the NHG avoids being seen as providing guidelines that are 'imposed from above'.

6.2.3. ORGANISATION OF CARE

Another aspect that helps explain how consensus can drive differences between guidelines is the discretion that guideline groups must decide on the organisation of care. In drafting a guideline, decisions must be made about which healthcare professionals can perform specific elements of the treatments of conditions: this is referred to as the organisation of care. NICE guidelines specifically exclude saying anything specific about organisation of care, restricting itself to indirectly influencing the influence of care through the prescription of training for healthcare professionals.[4] NHG guidelines take an explicit line on the organisation of care, which is easier as their guidance only concerns GPs and it can only indirectly affect other professionals if the guideline recommends that a patient should not be referred to a group of medical professionals.[5]

This aspect had some limited influence on the development of the guidelines, where the Dutch diabetes and back pain guidelines were more clearly concerned with (re)organising the organisation of care delivered by GPs, in contrast to the English guidelines that covered a larger range of

4 NICE, 'Developing NICE Guidelines' (Chapter 2, n 93).

5 As NHG guidelines are only written for GPs, they cannot influence the guidelines of other professionals directly.

medical specialities. Those aspects were, however, relatively minor in the overall text of the guideline.

6.2.4. CLINICAL PRACTICE

Clinical practice is one key area that informs consensus among guideline group members. A key finding here is that guidelines are more similar if the consensus in the group is directed towards a replication of current practice. On the surface this might look like a statement of the obvious, if guidelines replicate current practice and this practice is similar in the two countries, consequently the guidelines will be similar too. The defining factor, however, is that first a guideline group reaches consensus on the desirability of achieving a result that is close to current practice in the field and, in this light, the evidence is analysed. So, the formal process of evidence-based medicine is reversed. It is not the painstaking search for evidence that then informs the decision to choose to stick with current practice, rather as the evidence does not provide answers to which therapy is superior so it is wise to maintain the status quo. Rather than this being about clinical practice and evidence, the decisions made by the group were based on maintaining status quo in their recommendations and a prevailing attitude of consensus and agreement to comprise.

The Dutch lower back pain guideline provides a good illustration of this process. Early in the process of negotiating this guideline, several members left the group, mainly because they could not agree which of the possible treatment for lower back pain was the best. As a result, the group adopted a pragmatic view, where treatments were adopted as equal, even if some differences could be seen in the evidence underpinning them. As a result of the adoption of this principle to regard treatments as equal, consensus was achieved and as a result the Dutch guideline changed clinical practice in delivering lower back pain in only minor ways. This demonstrates that social consensus processes are linked to the outcomes of recommendations of guidelines.

This influence of clinical practice is not invariably directed towards replicating the status quo. A diametrically opposing case could be made when analysing the framing adopted by the Dutch diabetes group. While the Dutch diabetes guideline was conservative in only recommending a limited range of treatment this was driven by a desire to *change* clinical practice. The change in this case consisted of *reversing* the existing trend to prescribe newer diabetes medication.

It is not always possible to predict whether a guideline group will adopt a stance towards replicating current practice, or whether they seek a progressive guideline. Our case studies throw up somewhat surprising results. Both diabetes guidelines are progressive; they both seek to change existing practice, something that correlates with the quick change in this field of medicine. But while the English try to include new medication as much as possible, stretching the definition of cost-effectiveness in the process, the Dutch group seeks progress in reversing towards more classical diabetic treatment regimes. For the two back pain guidelines the relationship is murkier still, neither guideline group has access to an abundance of evidence to work with, so both end up largely replicating existing practice.

The existing guidelines in the relevant medical field, in combination with existing clinical practice does plausibly exert influence on the development of guidelines because it demarcates a starting position, the direction of this influence is, however, highly contextual. Conceptually this could be seen as only part of the wider frame in which guidelines groups evaluate evidence, in this sense these frames are necessarily multi-layered.

6.2.5. CONCEPTIONS OF DISEASE

Lying behind ideals of clinical practice sit the ideas and conceptions of disease by guideline makers. Guidelines will differ if guideline groups differ in their conception of illness or their conceptions of (the model) patient. The guidelines on lower back pain show that there is a slight difference in the way the different groups conceptualise lower back pain as a condition. The English group offers a more mechanical model were a potential (if unknown) physical cause of pain predominates. The Dutch place the stress on the physiological treatment of lower back pain and emphasise the need to deal with chronic pain in a holistic way. As a result, the recommendations of the guidelines are underpinned by different ideas and the consensus around those ideas, held by members of the drafting groups.

Another example of this is provided by the guidelines in diabetes. The different diabetes guideline groups do not differ in their conception of the disease, but they do differ in their conceptions of the (model of) patients with diabetes. The English guideline group driven by the need to reach consensus in the difficult area of glucose-lowering drugs does this successfully through defining the diabetes patient as consisting of a myriad of sub-groups. This allows all parties to come together behind a decision tree that is full of carefully crafted exceptions. The Dutch group sees diabetes patients as a uniform group, when it comes to prescribing glucose-lowering drugs. They see no need to differentiate between those of different sex, ethnicity or weight and believe that the diabetes population as a whole would benefit from a highly standardised approach, where exceptions (although they do occur) are rare. Different ideas behind the consensus making in the guideline groups resulted in real differences in the recommendations of the guidelines.

These different disease conceptions are one of the factors that can bring guideline groups to change recommendations even if the medical studies they base those on stay the same, the fuel a constant reinterpretation of scientific knowledge in the construction of guidelines, as from one guideline to another the underlying ideas of disease might shift.

6.2.6. PERCEPTIONS OF CHANGE IN EVIDENCE

Perceptions of evidence and the role this plays in the consensus reached by the guideline groups is an important function in the social construction of guidelines. There are two possibilities for guideline groups, they can either recommend a change or reaffirm existing practice. In this case, members of the guideline groups reaching consensus chose the status quo more often than they did not. This was because of a perception that the evidence underpinning their recommendation had not substantially changed. Evidence that is 'stable' is a prerequisite for the guideline group to endorse recommendations that reflect the status quo. This quality of stability or change of evidence is not related to the amount of studies being published or any other numerical value. Rather it is related to the perception by the guideline group of whether there is a *qualitative* change in the evidence. This change must be substantial and, for this to be the case, a threshold must be reached before a guideline group concludes the result of new studies warrants a change in recommendation. This *threshold* is dependent on the particular group and the medical field of which it is part.

The English lower back pain guideline showed an example of a situation where a guideline group is satisfied that a change in evidence warrants a change in recommendation. They recommended acupuncture based on an RCT conducted in England, which showed a beneficial effect for patients.[6] Here the threshold is quite low; one small RCT is enough to

6 Thomas and others (Chapter 4, n 21); Savigny and others (Chapter 4, n 3) 156–158.

overturn an earlier recommendation not to recommend acupuncture. This contrasts with the decision of the Dutch diabetes guideline group not to recommend the new glucose-lowering diabetic drugs, mainly because of lack of long-term data and safety concerns. In their case we can point to a host of new studies on these drugs, none of which were sufficient for the group to classify this as a change of evidence that required a change in recommendations.

What is important here, is that it not just evidence that drives choices it is the perception of qualitative change which forms the pivotal reason behind changing recommendations. This book suggests that these perceptions in choices are sometimes more important than the evidence that underpins them. This suggests that a numerical view of evidence (or the picture of an evidence base as a collection of studies) does not capture fully how guideline group members work.

These findings are broadly in line with those of Pagliari,[7] Hopthrow[8] and Berg,[9] in that participants of groups are not all equal, some contributing more than others. Hopthrow's processes of information sharing, systematic processing, group formation and process loss also map on the guideline-drafting processes. Those insights are not the most relevant findings to come out of this study as this earlier literature fails to fully understand the intimate connection between the participant's pre-existing knowledge before entering the group and how this understanding filters into the process that occurs within the group. This study would argue that these pre-existing notions or frames are vital. In this way differentiating from approaches that adopt a neat internal and external divide between the guideline group and 'the outside.'

6.2.7. THE CONSTRUCTION OF FRAMES

Moreira, in his discussion of repertoires of evaluation, places the focus on identifying several different repertoires that were all present in the deliberations of a guideline group.[10] This study shows that these 'repertoires' are not separate applications of knowledge as social action, but it is a mix of several of these 'repertoires' or frames that colour the appraisal of

---

7 Pagliari, Grimshaw and Eccles (Chapter 2, n 69).
8 Hopthrow, Feder and Michie (Chapter 1, n 7).
9 Berg, ter Meulen and Van den Burg (Chapter 2, n 102).
10 Moreira (Chapter 2, n 21).

evidence and structure the reaching of consensus in a guideline group. Moreira suggest that further research is needed into how these repertoires are 'blurred … coordinated and crystallised in the CPG [clinical practice guideline] document.'[11] This study suggests that we can understand this process by restating it as one of an interaction between a contextual mental frame of reference with medical knowledge, called evidence, leading to the pragmatic construction of 'facts' that form the basis for recommendations. How these frames are constructed can be illustrated by the following examples.

The analysis of the Dutch diabetes guideline shows how the participants put two principles up front: long-term effectiveness and safety. They adopted this frame *before* considering any of the evidence. Their outlook was informed by the culture of the institution they were a part of, the composition of the group and negative experiences with Rosiglitazone, one of the diabetes drugs that had to be taken off the market. They consistently applied this frame to the evidence they reviewed, which made them resistant to change (in evidence) that did not accord with those principles. These contingent factors are vital to grasping the specific interpretation of medical knowledge a guideline group employs, which varies with each set of individuals.

Consensus can therefore be a reason for differences between guidelines as well as steering convergence in guidelines. In conclusion, there are several elements that influence how consensus is reached by guideline makers – these have a limited but specific impact on the outcomes of the text of the guidelines. More importantly, the way in which reaching consensus operates depends on the multi-layered framing employed by the guideline group members. This frame depends on the institutional context in which the guideline is drafted, the composition of the guideline group and the position of the guideline in the wider healthcare system. However, these frames go beyond the social and consensus processes covered in this section and are also shaped by institutions and cultures of institutional practice.

6.3. INSTITUTIONS: CULTURES OF INSTITUTIONAL PRACTICE

Analysing the drafting of guidelines cannot be complete without considering the institutions that are responsible for publishing and

[11] Ibid, 1984.

endorsing the guidelines that guideline groups draft. The institutional environment of guideline production is important but is not addressed in the literature in this particular field. This study provides some insight into the myriad of ways guideline-making institutions shape guideline groups and by extension inform the guidelines they produce. Institutional factors provide part of the reason why guidelines differ, as their organisational set-up influences their drafting. However, the influence of institutions on guidelines goes further than this: it affects the role conflicts of interests have to play, it shapes the framing of the evidence through the perception of a specific cultural history by guideline makers, it influences the composition of the guideline group and it imparts specific directions on what guidelines are for and so what their proper role is in the relevant healthcare systems. These institutional influences inform the whole process of developing guidelines and they touch upon many relevant aspects of guideline drafting. These aspects will be further discussed in the following sections, before drawing out conclusions about how institutional factors influence the drafting of guidelines. This book will suggest that organisations form cultures of institutional practice which directly inform medical guidelines.

Institutions shape part of the framing of evidence by guideline group members. This framing influences the purpose and aims of the guidelines. How group members view evidence is partly due to how they view this institutional context and how that operates during the process of guideline drafting. This is partly informed by their understanding of earlier guidelines that have been produced. A sense of 'how we do things here' prevails throughout guideline making. A difficulty in ascertaining this influence is that the text of a guideline does not necessarily reflect this kind of institutional influence. Therefore, a reliance on interviews is necessary to reconstruct potential mechanisms of influence.

6.3.1. AUDIENCE

For example, the NHG guidelines are made by GPs for use by GPs. This starting point looks obvious but has implications for the framing of evidence in guideline groups. Both the lower back pain and diabetes guideline group stress the clinical relevance for GPs of their recommendations. This is driven by the mandate that they are given by the NHG to deliver answers to practical problems that have been put forward by other GPs. The lower back pain group prioritises the clinical relevance of studies over their statistical information.[12] while the Dutch diabetes group puzzles endlessly on the formulation of the treatment algorithm for the differentiation of blood sugar targets, so as to maximise the chances that GPs will understand and follow the visual information.[13] These observations provide some support for the fact that the overriding cultural influence on guideline groups that are part of the NHG is the production of practical knowledge for GPs. That guidelines are evidence-based is important and efforts are made to further formalise the searching and analysing of evidence, but this is less important than *useable knowledge*. This is achievable, as the Dutch guideline groups always include several practising GPs who have intimate knowledge about the clinical environment in which the guideline is going to be used. In the Dutch case, institutional pressures focus on the practicality and usability of guidelines rather than other motivations.

The NICE guidelines are part of an institution that has a different outlook. Guidelines are produced for the whole NHS, not one specific profession. NICE also has a duty to consider the cost-effectiveness of treatments within its guidelines. This leads to an approach which stresses the objectivity and robustness of formalised procedural measures, to help achieve consensus and weigh different interests. Evidence-based medicine is important: through the use of GRADE and other formalised measures to establish the technical robustness of evidence as well as economic studies, NICE tries to create conditions for a multidisciplinary group of medical professionals to reach consensus on recommendations. The robustness of the procedures that NICE employs is the main weapon it has to secure the legitimacy of the guidelines it produces. This means that the clinical relevance of the medical studies underpinning the guideline is relevant but, from an institutional perspective, the guideline group is incentivised to accord more weight to statistical results of medical studies. These differences in institutional context drive – albeit indirectly – the evidence and the recommendations in the various guidelines.

6.3.2. COMPOSITION OF THE GROUP

The composition of guideline groups is a further element where a specific institutional context matters. Institutional rules govern the composition of guideline groups and choice of participants in the group. While at the

12 As detailed in their discussion on educational materials.

13 Guideline group members claim they had four or five meetings about this one issue.

NHG selection of guideline group members is an informal process – with a preference for GPs with a doctorate in combination with GPs with an academic background – it always results in a group where the majority of the members are GPs. As a result, they will share a certain professional outlook and are orientated towards the interests of Dutch GPs. In forming the diabetes guideline group, certain guideline group members could also influence the choice of other members by 'putting forward names' to the NHG. The process at NICE seems to have changed over the years. While the members of the lower back pain guideline group are drawn from the various professional associations which treat lower back pain, the diabetes guideline selection process is more of a mix of people who are tied to professional associations and those that are not. The NICE groups feature a greater mix of professionals from different specialisms, compared to the Dutch groups. Participants in these guideline groups must strive to reach recommendations that are supported within and across several professional specialisms. It could be said institutional bodies directly dictate the composition of guideline groups and, through this influence, direct the resulting negotiations which, in turn, produce certain recommendations. These factors are all unrelated to considerations of evidence, but can be said to be critically important in practice. This suggests that some of the lead factors influencing the drafting of guidelines are not directly tied to evidence and are, in fact, determined by institutional configurations and specific socio-institutional cultural contexts.

6.3.3. CONFLICTS OF INTEREST

One additional way institutional power is demonstrated is through the institutional control exercised over the reporting and policing of conflicts of interest in guideline drafting. The reporting of conflicts of interest is mandated by the manuals produced by guideline making organisations such as the NHG and NICE.[14] Both organisations require the reporting of financial and non-financial conflicts of interest. There are some slight differences in procedure between the two institutions: for example, the time that must elapse after which a conflict of interest is long enough in the past to be deemed irrelevant. More relevant for this study, however, is

---

[14] NHG, 'Procedureboek 2010' (Chapter 2, n 82); NICE, 'Developing NICE Guidelines' (Chapter 2, n 93).

the institutional culture that shapes how conflicts of interest are dealt with in practice.

The NHG has adopted a strict line and is very vocal about wanting to avoid conflicts of interest as much as possible. The fact that the diabetes guideline group consisted of several people with conflicts of interest showed that it is not always successful in this aim. Nonetheless, members of both guideline groups interviewed, who conducted their work between 2003–2013, all stated that the NHG takes a strict line on conflicts of interest. So, regardless of the reality, there is at least a strong perception among all guideline group members that conflicts of interest should be avoided.

NICE policy on conflicts of interest has grown stricter over the years. While members of the 2008 guideline group on lower back pain were drawn from the relevant professional associations, in an informal way without a public vacancy, for recent guidelines, all position are formally advertised. The interpretation of conflict of interest has also become tighter. The guideline group that produced the 2016 guideline on diabetes has far fewer people with a conflict of interest than the 2008 and 2009 guidelines.[15] The main difference with the NHG is that the assessment of conflicts of interest relies on a formal assessment of the ties the potential guideline group members report, in contrast to a practice at the NHG where in selecting guideline group members social networks play a bigger role and an assessment of how independent someone is more depended on social relations.

The results of the case studies suggest that conflicts of interest are policed by institutional structures, but the true impact of this on the text of the guidelines remains unclear and difficult to trace. This study cautiously suggests that the NHG was more successful in promoting a guideline drafting culture that was critical of the pharmaceutical industry and its potential influence on guidelines. This clearly demonstrates that institutional choices shape guideline drafting, rather than choices being made in a vacuum and solely based on evidence.

6.3.4. INSTITUTIONAL MISSION

The final element that stands out if we analyse the results of the case studies is the perceptions guideline group members have of the purpose of institution. This relates to how the guideline drafters see the institution

[15] NICE, 'Type 2 Diabetes in Adults' (Chapter 5, n 5) s 4.

they are working for, its position in both the healthcare system and wider society and the ultimate reason for making a guideline in the first place. This is reflected most clearly in the existing publications and products produced by the Dutch and English institutions and other institutional documents which reflect the mission of the organisation.

The NHG guidelines are a part of a larger range of 'products' produced by the NHG aimed at Dutch GPs and other medical professionals working with GPs in primary care. The NHG produces protocols, handbooks and factsheets all aimed at improving several aspects of care by GPs. Guidelines are only one way the NHG uses to communicate with GPs; it is clear that they are seen as an educational and advisory tool for use by GPs and practice nurses and other health professionals. A further, but longer-term, effect of the guidelines has been that the standing of the GP profession has increased considerably over the years. Guidelines are now an integral part of training new GPs. Guideline group members are aware of these efforts, all of them have either worked with the NHG or attended one or more of its activities. The NHG diabetes guideline shows the influence of this institutional background. It deals explicitly with the question of whether NHG guidelines should dictate the organisation of diabetes care, or whether local guidelines should be followed. It recommends that the NHG organisational model of diabetes care delivery should be followed.[16] This shows how NHG guidelines are integrated in a package that influences the organisation of primary care in the Netherlands. In contrast, in England, a focus on advancing the position of a specific medical profession is understandably absent. The NICE mandate requires guidelines that include all professions and so does not result in strong institutional steering of specific products to further the interests of one profession. The English guidelines present a mixed bag of various documents influenced by the needs of the healthcare system as whole and represent a range of institutional priorities.

6.3.5. INSTITUTIONAL FRAMING

Important institutional differences emerge when considering the drafting of a guideline as a process. These institutional impacts not only occur *within* a guideline group but they are also intimately connected to

16 Rutten and others (Chapter 5, n 70) fn 101.

institutional factors *outside* the group. For example, the Dutch guidelines were produced as an educational tool for GPs in training with a view to either strengthening their profession or, at the very least, maintaining their current position in the medical field. Whereas NICE guidelines are more closely aligned to government goals of healthcare rationing and approach the NHS as a whole, these guidelines aim to improve care within the explicit constraint of cost-effectiveness. This institutional context results in markedly different guidelines, notwithstanding the fact that they consider the same medical condition.

This description points to the importance that institutional scripts have in driving participants in guideline groups to take certain decisions. These findings fit very well with Meyer's concept of 'agentic actors': our guideline group makers indeed describe themselves as being driven by ideals of medicine/clinical practice or other cultural ideas or goals, while also having a self-interest. Some of the interviews also provide evidence as to why the participants take part: some put themselves forward out of curiosity, others for career advancement while there are those who like the status associated with drafting a guideline. These references are, however, more muted and subtle; while outwardly they are biased towards the institution they are a part of, they only communicate in the language of evidence-based improvement of quality of care.

In conclusion, this suggests that institutional factors specifically and concretely influence the drafting of guidelines. Institutions achieve this through promulgating specific cultures of institutional practice, which directly inform medical guidelines. This opens up a fresh perspective to allow the consideration of professional self-regulation, such as guidelines, in a way which pays heed to the particular institutional embeddedness of the processes of standard setting and information gathering. However, this confirms existing scholarship on sociological institutionalism and its relevance for understanding the actions of guideline drafters.

6.4. EXTERNAL FACTORS: LIMITED INFLUENCE

This study found limited impacts of external factors on the final guideline texts. This omission can partly be explained by the fact that, after guidelines are published, commentary or criticism hardly has an effect. Any comments that are made by commentators before a guideline is published are not always public, as was the case in the Netherlands. Nonetheless, discussing external factors is valuable because it reveals some of the path-dependencies inherent in guideline development and provides contrasting empirical examples of its occurrence.

Guidelines are written to impact the delivery of care and to help improve the standard of care. Crucially they can also affect the organisation of care and the autonomy of healthcare professionals. To understand the mechanisms behind choices in the guideline drafting process looking at how a guideline is received after it is published is relevant.

The results of the case studies provide an interesting picture of guidelines that attract criticism and those that hardly received any response. By analysing these results in detail, it will become clear that path-dependency plays an important role in understanding the responses to guidelines and the choices made in guideline drafting. Path-dependency is defined here in a general way: 'most generally, path dependence means that where we go next depends not only on where we are now, but also upon where we have been'.[17] The responses to guidelines seem to have been driven by a resistance to change, as when historical choices have been (dramatically) changed by dropping or adding a treatment for a condition or disease. This resistance sometimes leads to the reinstatement of historical choices, despite the earlier contention that those choices are *inferior*.

A few examples for the case studies will help to explain this argument. Several of the guideline analysed in this study showed no external responses of disapproval by professional associations. The Dutch back pain and diabetes guideline was met with silence and support respectively. The English guidelines on diabetes were supported and although the pharmaceutical industry asked for a wider role for some medication,[18] medical professionals were supportive. The exception was the English guidelines on back pain. There was strong resistance to the idea of dropping injections in the back. The guideline group came under pressure to change the guideline, but it resisted and remained unchanged on this point. This shows how when a guideline group wants to deviate from a path of (in this case) treatments chosen in the past, this may lead to resistance that sometimes sees a return of the status quo.

The recent 2016 NICE guideline on diabetes,[19] updated the 2008 and 2009 guidelines analysed in this study, provides a further interesting

---

17 Stan J Liebowitz and Stephen E Margolis, 'Path Dependence' [1999] *Encyclopedia of Law and Economics* 981.

18 As could be gleaned from the consultation documents. 'Diabetes-Type-2-Update-Consultation-Table2 Cg-66.Pdf'. Available at: <https://www.nice.org.uk/guidance/cg66/documents/diabetes-type-2-update-consultation-table2>.

19 NICE, 'Type 2 Diabetes in Adults' (Chapter 5, n 5).

example of resistance to change and the wish to preserve historical choices. This example makes clear that historical choices and their results *make it harder to change those choices in the future*. The 2016 draft guideline favoured Repaglinide, a decision that caused uproar.[20] This resistance against changing the second step in blood sugar-lowering therapy from Sulfonylurea to Repaglinide was predicated (mainly) on the fact that it was prescribed in less than one per cent of cases of diabetes,[21] coupled with the fact that it was seen as being clinically inferior. Without giving any judgment on the evidence-base the guideline group used to make this recommendation, the fact that the drug was unpopular made it unfeasible that it could become a mainstream medication in treating diabetes. The historic choice not to favour Repaglinide made it very impractical to change this choice later on. The guideline group completely reversed their earlier choice for Repaglinide and relegated the drug to a small footnote in the algorithm they eventually agreed upon.

Repaglinide was perceived as being clinically inferior, so the cost-effectiveness arguments that led to its adoption as a preferred medication could not be sustained. The 2014 Osteoarthritis guideline provides a further good example of this process. In the draft of this guideline, the guideline group recommends that paracetamol should not be routinely offered in the treatment of osteoarthritis based on a combination of safety issues and the fact that it was less effective than no treatment in the economic assessment.[22] This – as with the diabetes guideline – led to a storm of protest[23] and the decision was reversed.[24]

The main reason was that the suggested alternatives to paracetamol, the Non-Steroidal Anti-Inflammatory Drugs and opioids, also had side-effects, so patients switching to these medications would be even worse off than when they used paracetamol. Here, the optimal choice could not be made: removing the choice of paracetamol was not a path that could be

20 Barnett (Chapter 5, n 55); Price (Chapter 2, n 132).

21 'British National Formulary'. Available at: <https://bnf.nice.org.uk/treatment-summary/type-2-diabetes.html>.

22 NICE, 'Osteoarthritis (Update): Draft Guideline' (2013) 410–416. Available at: <https://www.nice.org.uk/guidance/CG177/documents/osteoarthritis-update-draft-guideline2>.

23 NICE, 'Osteoarthritis (Update): Consultation Comments Table' (2013). Available at: <https://www.nice.org.uk/guidance/CG177/documents/osteoarthritis-update-consultation-comments-table2>.

24 NICE, 'Osteoarthritis About-This-Guideline'. Available at: <http://www.nice.org.uk/guidance/cg177/chapter/about-this-guideline>.

taken, because providing no treatment where historically treatment with paracetamol was provided was considered unacceptable. Coupled with the fact that paracetamol was (and is) a medication that is available over the counter, so that restrictions on its prescription might have consequences beyond this guideline, made this choice, in the given circumstances, impossible. External forces can have an influence when the choices suggested by the guideline makers are so radical that a sufficiently large number of people might reject the choice. Or the choices are perceived to have a future substantial impact, so guideline makers self-limit their choices. If a substantial number of people refused to accept the recommendation of a guideline, this would lead to a loss of legitimacy and this influences the drafters during and after the process of writing it. Therefore, external forces are a relevant factor, but only in limited circumstances where guidelines push for change.

These different experiences with critique on guidelines suggest that when guideline makers want to deviate from the status quo they can expect some resistance. This is something guideline group members are aware of and this affects the way they draft guidelines. In this way, this author would propose to extend the repertoire of politics as offered by Moreira[25] to not only include the government and pharmaceutical industry but also include in this category the politics of the medical professionals for whose benefit the guideline is written. Not only do medical professionals resist change if this affects the organisation of care, such as injections for the back, but they are equally poised to reject a limiting of choice in treatments without compelling justification. Guideline group members are, of course, part of these professions and are aware of the standard of care in the medical field in question. They therefore frame their decisions with reference to the expected response from their fellow medical professionals.

Differences between guidelines could therefore partly be explained by external factors, however, this has not been borne out by this study. In these case studies, none of the guidelines were changed as result of 'outside feedback'. This research has demonstrated that guideline drafters did react to the *potential* of feedback therefore, in most cases, avoided it. Guidelines are shaped by the specific configuration of medical professionals in the relevant medical field, their perceptions of external factors and institutional structures and how vocal they are in defending their (clinical) positions.

---

25 Moreira (Chapter 2, n 21).

6.5. CONFLICTS OF INTEREST: THE DIFFICULTIES OF ATTRIBUTION

The role of conflicts of interest in guidelines is a nuanced one. The presence of members of a guideline group that have a conflict of interest does not necessarily mean that this has influenced the drafting of the guideline. Nonetheless, this study has set out to establish if a conflict of interest has had a discernible influence on the development of guidelines. In some instances, the pharmaceutical industry has tried to influence guideline makers, but it remains unclear whether this ultimately affected the final guideline text.

There exists a sharp divide between guidelines on lower back pain and guidelines on diabetes. While conflicts of interest seem largely absent in the case of lower back pain, in diabetes they do play a role. Furthermore, there are important differences in how conflicts of interest have influenced guideline groups and it remains unclear whether a causal relationship between these conflicts and the recommendations in a guideline can be made.

The analysis of the results of the case studies on the back-pain guidelines shows that some members of the guideline groups report conflicts of interest. There is no evidence that these have had any influence on the recommendations in the guideline. Some evidence is co-authored by members of the English guideline group while, in the Dutch group, studies are cited that are authored by a member of the group. This might lead to a 'cognitive bias' where studies produced by one of the members of the group is given a higher weight then might be warranted based on the study itself. While there is no evidence that this bias has occurred, there is evidence that guideline group favour studies conducted in their own country, but this has not resulted in recommendations that differ between the lower back pain guidelines.

The picture for the diabetes guidelines is rather different. In the Dutch guideline group three of the seven members reported a conflict of interest. The central study cited in support of recommendations on medication to lower blood glucose was a study co-written by five of the seven members of the guideline group. The ingredients for a group that suffered from a cognitive bias as well as conflicts of interest were therefore present. The group did develop a bias, but this was more plausibly an anti-industry bias. The study conducted by five of the group members did receive significant weight; this led to a strong recommendation for the 'old' diabetic drugs and a very limited position for the drugs that had come on to the market more recently. The Dutch guideline on diabetes, therefore, is an international outlier and is one of the most restrictive when it comes to the newer diabetic drugs.

Equally interesting is what happened during the process of forming the guideline group that was going to write the Dutch diabetes guideline. One of the members discussed in great detail how a member of a pharmaceutical company he had contact with was already aware that he was going to be a member of the guideline group just two days after he had been approached, before this information was public. He went on to describe how this company had provided him with 'relevant trails' to make it 'easier' for him to do his work and, as he explained, to make sure the research on their drug was featured in the evidence selected for the guideline. This experience led him to conclude that he should further distance himself from the pharmaceutical industry. It shows that concerns about conflicts of interest are not just theoretical: attempts to influence guideline makers takes place in practice.

Several members of the English guideline group reported a conflict of interest. There is a very limited overlap between the studies cited in the guideline and any members of the guideline group, so the presence of a 'cognitive bias' seems unlikely. There is, however, some evidence that points to the guideline group weighing aspects of the new diabetic drugs, the potential for weight loss and avoidance of hypoglycaemia, as important, leading them to favour these drugs and give them a place in the treatment of diabetes. This does not mean that this was caused by a conflict of interest. It is just as likely that this was the result of a genuine consensus that these drugs were clinically superior in some specific clinical circumstances and therefore were given a place in the treatment of diabetes.

This suggests that if we limit ourselves to the text of the guidelines, conflicts of interest in these case studies are no more than a potential factor. It explains some of the differences in diabetes guidelines, specifically the different choices regarding medication for lowering blood glucose in the diabetes guideline. Conflicts of interest had a very limited role in the other guidelines and for the lower back pain case studies. This might be due to the difficulties in establishing a causal relationship between the disclosure of a conflict of interest and the final recommendations in a guideline.

Using a broader lens and looking at the development of guidelines as a whole it is clear from the example of the Dutch diabetes guideline that attempts at influencing guideline makers are made, even if they are not always successful.

6.6. COST-EFFECTIVENESS: TENSION BETWEEN IDEALS AND PRACTICE

Drafting guidelines often involves evaluating evidence on cost. This takes the form of medical studies that provide knowledge about the cost-effectiveness of treatments. A further category of evidence is economic evidence. This often takes the form of cost–benefit or cost-effectiveness analysis where the cost of medication or treatment is contrasted with their effectiveness in improving the health of patients. The way cost-effectiveness played a role in guidelines varied between the Netherlands and England and between guidelines. Cost-effectiveness modelling did not form a formal part of the drafting of guidelines in the Netherlands, but was a mandatory aspect in the drafting of the English guidelines.

This study explicitly considers the relationship between economic evidence considered by guideline groups and other evidence considerations. Analysing the role of economic evidence further reveals the consequences this might have for differences between guidelines, given the large differences in the Netherlands and England in dealing with issues of cost-effectiveness. First, analysing the Dutch guidelines in detail will show that an informal role for cost issues does not necessarily lead to decisions that are 'costly'. A review of the English guidelines in contrast to the Dutch experiences shows some potential unintended consequences of the formulation of thresholds in dealing with costs. But even between guidelines in one country differences occur in how cost evidence is handled and how it shapes the development of a guideline.

When analysing the results of the case study on the NHG lower back pain guideline the issue of cost was not mentioned. The case study on this guideline, therefore, does not include an assessment of costs or cost-effectiveness. This is due to the fact that the decision on which treatments are part of the package of insured care lies with the Zorginstituut.

The Dutch diabetes guideline contains a different picture. The institutional situation has not changed, but in this guideline, reference is made to costs. Not by using a formal model, but in a simple qualitative sense: by labelling drugs as 'cheap' or 'expensive'. The interviews with members of the guideline group show that they felt a general obligation to pay heed to the cost of the healthcare system as a whole in the choices they made in the guideline.[26] This author would suggest, however, that cost played a larger indirect role

---

26 Paragraph 5.14.

than the interviews would suggest. The Dutch guideline group justified their choice for the 'old' diabetic drugs by referring to safety data and a lack of long-term studies into the efficacy of the drugs. These considerations would plausibly be different if these newer drugs were not 30–50 times more expensive than the older ones. In this sense 'the responsibility for the cost of the healthcare system' did figure in their deliberations, as the guideline reflects that these drugs are 'expensive'.

The English guidelines provide a different picture: both guidelines are filled with references to economic studies and contain modelling of treatment choices based on a formal assessment of healthcare states. A specific technical jargon is employed which includes quality-adjusted life years (QALY's), incremental cost-effectiveness ratio (ICER) and EuroQol health-related utility values, which is a standardised measuring tool used in surveys to measure how patients score their future health state when confronted with symptoms of a disease.[27] The aim of this modelling is to quantify the cost to the NHS of providing a treatment that will give an average patient an average of one year of health.[28] NICE has set a threshold value, which reflects the NHS' willingness to pay to provide this 'average' patient with 'health', this threshold is £20,000–£30,000 per year of health. Knowing this background, we can evaluate the judgment made in the two NICE guidelines. The back-pain guideline includes economic studies in their evaluation of evidence, whenever one is available.[29] All these studies show the cost of the treatments recommended is below the threshold set by NICE (except for one treatment, spinal fusion, which cost more than £20,000).[30] The group responded to this result by limiting access to the treatment to those who had followed all other steps/treatments in the guideline within a year; they could then be referred for an *opinion* on getting spinal fusion. As members of the guideline group explained, they expected the group of people who would complete the guideline within one year to be so small that the cost of the treatment would not be an issue. As the treatments for lower back pain were all relatively cheap, these considerations did not force the guideline group to change their recommendations. The inclusion of economic evidence in the guideline

---

27 An example is the EuroQol for diabetes: Adrian Bagust and Sophie Beale, 'Modelling EuroQol Health-Related Utility Values for Diabetic Complications from CODE-2 Data' (2005) 14 *Health Economics* 217.

28 Health is 'quality-adjusted' to reflect the fact that the person has a disease, it is an expression of 'relative health' versus the condition without the treatment.

29 One example is Thomas and others (Chapter 4, n 21).

30 Savigny and others (Chapter 4, n 3) Appendix E.

did, however, make more explicit the additional cost of providing a course of acupuncture on the NHS, something which was used in the external response to the guideline after it was published.

They were asked to draft a guideline for anyone with back pain between six weeks and one year.[31] This excluded from their consideration people with chronic pain (defined as back pain for longer than a year). This was thus a guideline that was constructed for a very particular clinical condition, which allowed the guideline group to push to the background difficult questions of what the position of spinal surgery should be in *chronic back pain*. This experience underscores the need to see the drafting of a guideline within a specific institutional context and a particular medical field: the back-pain guideline was the result of specific institutional choices by NICE to define the scope in a (limited) way. This example shows how cost-effectiveness considerations can be neutralised in this case through declaring a specific treatment outside of the scope of the guideline and allowing the treatment to be recommended through other mechanisms.

Including cost-effectiveness is not uniform among all NICE guidelines. Those concerning diabetes were influenced by economic evidence to a greater extent than the back-pain guidelines. This can partly be explained by the nature of the medical condition: treating diabetes is complex, so the guideline group therefore had to make more complex decisions and faced various trade-offs in deciding about aspects of diabetes care. The group was helped by the fact that there were more economic studies that provided evidence of the cost-effectiveness of various diabetes treatments, as well as a model based on the UK Prospective Diabetes Study (UKPDS) to help calculate the cost and effectiveness of several blood sugar lowering drugs.

In this case study, the analysis focused on the decision the English group made concerning the use of Exenatide. This was not the only drug where economic evidence played a role, but it was chosen because it provides a clear example of the mechanisms behind the conflict between economic and clinical knowledge in drafting guidelines. Exenatide was not shown to be cost-effective in the original cost-effectiveness model.[32] The guideline group responded by attacking the assumptions underlying the modelling. They argued that the model did not sufficiently allow for the positive effects of the drug (reduction in hypoglycaemia and weight loss). In the

---

31 Ibid, Appendix A.

32 National Collaborating Centre for Chronic Conditions (Great Britain) and Royal College of Physicians of London (Chapter 5, n 4).

revised modelling, one instance was found where the drug was cost-effective. The resulting compromise tried to accommodate the economic evidence (which suggested that the drug would only be cost-effective in limited circumstances) with the clinical wish to be able to employ the drug to increase patient's quality of life. This resulted in a carefully phrased compromise where the drug could only be prescribed to people, who were obese and responded positively to the drug with a decrease in blood sugar level as well as weight loss.[33]

This aspect of guideline drafting neatly encapsulates several elements that make NICE guidelines on these aspects fundamentally different from NHG guidelines, while at the same time revealing the unintended consequences of trying to square healthcare rationing with producing clinical guidelines. In line with Goldberg, this suggests the use of economic modelling is the ideal location to see how guidelines are places where political questions are transformed into technical ones.[34] The operation of this mechanism can be shown through analysis of the underlying motivations in the debate surrounding Exenatide. For the English group, the conflict between the assumptions underlying the (original) economic modelling that concluded that Exenatide was not cost-effective clashed with the assumptions the group members held about what they considered to be good care. The members operationalised diabetes care as a continuous process, where Exenatide would provide an option to delay or even prevent the starting of insulin therapy. They thought about cost in a holistic way: the cost of insulin therapy, including assistance with injections and the monitoring of blood glucose levels all had to be considered. The result of these deliberations was that the clinical availability of Exenatide as a treatment option was of greater weight than considerations of cost.

The debate surrounding this issue appears to be a technical debate about the definition of costs and the calculation of benefits, but it is also a debate about *values*. By defining good care implicitly as a continuous process, as part of a management of a chronic and lifelong condition, providing drugs that are not strictly cost-effective is a perfectly rational choice and is in conformity with values about patient care. Due to the inclusion of economic evidence, the English diabetes group was forced to reveal some of these values more clearly, than a group who did not include this evidence in their debates.

33 Ibid, 124.
34 Goldenberg (Chapter 3, n 134).

The use of economic evidence has a potential unintended consequence, however, as we can glean from the debate surrounding Exenatide. The explicit definition of a threshold invites the guideline group to find a situation where the medication is (just) below the threshold so that it can merit the label of 'cost-effective.' As we have seen, a conception of diabetes care where Exenatide was a valuable drug led to its inclusion in the treatment algorithm with conditions attached to its use. At the same time, this meant that the option not to give advice on the use of the drug at all did not appear in the table because it was cheaper than the NICE threshold. This led to the paradoxical result that a 'cost-effective' NICE guideline recommends more expensive medication than the Dutch guideline that does not concern itself with cost (at least formally). The realisation that cost-effectiveness (in the sense of not reaching the NICE threshold) is not necessarily always the most cost-effective option is an important one. This result should be interpreted cautiously, however, because this one example might not apply to all NICE guidelines. It could be tied to the particular circumstances of the diabetes guideline.

The mixture of ways cost-effectiveness forms part of the drafting of a guideline does not allow for very general conclusions, but some underlying mechanisms can be established. The role of economic evidence forces guideline groups to explicitly consider two different conceptions of guidelines: as an instrument of healthcare rationing and for the highest possible quality of care. The English diabetes guideline group successfully resolved this tension by redefining the economic evidence in such a way that a compromise can be struck that satisfies clinical and economic considerations. In contrast, the Dutch guideline on back pain includes recommendations for treatments (physiotherapy) that are not covered under the basic health insurance package in the Netherlands, so the cost must be borne by patients (through additional insurance or cash payments). So, neither the cost to patients nor the cost to the healthcare system are formally considered. In this way, the Dutch back pain guideline avoids the conflict described here: it has as its sole purpose advice on the best quality of care.

Economic evidence, therefore, has the potential to counteract clinical evidence. If drugs are too expensive in relation to their effectiveness, they might not be recommended. The case studies provide no evidence that economic evidence forced guideline groups to actively change their recommendations to cheaper drugs.[35] There is evidence, however, that

---

[35] The draft 2016 guideline on diabetes was heavily influenced by cost-effectiveness considerations, as discussed in the controversy surrounding Repaglinide.

the prescribing of Exenatide was curtailed to accommodate the fact that the economic evidence showed that the drug was not cost effective if prescribed to all patients. Therefore, while cost evidence did not lead to the recommendation of cheaper drugs, there is some evidence that it did lead to more expensive drugs not being the first recommended choice. While the effect of economic evidence on differences in guidelines is small, the fact that the English guidelines are perceived as healthcare rationing instruments might influence their implementation.[36]

This study finds that the practice of considering economic evidence does not yet fully live up to the ideal of choosing treatments that are both clinically effective and cost-effective. Scientific evidence is never perfect or complete and, even if it was, it would not always be able to satisfy the joint requirements of treatments being both the cheapest and the best option. In the end it is always the clinician armed with practical knowledge about the true value of the treatment who can successfully mediate between these conflicting pressures. This helps to uncover one of the strengths of guidelines as a regulatory tool: they provide a clear, consultative, iterative and social dynamic process to thrash out complicated and thorny scientific questions. This is important, especially in the case of cost, because otherwise normative choices would be made arbitrarily by a spreadsheet based on the lowest cost option. It is proposed that it is more fruitful to understand the consideration of cost not only as a technical exercise, but also as an invitation to consider the relative weight of various values.

Evidence on cost-effectiveness, its use in the drafting of medical guidelines and analysis of that process through socio-legal methods can provide more clarity on the practices underpinning medical regulation. The way in which doctors and guideline drafters mediate cost pressures while maintaining appropriate clinical choices, helps to prioritise patient care and well-being. This blunts some of the neo-liberal drivers in this sector, characterised by an oversimplification of medical decisions to be a simple judgment of the lowest cost. This discussion of ideals and political motivations in medical healthcare regulation is a particularly salient and topical debate in current healthcare policy and is deserving of future research.

---

[36] A full appraisal of these effects falls outside the scope of this book.

6.7. CONCLUSION

In conclusion, cost-effectiveness considerations are a very important element of the discussions in English guideline groups. However, to date, they have played a limited role in the Dutch guidelines because of the current institutional context of the Dutch healthcare regulation system. As evidence on cost is likely to gain prominence in the Dutch system for future guidelines, this opens up possibilities for future research in this area. Posing questions as to the validity and value judgements implicitly made in cost choices early in the policy process, would enable decision makers to be self-reflexive about their evidence choices in healthcare guidelines.

CHAPTER 7
CONCLUSION

This concluding chapter aims to address what factors and mechanisms explain the differences between the development of evidence-based guidelines. The conclusions drawn from this study will be organised around the themes identified in the sub-questions of this book: What role does evidence play in creating differences and similarities in guidelines and what types of 'evidence' are used? How do institutional framings impact on guideline development? What is the role of group decision-making in the development of guidelines? What is the role of evidence on cost and cost-effectiveness in the formation of guidelines? How do external factors determine choices made in guideline development? And finally, how do these factors and mechanisms impact on guidelines as a form of professional self-regulation?

7.1. EVIDENCE

Evidence has been of central concern in this book. To study empirically how guideline groups, grapple with the fact that guidelines must be evidence-based has been a key theme in understanding the development of medical practice guidelines.

It turns out guidelines are not based on evidence in a straightforward sense; rather they are the result of a complex negotiation of social, economic, political and normative mechanisms that both select and shape evidence in various ways. The notion of cognitive framing turns out to be a powerful conceptual tool to describe this black box in detail.

A major conclusion of this book is that evidence-based guidelines are not as evidence-based as they claim to be; rather, the term 'evidence-based guideline' is used to justify subjective normative and political choices in professional self-regulation. This allows for a new understanding of how scientists construct and produce knowledge and how this is consequently presented as empirical truth. The analysis suggests that guidelines are an expression of a temporal closure of debate on the optimal medical choices regarding a specific condition.

This process of selecting evidence and evaluating the methodological soundness of evidence is relatively well understood. It has been shown how different guideline groups make different decisions. Some only include evidence of a certain quality (RCTs), others rely on summaries of studies (Cochrane Reviews One could stop there and consider that because guideline groups differ in their process of selecting evidence, this explains the differences in the development of guidelines. This is where existing scholarship is lacking as it fails to consider how this evidence is then used in a social and constructive process to make recommendations in a guideline. It is better to speak of 'evidence-informed' guidelines, where medical studies can inform the understanding of the likelihood of certain treatments being effective, but do not determine conclusively which recommendation should be drawn from that information and therefore which action should be taken. So even if the process of selecting evidence was the same and groups considered exactly the same medical studies, different inferences could still be drawn from the medical knowledge presented to them.

This book has clearly shown how the consideration of the evidence is a process in which *meaning is attributed* to the medical knowledge contained in medical studies through a social, discursive and iterative discussion. This discussion is fed by a context-dependent combination of principles of good care (that treatments should provide maximum of choice, with a minimum of harm to patients), deep knowledge of clinical practice and political considerations (who gets to do what and when and how). Guideline recommendations must fit within an existing *frame* of treatment of a given condition and, regardless of the strength of the evidence, consensus within the drafting groups, needs to be reached. It is only through the combination of these various factors that recommendations are reached and that guidelines can be said to be based on evidence.

It is through a detailed understanding of the interaction between a clinical cognitive frame that the appraisal of evidence is conducted. Evidence is thus not a form of knowledge that is mechanically applied to a well understood clinical set of circumstances. Rather, it is socially constructed in a discursive process that is context dependent. This explains why guidelines can be similar, notwithstanding large differences in the evidence cited and can be different, although the evidence used is similar. It is the framing, through a process of debate, which creates recommendations. This does not mean that guidelines can completely ignore evidence, medical studies do provide certain limitations on the arguments a group can make. However, it is through this argumentative process that evidence is imbued with meaning.

Guidelines exhibit a certain duality, a tension between their text and their drafting. Guidelines are attempts to mobilise practical knowledge to answer clinical questions, to provide *guidance*. Guidelines are part of a continuous dialogue between members of the medical profession(s) involved in the treatment of the medical condition of the guideline. This helps answer the question Moreira poses:[1] How can the text of a guideline can be so technical while the process of drafting is such an intensely messy and social enterprise? A possible answer to this question lies in the function a guideline performs in the dialogue with other professionals. To be able to be perceived as convincing and *legitimate*, the subjective elements of its construction must, as far as possible, remain hidden from view: calling a guideline 'evidence-based' provides such a device.

This rhetoric move within the context of guideline drafting has two separate effects. Firstly, it changes the terms under which other 'participants' in the debate on the condition or disease can attack (recommendations in) a guideline. Only if people who criticise the guideline can point to conflicting evidence (in the form of medical studies) will the criticism be accepted as legitimate. This conveniently deflects attention from some of the 'non-evidentiary justifications' guideline groups use to make decisions. Are these are also decisions captured by and protected within the 'evidence-based' framing they are partly immune from legitimate criticism. This rhetoric achieves 'closure' of the debate on the optimal treatment of a given condition by delegitimising critique that cannot muster compelling medical studies to directly challenge the guidelines' recommendations. This has the effect of shutting out some voices from the debate and restricting the boundaries of those who can provide input to this process and those who are excluded.

The second effect of the rhetoric move towards objectivity is probably the most profound, if the hardest to substantiate, as it results in the transformation of a messy contextualised social process of negotiation into a guideline whose recommendations can claim to be objective. This is not objectivity in the form of a universal and objective truth, but it does enable a temporary claim that legitimate scientific knowledge is being used to address clinical questions. What makes this particular claim special is the

1 Moreira (Chapter 2, n 21).

fact that it is believed and supported by a methodology: evidence-based guideline making. It is because of the belief in this methodology that guidelines can claim that their recommendations have legitimacy. What is peculiar is that it does not matter whether guidelines actually follow this evidence-based model closely in practice; it is enough to claim that they are evidence-based. The text of the guidelines, in varying degrees, provides the assurance that the correct procedures were followed. It is for this reason that, especially in the case of the NICE guidelines, extensive appendices are included at the end of the text. The main function of these appendices is to reassure the reader and provide sources of information. If a person chose to read the entire guideline, the appendices would reassure them that the correct methodological approach has been undertaken. The Dutch guidelines are less ostentatious in displaying their underlying methodological choices and the NHG guidelines are much shorter. Nonetheless, the Dutch guidelines make the same claim and nominally employ the same methodology as their English counterparts. The reason the Dutch guidelines are less explicit about methodology is that they have another important source of legitimacy, one that trumps considerations of evidence-based medicine: the reputation of the NHG, which authorises the guidelines. The broad support and virtually universal membership of the NHG by GPs in the Netherlands guarantees the legitimacy of the guidelines.

In conclusion, the analysis here suggests that medical communities have limited reliable medical knowledge and that, despite their claim of being evidence-based, guidelines are still the result of consensus between medical experts. This contradicts the founding claim of evidence-based guideline-making that the process is no longer based on the subjective knowledge of medical professionals, but on solid empirical evidence.

The criticism of the evidence hierarchy such as those voiced by Chin[2] is therefore well founded. Guideline group members might occasionally mention the evidence hierarchy but interpret this is very different ways: in some cases, excluding some types of cases from consideration, in others, preferring a different hierarchy entirely. More importantly, this book has shown how drafting evidence-based guidelines goes beyond merely following an evidence framework by using a complementary knowledge framework.

2 Chin-Yee (Chapter 2, n 17).

In line with the work of Cambrosio et al,[3] regulatory objectivity is a good term to describe the process of guideline making, a collective process where people (guideline makers) and objects (medical knowledge/evidence) are connected by specific coordination regimes. This book builds on Cambrosio's work by providing empirical examples of how these coordination regimes might function. This author would argue that every guideline group creates a distinct framework that draws upon various sources of knowledge such as clinical practice, institutional culture and medical knowledge to formulate the 'coordination regime' for a specific guideline.

The earlier work of Moreira on guidelines suggests two repertoires of evaluation: process and practice.[4] In his work he suggests guideline groups should consider both the technical aspects of the knowledge they gather, the quality of the medical studies and their methodological soundness, as well as the practical usability of this medical knowledge. This book supports Moreira's findings insofar as the groups do indeed discuss those aspects in their development of medical guidelines. Moreira, however, neither acknowledges the importance of institutional factors nor considers the specific position the guideline has vis-à-vis other medical professionals. It is argued here that these frameworks are equally important. A further limitation of Moreira's study is that he does not consider the preconceptions guideline makers bring to the negotiation table *before* the drafting process begins. This book has shown how making sense of evidence in a guideline group is closely connected to a frame of reference that is comprised of pre-existing knowledge and clinical expertise.

This book would therefore argue for calling guidelines 'evidence informed' while being mindful of the subjective and contextual process of constructing meaning and 'facts' from evidence.

7.2. INSTITUTIONS

We have highlighted the importance of addressing the institutional factors influencing guideline drafting. Institutional impacts are multi-layered and range from direct influence on the composition of guideline groups, to a steering of the management of conflicts of interest, to creating a specific institutional culture of guideline drafting.

---

3 Cambrosio and others (Chapter 2, n 24).

4 Moreira (Chapter 2, n 21).

Institutions are important in the process of publishing and endorsing the guidelines that guideline groups draft. The institutional environment of guideline production can shape and form the initial terms and scope of the guideline, the outputs of the searching for evidence and how it is received by external audiences. This book provides some insight into how guideline-making institutions shape guideline groups and inform the guidelines they produce. Institutional factors are a critical part of the reason why guidelines differ, as the organisational set-up of guidelines influences their drafting.

Critically, the influence of institutions on guidelines is at the centre of the guideline drafting process: it affects the role conflicts of interests have to play, shapes the framing of the evidence through the perception of a specific cultural history by guideline makers, influences the composition of the guideline group and imparts specific directions as to what guidelines are for and their proper role in the relevant healthcare systems.

Institutions also shape the framing of evidence by guideline group members. This framing influences the purpose and aims of the guidelines and of the guideline-making process. How e group members view evidence is partly due to how they view the institutional context within which they must operate during the drafting process. Evidence and institutional factors are here presented as analytically separate categories but, in reality, they are tied very closely together. A frame that a guideline group employs is, at least partly, informed by an understanding of what the institutions 'demands', what its processes and resources are and how it conceptualises guidelines as part of an institutional mission.

The position of a guideline within a healthcare system in a wider sense is steered by a perception of an institutional mission. Who are we making guidelines for? Just one profession, or the whole healthcare system? These considerations will shape the approach a guideline group will take in the development of a guideline.

Institutions exert control by deciding who can join guideline groups. These decisions matter, as the presence of guideline group members with specific expertise can be linked to the inclusion of treatments they are experts in.

All these aspects taken together have the effect of creating cultures of institutional practice that place demands on medical professionals while they are drafting guidelines. Institutions achieve this through promulgating rules and specific cultures of institutional practice, which directly inform the medical guidelines produced. This research provides a fresh perspective on how guidelines are considered, in a way that heeds the particular institutional embeddedness of the processes of their development and other instruments developed by professionals.

This book has shown that institutional culture is more important for guidelines than has been realised before. Drafting a guideline is something that happens within an institution that provides at least some of the 'cultural scripts',[5] which steer the choices in the development of guidelines.

7.3. GROUP DECISION-MAKING

Recommendations in a guideline are the result of the consideration of evidence within a frame of understanding, embedded in the wider institutional context. The process of group decision-making within a guideline provides the 'glue' or the bridge between the wider institutional frame and the consideration of the evidence. This book presents several factors of the decision-making process that together form part of the frame employed by the guideline group. Some of these are present before the group start to develop the guideline, others are constructed anew by each different guideline group; their uniqueness provides the key to explaining differences in the development of guidelines.

Four factors are prominent in the discussions of all the guideline groups, although their intensity varies: organisation of care; clinical practice; conceptions of disease; and perceptions of change in evidence.

A relatively minor factor are the discussions within a guideline group on the organisation of care. This not only involves recommending a certain treatment or advising against one but can also mean that the guideline group makes clear who should provide the treatment. When a guideline group would like to change the organisation of care, they will interpret the evidence with this goal in mind, stressing the factors that support their position.

Of greater importance is the specific backdrop of clinical practice in existence before a guideline is developed. It has been shown here how the wish to change clinical practice might cause resistance within a guideline group. If a group wants to (radically) change current practice by including new treatments, or wants to drop existing treatments that are widely used, a *qualitative* assessment of the evidence will be made to ascertain whether

5 Meyer and Jepperson (Chapter 2, n 76).

the group feels the threshold to recommend a change in practice has been reached. These discussions can be very heated, sometimes leading to a breakdown within a group, as, in the eyes of medical professionals, the organisation of a pathway of care is the defining feature of a guideline.

Underlying the discussion on the best organisation of care or the wish to change clinical practice are ideas about the nature of the disease at hand. Subtler, harder to show, but nonetheless important are the subtle differences between guideline groups in the ideas they have about the model patient or the exact nature of the disease. The diabetes guideline provides a pertinent illustration as the differences in ideas about the (model) patient drove the two guidelines in very different directions. A model of diabetes care that prioritises the tailoring of care will steer the group in the direction of a highly tailored guideline with many exceptions, as happened in England. The Dutch approach was heavily steered towards a uniform model of diabetes care, purposefully restricting choice in furtherance of this aim.

These different considerations play out while medical knowledge moves forward. As part of the work of creating a new guideline, the group will refer to the previously published guideline. One aspect on which the group needs to reach consensus is whether the evidence has changed sufficiently to warrant a change in a guideline. This assessment is qualitative in nature and some guideline groups have very different ideas about the evidence required to change a recommendation.

The literature on group decision-making suggests that the composition of and power differences within a guideline group affect its process of decision making.[6] This argument has found limited support in this strand of literature. Power differences in groups have less of an influence in this book than might have been expected based on the literature. The collective nature of group decision-making provides a moderating influence which prevents differences in seniority between group members from influencing the final recommendations in a guideline. There are some instances, however, that prove the exception to the rule: the presence of a specialist in acupuncture in the English back pain guideline group drove the recommendation for that treatment. Even in that case, the composition of the group itself was only a minor factor, other aspects that helped create a multi-layered frame of meaning were more predominant.

The literature on medical politics and healthcare interrogates the link between power and knowledge in healthcare. Guidelines can be tools to

6 Pagliari, Grimshaw and Eccles (Chapter 2, n 69); Hopthrow, Feder and Michie (Chapter 1, n 7).

convert political questions into technical questions.[7] This book has given empirical support to these claims. Calling guidelines evidence-based is a rhetorical device to transform normative questions into technical ones. Contentious issues and subjective decisions taken in guideline groups can be hidden from view by employing of the language of evidence-based medicine. The case studies have also shown how criticism of guidelines can be defeated purely by reference to medical studies, claiming the guideline is thus evidence-based, ignoring critique that asks guideline groups to make more explicit the values (or frames) on which they have based their decisions.

The institutional theory provided by Meyer and Jepperson on 'agentic actors'[8] turns out to fit very well with the position and behaviour of guideline makers. They all described their work in terms of achieving societal goods: better quality care. The case studies provide ample evidence, however, that self-interest in pursuing a position in a guideline motivated most actors. This fits neatly with Meyer and Jepperson's thesis that actors need to describe their actions as driven by ideals to gain high(er) status in society while masking their self-interest.

These different strands of literature fail to acknowledge the specific collective nature of the construction of frames in guideline groups. While guideline makers might be self-interested, they are forced to work together to create a collective idea of the task at hand and systematically make decisions within those parameters.

7.4. COSTS

There is hardly any literature that conceptualises cost and cost-effectiveness studies as an integral part of guideline development. The differences in institutional positioning of considerations of cost in the English and Dutch healthcare system have nonetheless influenced guidelines. It has been shown here how evidence on cost matters is an extra aspect that drives guidelines groups and could be seen as a specific form of evidence.

The fact that cost considerations are integral to deliberations of the English guideline groups might plausibly mean that they would recommend cheaper treatments, limited by what they could do because of specific

7 Belkin (Chapter 2, n 111); Goldenberg (Chapter 2, n 17); Rodwin (Chapter 2, n 114).
8 Meyer and Jepperson (Chapter 2, n 76).

institutional concerns. Dutch groups, not limited in that way, would be free to recommend more expensive treatments. The real picture was different from this simplified model. English groups found ways around cost constraints and recommended more expensive treatments in some guidelines. The Dutch groups used cost as an informal argument in the discussion to reject some more expensive treatments. The example of the use of Exenatide in the English Diabetes group was particularly relevant to show how guideline groups can stretch the definition of cost-effective to accommodate clinical choices that satisfy their preferences.

Guidelines not only consider medical evidence, they also deploy economic evidence using various degrees of formality as the case studies show. Guideline makers must make choices and compromises, to be able to square ideas on the optimal clinical treatments with that of optimal cost-effectiveness. The cost of advising for drugs that are not cost-effective is high, as guideline groups, especially in England, will be under institutional pressure to thoroughly justify that choice. In response, guideline groups restrict patient access to some expensive treatments to be able to justify those treatments as cost-effective. Consequently, evidence from medical studies is not the only factor steering recommendations in guidelines and its role is smaller when treatments are more expensive. The role of cost remains an underexplored area. It is likely to become more prominent in the future as healthcare resources remain scarce.

7.5. EXTERNAL FACTORS

While guidelines are nominally independent, external factors might plausibly affect their development. In this book, two particular sources of potential influence have been considered: external commentaries on guidelines and conflicts of interest.

The external commentary on certain guidelines has not led to changes in their text. In some instances, certain critique might plausibly affect a future guideline, but not those that are currently being developed. One of the reasons for external factors having a lack of impact on the text of a guideline is the vested interest guideline-making institutions have in retaining their independence. The institutions do not want to be seen to 'give in'. An important tool in this respect is the fact that institutions can refer to the evidence-based methodology they have employed in drafting the guideline, limiting the amount of 'valid criticism' that can be made.

The work of Goldacre[9] has been influential in drawing attention to the potential corrupting influence of conflicts of interest on the development of guidelines. This book has indeed found examples of attempts by the pharmaceutical industry to influence guideline makers, showing the continued relevance of Goldacre's critique. The detailed descriptions of attempts to influence members of the Dutch diabetes group reflects this. Nonetheless, within the limits here, it has not been possible to adduce a causal relationship between any conflicts of interest group members declared and the resulting text of a guideline. Only a correlation between the number of members who report a conflict of interest and the amount of expensive medication they recommend can be established, but this is not sufficient to say that conflicts of interest had an actual influence on any of the guidelines in this book.

7.6. REGULATION

It has been suggested here that guidelines could be conceptualised as being both tools of mandated self-regulation and at the same time an instrument of control for governments to control medical professionals. This inherent tension in the development of a guideline has indeed played out in the case studies discussed in this book. Guideline can be placed on a continuum from guidelines that are 'purely self-regulation' of medical professionals to those that are 'exclusively instruments of control' for governments.

Transparency of professional practice for outside observers is one of the effects of developing guidelines. This can illustrate the argument that guidelines provide a double function: providing increased autonomy for the professional, while at the same time permitting more control. Levay and Waks suggest that the transparency that guidelines bring can be a positive development for the professional.[10] The results of the case studies provide some support for this positive view. One of the main reasons for professionals to engage in guideline making efforts is to remain in control of the criteria of evaluation of their work as professionals. In that sense all the guidelines studied were successful, the definitions provided by professionals of what 'counts' as good clinical practice remains the standard the profession is judged on. These aspects have not been displaced in either country by government-defined initiatives.

---

9 Goldacre (Chapter 2, n 130).

10 Levay and Waks (Chapter 2, n 58).

Complicating that picture is the finding that guidelines perform both functions at the same time, while one of these aspects might be seen as dominant. The English diabetes guidelines were perceived as being influenced by government-mandated rationing, through the extensive use of cost-effectiveness data. The Dutch back pain guideline was more closely linked to professional aims of self-regulation and organisation of care. But all the guidelines contained aspects of both dimensions, which leads to the conclusion that guidelines are indeed specific regulatory tools that embody this duality.

The work of Evetts[11] and especially Fournier[12] on professionalisation is particularly relevant. Fournier's assessment of professionalisation initiatives, which include guidelines as disciplinary tools, chimes with this research. Guidelines can indeed be seen as disciplinary tools, as the resistance to the English back pain guideline has demonstrated. It was suggested corporatist healthcare systems, such as the Dutch one, would allow for less clinical change through guidelines. This assumption turns out to be untrue, the opposite has been shown to be correct. In the Dutch system, a more dispersed system of guideline making creates a closer relationship between professional and guideline makers which allows for greater clinical change, because the legitimacy of the guideline is greater.

Conceptualising guidelines as regulation has not been a central plank of this book, nonetheless it holds potential for comparative study of forms of regulation by different experts in different domains of public policy making.

7.7. CONCLUDING REMARKS

We can best describe guidelines as technical, dry and, frankly, boring documents. This façade of technical, uncontroversial guidance is, however, one of the central claims to their success. It allows political questions to be transformed into technical issues and for these to be solved by technical experts: the healthcare professionals themselves. It turns out that the more normal and uncontroversial the text of the guideline might look, the more controversial and heated were the discussions that went into producing them. The world of guidelines is fascinating, sometimes weird, but always

11 Evetts (Chapter 2, n 49).

12 Fournier (Chapter 2, n 55).

interesting. The focus of this book might have started with observing the differences in text despite similarities in circumstance, but it has moved deeper to try to understand the social world behind these words on paper, the lived reality of creating regulation and what this means for the people involved.

The results here do not provide a uniform answer that can explain the similarities and differences in guidelines. There is an argument that guidelines are a way for social and normative choices to be presented as technical choices hiding behind the 'evidence-based' label. Guidelines provide specific forms and formal symbolic practices to be able to justify and legitimise the making of choices on optimal healthcare. The searching for evidence, the extensive modelling of economic choices, the institutional hurdles that have to be cleared, all work towards the goal of mystifying the fact that a group of men and women in a room have to use their own judgement to make choices that will affect other healthcare professionals, without being able to claim a position of authority over them. In the evidence-based literature it is often lamented that guidelines are ineffective, not implemented, etc. While this might be true, the truly remarkable thing about the process of drafting guidelines is that so many of them are successful.

Evidence-based guidelines are better characterised as evidence-informed guidelines. Not because the decisions by guideline groups are taken on a whim, without regard to scientific knowledge, far from it, rather because it is the social process and the cognitive frames that guide this process that provide the real impetus that results in guideline texts.

Guidelines are highly contextual creations, where replication of 'results' is virtually impossible, because in every new guideline group a new frame of understanding is created, in such a way that even if 'evidence' could be said to be completely the same[13] new and different understandings would be reached every time. The similarity between guidelines is therefore even more striking than the differences because guidelines across countries are closely tied to the medical field to which they speak and that similarities exist, despite sometimes large differences in the medical studies selected.

The resulting guideline text claims (or can be perceived to claim) objective results of robust and impartial assessment of all medical knowledge available, to enable practitioners to trust their judgements and apply them in clinical practice as if they were their own.

---

13 Ignoring, for the moment, how unlikely this is in practice.

Guidelines have been shown to be remarkable documents, concealing a varied, complex and interesting world of colliding interests, characters, values and principles behind their patient words. In conclusion, the development of evidence-based guidelines has been critically analysed and it is argued that guidelines are context dependent, socially constructed and negotiated regulatory documents.

BIBLIOGRAPHY

Alonso-Coello P and others, 'The Quality of Clinical Practice Guidelines over the Last Two Decades: A Systematic Review of Guideline Appraisal Studies' (2010) 19 *Quality and Safety in Health Care* 1.

Armstrong D, 'Clinical Autonomy, Individual and Collective: The Problem of Changing Doctors' Behaviour' (2002) 55 *Social Science & Medicine* 1771.

Armstrong D and others, 'Development of Clinical Guidelines in a Health District: An Attempt to Find Consensus' (1992) 1 *Quality in Health Care* 241.

Asch SE, 'Opinions and Social Pressure' (1955) 193 *Scientific American* 31.

Atkin S and Walton C, 'Commentary: Controversies in NICE Guidance on Management of Type 2 Diabetes' (2008) 336 *BMJ* 1308.

Atkins L and others, 'The Process of Developing Evidence-Based Guidance in Medicine and Public Health: A Qualitative Study of Views from the Inside' (2013) 8 *Implementation Science* 101.

Bagust A and Beale S, 'Modelling EuroQol Health-Related Utility Values for Diabetic Complications from CODE-2 Data' (2005) 14 *Health Economics* 217.

Banta D, 'The Development of Health Technology Assessment' (2003) 63 *Health Policy* 121.

Barnett AH, 'NICE Draft Type 2 Diabetes Guidelines: A Cause for Concern' (2015) 3 *The Lancet Diabetes & Endocrinology* 403.

Belkin GS, 'The Technocratic Wish: Making Sense and Finding Power in the "Managed" Medical Marketplace' (1997) 22 *Journal of Health Politics, Policy and Law* 509.

Berg M, ter Meulen R and Van den Burg M, 'Guidelines for Appropriate Care: The Importance of Empirical Normative Analysis' (2001) 9 *Health Care Analysis* 77.

Black J, 'Constitutionalising Self-Regulation' (1996) 59 *The Modern Law Review* 24.

——, 'Critical Reflections on Regulation' (January 2002). Available at: <http://www.lse.ac.uk/CARR>.

——, 'Constructing and Contesting Legitimacy and Accountability in Polycentric Regulatory Regimes' (2008) 2 *Regulation & Governance* 137.

Black J and Rouch D, 'The Development of the Global Markets as Rule-Makers: Engagement and Legitimacy' (2008) 2 *Law and Financial Markets Review* 218.

Black N and others, 'Consensus Development Methods: A Review of Best Practice in Creating Clinical Guidelines' (1999) 4 *Journal of Health Services Research & Policy* 236.

Board HC, 'Standing Group on Health Technology' (1998) 2 *Health Technology Assessment* 16.

'Boeterapport NMa' (*Report of a Fine by the Dutch Competition Authority*). Available at: <https://www.acm.nl/sites/default/files/old_publication/bijlagen/4595_6888BLD.pdf>.

Boffey D, 'NHS Chief Admits to Dismay at Jeremy Hunt's Meddling' *The Guardian* (21 December 2013). Available at: <http://www.theguardian.com/society/2013/dec/21/nhs-service-jeremy-hunt-malcolm-grant>.

Boltanski L and Thévenot L, 'The Reality of Moral Expectations: A Sociology of Situated Judgement' (2000) 3 *Philosophical Explorations* 208.

Braithwaite J, 'Enforced Self-Regulation: A New Strategy for Corporate Crime Control' (1982) 80 *Michigan Law Review* 1466.

——, 'The New Regulatory State and the Transformation of Criminology' (2000) 40 *British Journal of Criminology* 222.

'British National Formulary'. Available at: <https://bnf.nice.org.uk/treatment-summary/type-2-diabetes.html>.

Brouwers MC and others, 'AGREE II: Advancing Guideline Development, Reporting and Evaluation in Health Care' (2010) 63 *Journal of Clinical Epidemiology* 1308.

Burgers JS and others, 'Inside Guidelines Comparative Analysis of Recommendations and Evidence in Diabetes Guidelines from 13 Countries' (2002) 25 *Diabetes Care* 1933.

——, 'Characteristics of Effective Clinical Guidelines for General Practice' (2003) 53 *The British Journal of General Practice* 15.

——, 'Towards Evidence-Based Clinical Practice: An International Survey of 18 Clinical Guideline Programs' (2003) 15 *International Journal for Quality in Health Care* 31.

Burgers JS and Everdingen JJE van, 'Evidence-based richtlijnontwikkeling in Nederland: het EBRO-platform' (2004) 148 *Nederlands Tijdschrift voor Geneeskunde* 2057.

Burton AK and others, 'Information and Advice to Patients with Back Pain Can Have a Positive Effect: A Randomized Controlled Trial of a Novel Educational Booklet in Primary Care' (1999) 24 *Spine* 2484.

Cambrosio A and others, 'Regulatory Objectivity and the Generation and Management of Evidence in Medicine' (2006) 63 *Social Science & Medicine* 189.

Campbell D, '"Control Freak" Jeremy Hunt Accused of Manipulating NHS for Political Ends' *The Guardian* (27 March 2014). Available at: <http://www.theguardian.com/society/2014/mar/27/jeremy-hunt-control-freak-manipulating-nhs>.

Caporaso JA and others, 'Still a Regulatory State? The European Union and the Financial Crisis' (2015) 22 *Journal of European Public Policy* 889.

Carpenter DP and Moss DA (eds), *Preventing Regulatory Capture: Special Interest Influence and How to Limit It* (Cambridge University Press 2014).

Centre for Health Economics, The University of York, 'NICE Threshold'. Available at: <http://www.york.ac.uk/che/research/teehta/thresholds/>.

Chalmers I, 'The Cochrane Collaboration: Preparing, Maintaining, and Disseminating Systematic Reviews of the Effects of Health Care' (1993) 703 *Annals of the New York Academy of Sciences* 156.

Chin-Yee BH, 'Underdetermination in Evidence-Based Medicine' (2014) 20 *Journal of Evaluation in Clinical Practice* 921.

City and Hackney CCG, 'End of Life Contract – Service Specification 2017. Pdf' (City and Hackney CCG). Available at: <http://onel.nhs.sitekit.net/ONELCityHackney/Downloads/About%20Us/Tenders%20procurements%20contracts/2017%20contracts/End%20of%20Life%20%20contract%20-%20Service%20Specification%20%202017.pdf>.

Claxton K and others, 'Discounting and Cost-Effectiveness in NICE – Stepping Back to Sort out a Confusion' (2006) 15 *Health Economics* 1.

——, *Methods for the Estimation of the NICE Cost Effectiveness Threshold* (University of York, Centre for Health Economics 2013). Available at: <http://www.york.ac.uk/media/che/documents/reports/resubmitted_report.pdf>.

Clinical Standards Advisory Group, *Back Pain* (HMSO 1994).

Cochrane AL, *Effectiveness and Efficiency: Random Reflections on Health Services* (Nuffield Provincial Hospitals Trust 1972).

Cochrane AL, Cox JG and Jarman TF, 'Pulmonary Tuberculosis in the Rhondda Fach' (1952) 2 *British Medical Journal* 843.

Cohen AM, Stavri PZ and Hersh WR, 'A Categorization and Analysis of the Criticisms of Evidence-Based Medicine' (2004) 73 *International Journal of Medical Informatics* 35.

Committee on Conflict of Interest in Medical Research, Education and Institute of Medicine (US), *Conflict of Interest in Medical Research, Education, and Practice* (Bernard Lo and Marilyn J Field (eds), National Academies Press 2009).

'Contributed Poster Presentations' (2006) 9 *Value in Health* A24.

Costa-Font J, Courbage C and McGuire A, *The Economics of New Health Technologies* (Oxford University Press 2009).

Currie CJ and others, 'Survival as a Function of HbA1c in People with Type 2 Diabetes: A Retrospective Cohort Study' (2010) 375 *The Lancet* 481.

Davidoff F and others, 'Evidence-based Medicine' (1995) 310 *BMJ* 1085.

De Amersfoortse, 'Protocol Voetonderzoek Bij Diabetes Mellitus 1.3.Pdf'. Available at: <https://www.amersfoortse.nl/api/pod/getpdf?uri=/POD/r/Pdf/42701.pdf>.

De Friesland Zorgverzekeraar, 'Basisverzekering Online Verzorgd Polis 2014' (*Basic Health Policy Online Care Policy 2014*). Available at: <https://www.defriesland.nl/Images/Basisverzekering-Online-Verzorgd-Polis-2014-11650.pdf>.

'De relatie tussen volume en kwaliteit van zorg: tijd voor een brede benadering' (Consortium Onderzoek Kwaliteit van Zorg 2012).

Department of Health, *Equity and Excellence: Liberating the NHS* (Stationery Office 2010).

'Developing NICE Clinical Guidelines'. Available at: <http://www.nice.org.uk/aboutnice/howwework/developingniceclinicalguidelines/developing_nice_clinical_guidelines.jsp>.

'Development and Validation of an International Appraisal Instrument for Assessing the Quality of Clinical Practice Guidelines: The AGREE Project' (2003) 12 *Quality and Safety in Health Care* 18.

Devlin N and Parkin D, 'Does NICE Have a Cost-Effectiveness Threshold and What Other Factors Influence Its Decisions? A Binary Choice Analysis' (2004) 13 *Health Economics* 437.

'Diabetes-Type-2-Update-Consultation-Table2 Cg-66.Pdf'. Available at: <https://www.nice.org.uk/guidance/cg66/documents/diabetes-type-2-update-consultation-table2>.

DiMaggio PJ and Powell WW, 'The Iron Cage Revisited: Institutional Isomorphism and Collective Rationality in Organizational Fields' (1983) 48 *American Sociological Review* 147.

Dodek P, Cahill NE and Heyland DK, 'The Relationship Between Organizational Culture and Implementation of Clinical Practice Guidelines A Narrative Review' (2010) 34 *Journal of Parenteral and Enteral Nutrition* 669.

Driskell JE and Mullen B, 'Status, Expectations, and Behavior: A Meta-Analytic Review and Test of the Theory' (1990) 16 *Personality and Social Psychology Bulletin* 541.

Duckworth W and others, 'Glucose Control and Vascular Complications in Veterans with Type 2 Diabetes' (2009) 360 *New England Journal of Medicine* 129.

Duhem PMM, *The Aim and Structure of Physical Theory* (Princeton University Press 1991).

'Dutch Cochrane Centre' <http://dcc.cochrane.org/>.

EADV/NAD, 'Een Multidisciplinaire Richtlijn over Zelfcontrole van Bloedglucosewaarden Door Mensen Met Diabetes.Pdf' <http://www.venvndiabeteszorg.nl/kennisbank%20documenten/Kennisbank-open-zelfcontrole/Een%20multidisciplinaire%20richtlijn%20over%20zelfcontrole%20van%20bloedglucosewaarden%20door%20mensen%20met%20diabetes.pdf>.

Eagly AH, 'Gender and Social Influence: A Social Psychological Analysis.' (1983) 38 *American Psychologist* 971.

Egeler C, 'NICE Guidline on Backpain Is Misleading' *BMJ*. Available at: <http://www.bmj.com/rapid-response/2011/11/02/nice-guidline-backpain-misleading>.

Elwyn G and others, 'Shared Decision Making: A Model for Clinical Practice' (2012) 27 *Journal of General Internal Medicine* 1361.

EMA, 'European Medicines Agency Recommends Suspension of Avandia, Avandamet and Avaglim. Anti-Diabetes Medication to Be Taken off the Market.' Available at: <http://www.ema.europa.eu/docs/en_GB/document_library/Press_release/2010/09/WC500096996.pdf>.

Everdingen JJE van, *Consensusontwikkeling in de geneeskunde* (Bohn, Scheltema en Holkema 1988).

——, *Evidence-based richtlijnontwikkeling: een leidraad voor de praktijk* (Bohn Stafleu Van Loghum 2004).

——, *Handboek evidence-based richtlijnontwikkeling: een leidraad voor de praktijk* (Bohn Stafleu van Loghum, Springer Media 2014).

Evetts J, 'Sociological Analysis of Professionalism: Past, Present and Future' (2011) 10 *Comparative Sociology* 1.

Evidence-Based Medicine Working Group, 'Evidence-Based Medicine: A New Approach to Teaching the Practice of Medicine' (1992) 268 *JAMA* 2420.

Farma Magazine, 'Herziene NHG-Standaard Diabetes Mellitus' (2015). Available at: <http://farma-magazine.nl/nhg-standaard-diabetes-mellitus-type-2/>.

Feinstein MD AR and Horwitz MD RI, 'Problems in the "Evidence" of "Evidence-Based Medicine"' (1997) 103 *American Journal of Medicine* 529.

Feyerabend P, *Against Method* (Verso 2010).

Field MJ and others, *Clinical Practice Guidelines Directions for a New Program* (National Academy Press 1990).

Fournier V, 'The Appeal to "Professionalism" as a Disciplinary Mechanism' (1999) 47 *Sociological Review* 280.

Freidson E, *Professionalism, the Third Logic* (University of Chicago Press 2001).

Fritz JM, Delitto A and Erhard RE, 'Comparison of Classification-Based Physical Therapy with Therapy Based on Clinical Practice Guidelines for Patients with Acute Low Back Pain: A Randomized Clinical Trial' (2003) 28 *Spine* 1363.

Gale EAM, 'Conflicts of Interest in Guideline Panel Members' (2011) 343 *BMJ* d5728.

General Medical Council, 'Good Medical Practice (2013)'. Available at: <https://www.gmc-uk.org/-/media/documents/good-medical-practice---english-1215_pdf-51527435.pdf?la=en>.

George JN, Vesely SK and Woolf SH, 'Conflicts of Interest and Clinical Recommendations Comparison of Two Concurrent Clinical Practice Guidelines for Primary Immune Thrombocytopenia Developed by Different Methods' (2014) 29 *American Journal of Medical Quality* 53.

GIP Databank, 'Databank'. Available at: <https://www.gipdatabank.nl/databank#/g//85_dia/ddd/bijlage>.

'Goedkeuringsbesluit Kaderbesluit En Drie Specifieke Besluiten van de CHVG Betreffende Huisartsgeneeskunde, Verpleeghuisgeneeskunde En Medische Zorg Voor Verstandelijk Gehandicapten' (*Ratification of the decision by the commission for GP care, social care and care for the mentally disabled on the training requirements*). Available at: <http://wetten.overheid.nl/BWBR0017529>.

Goldacre B, *Bad Pharma: How Drug Companies Mislead Doctors and Harm Patients* (Fourth Estate 2012).

——, 'COMPare: A Prospective Cohort Study Correcting and Monitoring 58 Misreported Trials in Real Time' (2019) 20 *Trials* 118.

——, 'COMPare: Qualitative Analysis of Researchers' Responses to Critical Correspondence on a Cohort of 58 Misreported Trials' (2019) 20 *Trials* 124.

Goldacre B and Heneghan C, 'How Medicine Is Broken, and How We Can Fix It' (2015) 350 *BMJ* h3397.

Goldenberg MJ, 'On Evidence and Evidence-Based Medicine: Lessons from the Philosophy of Science' (2006) 62 *Social Science & Medicine* 2621.

——, 'Iconoclast or Creed? Objectivism, Pragmatism, and the Hierarchy of Evidence' (2009) 52 *Perspectives in Biology and Medicine* 168.

Gorter KJ and others, 'Diabetes: Glycaemic Control in Type 2 (Drug Treatments)' (2012) *BMJ Clinical Evidence* 0609.

'Grading Quality of Evidence and Strength of Recommendations' (2004) 328 *BMJ* 1490.

Grol R and others, 'Implementatie van NHG-Standaarden: Succes of Probleem?' (2010) 53 *Huisarts en wetenschap* 42.

Group TAC, 'Intensive Blood Glucose Control and Vascular Outcomes in Patients with Type 2 Diabetes' (2008) 358 *New England Journal of Medicine* 2560.

Group TAS, 'Long-Term Effects of Intensive Glucose Lowering on Cardiovascular Outcomes' (2011) 364 *New England Journal of Medicine* 818.

Guyatt GH, 'Evidence-Based Medicine' [1991] ACP J Club A.

Guyatt GH and others, 'GRADE: An Emerging Consensus on Rating Quality of Evidence and Strength of Recommendations' (2008) 336 *BMJ* 924.

Harari E, 'Whose Evidence? Lessons from the Philosophy of Science and the Epistemology of Medicine' (2001) 35 *Australian and New Zealand Journal of Psychiatry* 724.

Harrison MI, *Implementing Change in Health Systems: Market Reforms in the United Kingdom, Sweden, and the Netherlands* (SAGE 2004).

Health Consumer Powerhouse, 'European Health Consumer Index'. Available at: <http://www.healthpowerhouse.com/files/EHCI_2015/EHCI_2015_report.pdf>.

Healy D, *Let Them Eat Prozac: The Unhealthy Relationship Between the Pharmaceutical Industry and Depression* (NYU Press 2006).

Hemingway H and others, 'Appropriateness Criteria for Coronary Angiography in Angina: Reliability and Validity' (2008) 149 *Annals of Internal Medicine* 221.

Hester JB, 'Official Statement from the British Pain Society'. Available at: <http://www.bmj.com/rapid-response/2011/11/02/official-statement-british-pain-society>.

'Hoe de Farmaceutische Marketingmachine Medische Richtlijnen Manipuleert' *De Correspondent*. Available at: <https://decorrespondent.nl/467/Hoe-de-farmaceutische-marketingmachine-medische-richtlijnen-manipuleert/14363052-1f180d9f>.

Hood C and others, *Regulation inside Government: Waste Watchers, Quality Police, and Sleaze-Busters* (Oxford University Press 1999).

Hopthrow T, Feder G and Michie S, 'The Role of Group Decision Making Processes in the Creation of Clinical Guidelines' (2011) 23 *International Review of Psychiatry* 358.

Hout FAG, 'The Dutch Disciplinary System for Health Care: An Empirical Study' (Institute for Research in Extramural Medicine (EMGO institute) at the dept of Public and Occupational Health VU University Medical Center (VUMC) 2006).

Huang ES and others, 'Glycemic Control, Complications, and Death in Older Diabetic Patients: The Diabetes and Aging Study' (2011) 34 *Diabetes Care* 1329.

'Huisarts Boycot Dure Diabetespil, Farmaceuten Lopen Geld Mis' *de Volkskrant* (8 April 2016). Available at: <http://www.volkskrant.nl/economie/huisarts-boycot-dure-diabetespil-farmaceuten-lopen-geld-mis~a4351320/>.

Hutchings A and Raine R, 'A Systematic Review of Factors Affecting the Judgments Produced by Formal Consensus Development Methods in Health Care' (2006) 11 *Journal of Health Services Research & Policy* 172.

Ibrahim T, Tleyjeh IM and Gabbar O, 'Surgical versus Non-Surgical Treatment of Chronic Low Back Pain: A Meta-Analysis of Randomised Trials' (2008) 32 *International Orthopaedics* 107.

Insitituut voor Verantwoord Medicijngebruik, 'Kosten Bloedglucoseverlagende Middelen Nederland versus Duitsland'. Available at: <http://www.medicijnbalans.nl/content/userfiles/files/Kosten%20bloedglucoseverlagende%20middelen%20Nederland%20versus%20Duitsland(1).pdf>.

'International Guideline Library – Guidelines International Network'. Available at: <http://www.g-i-n.net/library/international-guidelines-library>.

Janis IL, *Victims of Groupthink: A Psychological Study of Foreign-Policy Decisions and Fiascoes* (Houghton Mifflin 1972).

Jones DJ and others, 'Conflicts of Interest Ethics: Silencing Expertise in the Development of International Clinical Practice Guidelines' (2012) 156 *Annals of Internal Medicine* 809.

'Kennisinstituut van Medisch Specialisten – Het Belang van Een Goede Richtlijn' (*Knowledge Institute of Medical Specialists – The importance of a good guideline*). Available at: <http://kims.orde.nl/het-kennisinstituut-voor-u/richtlijnen/het-belang-van-een-goede-richtlijn.html>.

Klazinga N, 'Compliance with Practice Guidelines: Clinical Autonomy Revisited' (1994) 28 *Health Policy* (Amsterdam, Netherlands) 51.

——, 'Quality Management of Medical Specialist Care in the Netherlands. An Explorative Study of its Nature and Development' (Erasmus Universiteit Rotterdam 1996).

Kmietowicz Z, 'President of British Pain Society is Forced from Office after Refusing to Denounce NICE Guidance on Low Back Pain' (2009) 339 *BMJ* b3049.

Knaapen L, 'European Regulation and Harmonization of Clinical Practice Guidelines', *European Union Public Health Policy: Regional and Global Trends* (Routledge 2013).

——, 'Being "Evidence-Based" in the Absence of Evidence: The Management of Non-Evidence in Guideline Development' (2013) 43 *Social Studies of Science* 681.

——, 'Pragmatic Evidence and Textual Arrangements: A Case Study of French Clinical Cancer Guidelines' (2010) 71 *Social Science & Medicine* 685.

Knaapen LA, 'In Search of Standards That Avoid Standardization: The Production and Regulation of Evidence Based Guidelines' (PhD, McGill University 2013). Available at: <http://digitool.library.mcgill.ca/webclient/StreamGate?folder_id=0&dvs=1416319090786~744>.

KNMG/KNMP, 'KNMG/KNMP Richtlijn Uitvoering Euthanasie En Hulp Bij Zelfdoding'. Available at: <https://www.knmp.nl/praktijkvoering/richtlijnen/multidisciplinaire-richtlijnen/richtlijn-uitvoering-euthanasie-en-hulp-bij-zelfdoding>.

Koes BW and others, 'Clinical Guidelines for the Management of Low Back Pain in Primary Care: An International Comparison' (2001) 26 *Spine* 2504.

Koes BW, Sanders RJ and Tuut MK, 'CBO-Richtlijn Voor Diagnostiek En Behandeling van Acute En Chronische Aspecifieke Lage Rugklachten' (2004) 148 *Nederlands Tijdschrift voor Geneeskunde* 310.

Kuhn TS, *The Structure of Scientific Revolutions* (University of Chicago Press 1970).

Kulkarni AV, 'The Challenges of Evidence-Based Medicine: A Philosophical Perspective' (2005) 8 *Medicine, Health Care and Philosophy* 255.

Lakatos I, *The Methodology of Scientific Research Programmes* (Cambridge University Press 1999).

Landman GW and others, 'The Relationship between Glycaemic Control and Mortality in Patients with Type 2 Diabetes in General Practice (ZODIAC-11)' (2010) 60 *British Journal of General Practice* 172.

Latour B, *Reassembling the Social: An Introduction to Actor-Network-Theory* (OUP Oxford, 2005).

Lehoux P and Blume S, 'Technology Assessment and the Sociopolitics of Health Technologies' (2000) 25 *Journal of Health Politics, Policy and Law* 1083.

Leng G and Baker M, 'NICE Accredits Guidelines Using International AGREE Criteria' (2013) 347 *BMJ* f4771.

Levay C and Waks C, 'Professions and the Pursuit of Transparency in Healthcare: Two Cases of Soft Autonomy' (2009) 30 *Organization Studies* 509.

Levi-Faur D, 'The Rise of Regulatory Capitalism: The Global Diffusion of a New Order' (2005) 598 *Annals of the American Academy of Political and Social Science* 200.

Liebowitz SJ and Margolis SE, 'Path Dependence' [1999] Encyclopedia of Law and Economics 981.

Lincoff A and others, 'Pioglitazone and Risk of Cardiovascular Events in Patients with Type 2 Diabetes Mellitus: A Meta-Analysis of Randomized Trials' (2007) 298 *JAMA* 1180.

Loveman E and others, 'The Clinical and Cost-Effectiveness of Patient Education Models for Diabetes: A Systematic Review and Economic Evaluation' (2003) 7 *Health Technology Assessment* 22.

Majone G, 'The Rise of the Regulatory State in Europe' (1994) 17 *West European Politics* 77.

Marshall C, *Designing Qualitative Research* (SAGE 2006).

May C, 'Mobilising Modern Facts: Health Technology Assessment and the Politics of Evidence' (2006) 28 *Sociology of Health & Illness* 513.

McDonald R and Harrison S, 'The Micropolitics of Clinical Guidelines: An Empirical Study' (2004) 32 *Policy & Politics* 223.

McGuire DK and others, 'Association Between Sitagliptin Use and Heart Failure Hospitalization and Related Outcomes in Type 2 Diabetes Mellitus: Secondary Analysis of a Randomized Clinical Trial' (2016) 1 *JAMA Cardiology* 126.

McKinlay JB and Arches J, 'Towards the Proletarianization of Physicians' (1985) 15 *International Journal of Health Services* 161.

McKinlay JB and Stoeckle JD, 'Corporatization and the Social Transformation of Doctoring' (1988) 18 *International Journal of Health Services* 191.

Medicijnbalans, 'NHG-Standaard Diabetes Mellitus Type 2, December 2013'. Available at: <http://medicijnbalans.nl/video/40243>.

'Medische Richtlijnen per Organisatie' (*Medical Guidelines by Organisation*). Available at: <http://www.artsennet.nl/Richtlijnen/Per-organisatie.htm>.

Melander H and others, 'Evidence b(i)Ased Medicine – Selective Reporting from Studies Sponsored by Pharmaceutical Industry: Review of Studies in New Drug Applications' (2003) 326 *BMJ* 1171.

Meyer JW, 'Reflections on Institutional Theories of Organizations', *The SAGE Handbook of Organizational Institutionalism* (SAGE 2008).

Meyer JW and Jepperson RL, 'The "Actors" of Modern Society: The Cultural Construction of Social Agency' (2000) 18 *Sociological Theory* 100.

Milgram S, 'Some Conditions of Obedience and Disobedience to Authority' (1965) 18 *Human Relations* 57.

Miller D, 'Some Hard Questions for Critical Rationalism' (2014) 15 *Discusiones Filosóficas* 15.

'Mirror, Mirror on the Wall, 2014 Update: How the U.S. Health Care System Compares Internationally – The Commonwealth Fund'. Available at: <http://www.commonwealthfund.org/publications/fund-reports/2014/jun/mirror-mirror>.

Mirza SK and Deyo RA, 'Systematic Review of Randomized Trials Comparing Lumbar Fusion Surgery to Nonoperative Care for Treatment of Chronic Back Pain' (2007) 32 *Spine* 816.

Moran M, *The British Regulatory State: High Modernism and Hyper-Innovation* (Oxford University Press 2003).

Moreira T, 'Diversity in Clinical Guidelines: The Role of Repertoires of Evaluation' (2005) 60 *Social Science & Medicine* 1975.

Mulder JD and others, 'NHG Standaard Diabetes Mellitus Type II' (1989) 32 *Huisarts en Wetenschap* 509.

Mykhalovskiy E and Weir L, 'The Problem of Evidence-Based Medicine: Directions for Social Science' (2004) 59 *Social Science & Medicine* 1059.

National Collaborating Centre for Chronic Conditions (Great Britain) and Royal College of Physicians of London, *Type 2 Diabetes National Clinical Guideline for Management in Primary and Secondary Care (Update)* (Royal College of Physicians 2008). Available at: <http://www.ncbi.nlm.nih.gov/books/NBK53885/>.

NHG, 'Klacht NHG Tegen MSD Gegrond Verklaard' (Herziene NHG-Standaard Diabetes Mellitus Type 2). Available at: <https://www.nhg.org/actueel/nieuws/klacht-nhg-tegen-msd-gegrond-verklaard>.

——, 'NHG-Standaard Aspecifieke Lagerugpijn'. Available at: <https://www.nhg.org/standaarden/volledig/nhg-standaard-aspecifieke-lagerugpijn>.

——, 'Procedureboek 2010'. Available at: <https://www.nhg.org/sites/default/files/content/nhg_org/uploads/procedureboek_versie_090810.pdf>.

'NHG-Standaard Aspecifieke Lagerugpijn, Een Herziening?' 2005 *Huisarts en Wetenschap* 526.

'NHG-Standaarden' (*Standards of the Dutch Scientifc Association of General Practicioners*). Available at: <https://www.nhg.org/nhg-standaarden>.

NHS Employers, BMA, NHS England, 'General Medical Services (GMS) Contract Quality and Outcomes Framework' 08157. Available at: <https://www.nhsemployers.org/-/media/Employers/Documents/Primary-care-contracts/QOF/2018-19/2018-19-QOF-guidance-for-stakeholders.PDF?la=en&hash=6A53571FC0F7A63FA7354951C733B9E6011EC2CD>.

NHS England, 'CCG Authorisation'. Available at: <https://www.england.nhs.uk/2012/09/auth-decision/>.

NICE, 'Developing NICE Guidelines: The Manual' (2009). Available at: <http://www.ha-ring.nl/download/literatuur/The_NICEguidelines_manual_2009_-_All_chapters.pdf>.

——, 'Guide to the Methods of Technology Appraisal 2013' (2013). Available at: <https://www.nice.org.uk/process/pmg9/chapter/1-foreword>.

——, 'Osteoarthritis (Update): Consultation Comments Table' (2013). Available at: <https://www.nice.org.uk/guidance/CG177/documents/osteoarthritis-update-consultation-comments-table2>.

——, 'Osteoarthritis (Update): Draft Guideline' (2013). Available at: <https://www.nice.org.uk/guidance/CG177/documents/osteoarthritis-update-draft-guideline2>.

——, 'Developing NICE Guidelines: The Manual' (2014). Available at: <https://www.nice.org.uk/process/pmg20/resources/developing-nice-guidelines-the-manual-2014-edition-pdf-6596134525>.

——, 'Developing NICE Guidelines: The Manual' (2018). Available at: <https://www.nice.org.uk/process/pmg20/chapter/introduction-and-overview>.

——, 'The NICE Menu of General Practice and Clinical Commissioning Group Indicators' (2018). Available at: <https://www.nice.org.uk/Media/Default/Standards-and-indicators/indicator-menu-update.pdf>.

——, 'Code of Practice for Declaring and Managing Conflicts of Interest'. Available at: <https://www.nice.org.uk/Media/Default/About/Who-we-are/Policies-and-procedures/code-of-practice-for-declaring-and-managing-conflicts-of-interest.pdf>.

——, 'Osteoarthritis About-This-Guideline'. Available at: <http://www.nice.org.uk/guidance/cg177/chapter/about-this-guideline>.

——, 'Type 2 Diabetes in Adults: Management | Guidance and Guidelines'. Available at: <https://www.nice.org.uk/guidance/ng28>.

——, 'Type 2 Diabetes: Newer Agents'. Available at: <http://www.nice.org.uk/guidance/cg87/resources/cg87-type-2-diabetes-newer-agents-a-partial-update-of-cg66-short-guideline2>.

'NICE Outraged by Ousting of BPS President' *BMJ*. Available at: <http://www.bmj.com/rapid-response/2011/11/02/nice-outraged-ousting-bps-president>.

Nissen SE and Wolski K, 'Effect of Rosiglitazone on the Risk of Myocardial Infarction and Death from Cardiovascular Causes' (2007) 356 *New England Journal of Medicine* 2457.

Norris SL and others, 'Conflict of Interest in Clinical Practice Guideline Development: A Systematic Review' (2011) 6 *PLoS* S570–S580.

Ogus A, 'Rethinking Self-Regulation' (1995) 15 *Oxford Journal of Legal Studies* 97.

'Oncoline'. Available at: <http://www.oncoline.nl/>.

'Orde van Medisch Specialisten – Stichting Kwaliteitsgelden Medisch Specialisten (SKMS)'. Available at: <http://www.orde.nl/over-oms/wat-doet-de-oms/stichting-kwaliteitsgelden-medisch-specialisten-skms.html>.

'Overzicht Zorgverzekeraars in Nederland' (*List of Health Insurers in the Netherlands*). Available at: <http://www.zorginstituutnederland.nl/binaries/content/documents/zinl-www/documenten/rubrieken/verzekering/1302-overzicht-zorgverzekeraars-in-nederland/Overzicht+zorgverzekeraars+%28in+Nederland%29.pdf>.

Pagliari C and Grimshaw J, 'Impact of Group Structure and Process on Multidisciplinary Evidence-Based Guideline Development: An Observational Study' (2002) 8 *Journal of Evaluation in Clinical Practice* 145.

Pagliari C, Grimshaw J and Eccles M, 'The Potential Influence of Small Group Processes on Guideline Development' (2001) 7 *Journal of Evaluation in Clinical Practice* 165.

'Pallialine'. Available at: <http://www.pallialine.nl/>.

Palmer AJ and others, 'The CORE Diabetes Model: Projecting Long-Term Clinical Outcomes, Costs and Cost-Effectiveness of Interventions in Diabetes Mellitus (Types 1 and 2) to Support Clinical and Reimbursement Decision-Making' (2004) 20 *Suppl 1 Current Medical Research and Opinion* S5.

Papageorgiou AC and others, 'Estimating the Prevalence of Low Back Pain in the General Population: Evidence from the South Manchester Back Pain Survey' (1995) 20 *Spine* 1889.

Pope C, 'Resisting Evidence: The Study of Evidence-based Medicine as a Contemporary Social Movement' (2003) 7 *Health* 267.

Popper KR, *The Logic of Scientific Discovery* (Psychology Press 2002).

Powell WW and DiMaggio PJ, *The New Institutionalism in Organizational Analysis* (University of Chicago Press 1991).

Power M, *The Audit Society* (Oxford University Press 1997).

Price C, 'NICE Risks Making Itself a "Laughing Stock" over Guidance on Metformin Alternatives, Say Experts' (*Pulse Today*). Available at: <http://www.pulsetoday.co.uk/clinical/diabetes/nice-risks-making-itself-a-laughing-stock-over-guidance-on-metformin-alternatives-say-experts/20009139.article>.

'Published Clinical Guidelines'. Available at: <https://www.nice.org.uk/guidance/published?type=cg>.

Quine WV, 'Main Trends in Recent Philosophy: Two Dogmas of Empiricism' (1951) 60 *The Philosophical Review* 20.

Raine R and others, 'An Experimental Study of Determinants of Group Judgments in Clinical Guideline Development' (2004) 364 *The Lancet* 429.

Rashidian A, Eccles MP and Russell I, 'Falling on Stony Ground? A Qualitative Study of Implementation of Clinical Guidelines' Prescribing Recommendations in Primary Care' (2008) 85 *Health Policy* 148.

'Richtlijnen // Diliguide.Nl'. Available at: <http://www.diliguide.nl/>.

'Richtlijnendatabase'. Available at: <http://kims.orde.nl/het-kennisinstituut-voor-u/richtlijnen/richtlijnendatabase.html>.

Rodwin MA, 'Commentary: The Politics of Evidence-Based Medicine' (2001) 26 *Journal of Health Politics, Policy and Law* 439.

——, 'Conflicts of Interest, Institutional Corruption, and Pharma: An Agenda for Reform' (2012) 40 *The Journal of Law, Medicine & Ethics* 511.

Rutten G and others, 'NHG-Standaard Diabetes Mellitus Type 2 (Derde Herziening)' (2013) 56 *Huisarts en Wetenschap* 512.

Sackett DL and others, 'Evidence based Medicine: What It Is and What It Isn't' (1996) 312 *BMJ* 71.

Savigny P and others, 'Low Back Pain: Early Management of Persistent Non-Specific Low Back Pain' (National Collaborating Centre for Primary Care and Royal College of General Practitioners 2009). Available at: <http://www.atencionprimaria.imib.es/docmanager/Low_back_pain_guia_NICE_2009.pdf>.

Schott G and others, 'Does the Pharmaceutical Industry Influence Guidelines?: Two Examples from Germany' (2013) 110 *Deutsches Ärzteblatt International* 575.

Schulz KF, Altman DG and Moher D, 'CONSORT 2010 Statement: Updated Guidelines for Reporting Parallel Group Randomised Trials' (2010) 340 *BMJ* c332.

Shin JH, Haynes RB and Johnston ME, 'Effect of Problem-Based, Self-Directed Undergraduate Education on Life-Long Learning' (1993) 148 *Canadian Medical Association Journal* 969.

Spyridonidis D and Calnan M, 'Opening the Black Box: A Study of the Process of NICE Guidelines Implementation' (2011) 102 *Health Policy* 117.

Steinbrook R and Lo B, 'Medical Journals and Conflicts of Interest' (2012) 40 *The Journal of Law, Medicine & Ethics* 488.

Stelfox Henry Thomas, Choudhry Niteesh K and Allen S Detsky, 'Relationships between Authors of Clinical Practice Guidelines and the Pharmaceutical Industry' (2002) 287 *JAMA* 612.

Stephenson J, 'Nurses Claim NICE Diabetes Guidance Will Put Patients at Risk' *Nursing Times* (15 September 2015). Available at: <https://www.nursingtimes.net/clinical-archive/diabetes/nurses-claim-nice-diabetes-guidance-will-put-patients-at-risk/5090329.article>.

Stigler GJ, 'The Theory of Economic Regulation' (1971) 2 *The Bell Journal of Economics and Management Science* 3.

Stone PW, Curran CR and Bakken S, 'Economic Evidence for Evidence-Based Practice' (2002) 34 *Journal of Nursing Scholarship* 277.

Strathern M, 'The Tyranny of Transparency' (2000) 26 *British Educational Research Journal* 309.

Stratton IM and others, 'Association of Glycaemia with Macrovascular and Microvascular Complications of Type 2 Diabetes (UKPDS 35): Prospective Observational Study' (2000) 321 *BMJ* 405.

Sur RL and Dahm P, 'History of Evidence-Based Medicine' (2011) 27 *Indian Journal of Urology* 487.

The Action to Control Cardiovascular Risk in Diabetes Study Group, 'Effects of Intensive Glucose Lowering in Type 2 Diabetes' (2008) 358 *New England Journal of Medicine* 2545.

Thomas KJ and others, *Longer Term Clinical and Economic Benefits of Offering Acupuncture Care to Patients with Chronic Low Back Pain* (Gray 2005).

Thomson S and others, 'International Profiles of Health Care Systems, 2013' (Commonwealth Fund). Available at: <http://www.commonwealthfund.org/~/media/Files/Publications/Fund%20Report/2013/Nov/1717_Thomson_intl_profiles_hlt_care_sys_2013_v2.pdf>.

Tsoukas H, 'The Tyranny of Light: The Temptations and the Paradoxes of the Information Society' (1997) 29 *Futures* 827.

UK BEAM Trial Team, 'United Kingdom Back Pain Exercise and Manipulation (UK BEAM) Randomised Trial: Effectiveness of Physical Treatments for Back Pain in Primary Care' (2004) 329 *BMJ* 1377.

van Herk R, 'Artsen onder druk. Het kwaliteitsbeleid van de medische beroepen in Groot-Brittannië, Nederland en België tussen 1970 en 1996, als gevolg van de interne en externe druk op de zelfregulering van artsen.' (Erasmus Universiteit Rotterdam 1997).

van Herk R, Schepers R and Casparie AF, 'Huisartsen en zelfregulering. De ontwikkeling van intercollegiale toesting en standaarden voor huisartsen tussen 1970 en 1990' (1994). Available at: <https://lirias.kuleuven.be/handle/123456789/161090>.

Vos C de, 'Kwaliteit, disciplinering en sturing. Een historisch sociologisch onderzoek naar de vormgeving van kwaliteit van zorg in ziekenhuizen = Quality, Discipline and Governance. An Historical Sociological Study into the Design of Quality of Care in Hospitals' (Erasmus Universiteit Rotterdam 2014).

Walker BF, 'The Prevalence of Low Back Pain: A Systematic Review of the Literature from 1966 to 1998' (2000) 13 *Journal of Spinal Disorders* 205.

Watine JC and Bunting PS, 'Mass Colorectal Cancer Screening: Methodological Quality of Practice Guidelines is Not Related to Their Content Validity' (2008) 41 *Clinical Biochemistry* 459.

'Werkgroep Infectiepreventie (WIP)'. Available at: <http://www.rivm.nl/Onderwerpen/W/Werkgroep_Infectiepreventie_WIP>.

Wilson N and others, 'Governing Healthcare: Finding Meaning in a Clinical Practice Guideline for the Management of Non-Specific Low Back Pain' (2014) 102 *Social Science & Medicine* 138.

Wincott D, 'European Political Development, Regulatory Governance, and the European Social Model: The Challenge of Substantive Legitimacy' (2006) 12 *European Law Journal* 743.

Worrall J, 'What Evidence in Evidence-based Medicine?' (2002) 69 *Philosophy of Science* S316.

Wright JSF, 'The Regulatory State and the UK Labour Government's Re-Regulation of Provision in the English National Health Service' (2009) 3 *Regulation & Governance* 334.

'ZonMw – A Randomised Cost-Effectiveness Study on the Surgical versus Conservative Treatment of Sciatica'. Available at: <http://www.zonmw.nl/nl/projecten/project-detail/a-randomised-cost-effectiveness-study-on-the-surgical-versus-conservative-treatment-of-sciatica/hoe-nu-verder/>.

Zorginstituut Nederland, 'Kosteneffectiviteit in de Praktijk'. Available at: <https://www.zorginstituutnederland.nl/binaries/content/documents/zinl-www/documenten/publicaties/rapporten-en-standpunten/2015/1506-kosteneffectiviteit-in-de-praktijk/1506-kosteneffectiviteit-in-de-praktijk/Kosteneffectiviteit+in+de+praktijk.pdf>.

——, 'Kwaliteit' (*Quality*). Available at: <http://zorginstituutnederland.nl/kwaliteit>.

'Zorgverzekeraars in Nederland' (*Health Insurers in the Netherlands*). Available at: <http://www.zorghulpatlas.nl/zorghulpwereld/zorgverzekering/zorgverzekeraars-in-nederland/>.

'Zorgverzekeraars Nederland – Nieuwsbericht'. Available at: <https://www.zn.nl/338067458/Nieuwsbericht?newsitemid=1673035776>.

Zuiderent-Jerak T and others, 'Variatie in richtlijnen. Wat is het probleem?'. Available at: <http://www.pgosupport.nl/mailings/FILES/plugin_content/176/Regieraad_rapport_variatie_in_richtlijnen.pdf>.

INDEX

ABOUT THE AUTHOR

Friso Johannes Jansen is a Senior Lecturer in Law at Birmingham City University. Before joining the Birmingham City University Law Faculty he taught public law and social security law at the Applied Science University of Amsterdam and the University of Groningen. He is interested in the intersections of law and science and especially the growing role of (scientific) experts in shaping laws and regulation. His recent research focusses on the role of medical guidelines in decisions taken by medical tribunals and the motivations of vaccine sceptics in refusing vaccination.

www.ingramcontent.com/pod-product-compliance
Ingram Content Group UK Ltd.
Pitfield, Milton Keynes, MK11 3LW, UK
UKHW021844100926
8556IPUK00019B/1050

9 781780 688190